Cross LoC

Confidence Building Measures in India and Pakistan

Cross LoC

Confidence Building Measures in India and Pakistan

Brig. S. D. Lal (Retd.)

Gaurav Book Centre Pvt Ltd

Delhi

Publisher
GAURAV BOOK CENTRE PVT LTD
4832/24,Prahlad Lane,S-207 Ansari
Road, Daryaganj, Delhi-110002
Ph.: 43570976, 23278261
Email: gauravbookcentre@gmail.com

Edition: 2015

© Author

ISBN: 978-93-83316-19-9

Laser Typesetting
JEE-VEE Graphics, Delhi

Price: 1295/-

Printed
Vikas Computers, Delhi

Preface

The Line of Control divided Kashmir into two parts and closed the Jehlum valley route, the only entrance and exit of the Kashmir Valley at that time. This territorial division which, to this day still exists severed many villages and separated family members from each other.

The landmines planted by the Army alongsides of the line have killed scores of innocent people and left thousands as disabled. Without compensation, these disabled persons in the Indian Kashmir are fighting hard for their survival.

During 2008 Kashmir unrest, the Hindu extremist groups and the supporters of Bharatiya Janata Party blocked the Srinagar-Jammu National highway (NH 1A). The only national highway which today connects Kashmir Valley to the rest of India remained closed for several days which put essential commodities on halt and resulted in widespread protest against the Indian control. In response to the blockade, on 11 August 2008, under the leadership of Sheikh Abdul Aziz, 50,000 to 250,000 Kashmiri protesters attempted to cross the Line of Control to Muzaffarabad.

The protesters were stopped at Uri which resulted in killing of fifteen people and hundreds injured when police and Indian paramilitary forces fired on protesters. A slogan raised by the protesters was, *Khooni lakir tod do aar paar jod do* (Break down the blood-soaked Line of Control let Kashmir be united again).

This book contains the fundamental and basic information of the subject and useful for teachers, students and researchers.

—*Editor*

Contents

Contents

1

Line of Control

The term Line of Control (LOC) known as *Asia's Berlin wall,* refers to the military control line between the Indian and Pakistani-controlled parts of the former princely state of Jammu and Kashmir—a line which, to this day, does not constitute a legally recognized international boundary but is the de facto border. Originally known as the "Cease-fire Line", it was redesignated as the "Line of Control" following the Simla Agreement, which was signed on 3 July 1972. The part of the former princely state that is under Indian control is known as the State of Jammu and Kashmir. The two parts of the former princely state that are under Pakistani control are known as Gilgit–Baltistanand Azad Jammu and Kashmir (AJK). Its northernmost point is known as the NJ9842.

Another cease-fire line, one that separates the Indian-controlled state of Jammu and Kashmir from the Chinese-controlled area known as Aksai Chin, lies further to the east and is known as the Line of Actual Control (LAC). It has been referred to as one of the most dangerous places in the world.

LEGACY

The Line of Control divided Kashmir into two parts and closed the Jehlum valley route, the only entrance and exit of the Kashmir Valley at that time. This territorial division which, to this day still exists severed many villages and separated family members from each other. The landmines planted by the Army alongsides of the line have killed scores of innocent people and left thousands as disabled. Without compensation, these disabled persons in the Indian Kashmir are fighting hard for their survival. During 2008 Kashmir unrest, the Hindu extremist groups and the supporters of Bharatiya Janata Party blocked the Srinagar-Jammu National highway (NH 1A). The only national highway which today connects Kashmir Valley to the rest of India remained closed for several days which put essential commodities on halt and resulted in widespread protest against the Indian control. In response to the blockade, on 11 August 2008, under the leadership of Sheikh Abdul Aziz, 50,000 to 250,000 Kashmiri protesters attempted to cross the Line of Control to Muzaffarabad. The protesters were stopped at Uri which resulted in killing of fifteen people and hundreds injured when police and Indian paramilitary forces fired on protesters. A slogan raised by the protesters was, *Khooni lakir tod do aar paar jod do* (Break down the blood-soaked Line of Control let Kashmir be united again).

PAKISTANI AND INDIAN POSITIONS

Pakistani position

The Pakistan Declaration of 1933 had envisioned the princely state of Jammu and Kashmir as one of the "five Northern units of India" that were to form the new nation of Pakistan, on the basis of its Muslim majority. Pakistan still claims the whole of Kashmir as its own territory, including Indian-controlled Kashmir. India has a different perspective on this interpretation.

Indian position

Maharaja Hari Singh, King of the princely state of Jammu and Kashmir agreed toGovernor-General Mountbatten's suggestion to sign the Instrument of Accession India demanded accession in return for assistance. India claimed that the whole territory of the princely state of Jammu and Kashmir had become Indian territory (India's official posture) due to the accession, it claims the whole region including Azad Kashmir territory as its own.

Indian Line of Control fencing

The *Indian Line of Control fencing* is a 550 km (340 mi) barrier along the 740 km (460 mi) disputed 1972 *Line of Control* (or ceasefire line). The fence, constructed by India, generally remains about 150 yards on the Indian-controlled side. Its stated purpose is to exclude arms smuggling and infiltration by Pakistani-based separatist militants.

The barrier itself consists of double-row of fencing and concertina wire eight to twelve feet (2.4–3.7 m) in height, and iselectrified and connected to a network of motion sensors, thermal imaging devices, lighting systems and alarms. They act as "fast alert signals" to the Indian troops who can be alerted and ambush the infiltrators trying to sneak in. The small stretch of land between the rows of fencing is mined with thousands of landmines.

The construction of the barrier was begun in the 1990s, but slowed in the early 2000s as hostilities between India and Pakistan increased. After a November 2003 ceasefire agreement, building resumed and was completed in late 2004. LoCfencing was completed in Kashmir Valley and Jammu region on 30 September 2004. According to Indian militarysources, the fence has reduced by 80% the numbers of militants who routinely cross into the Indian side of the disputed state to attack soldiers.

Pakistan has criticized the construction of the barrier, saying it violates both bilateral accords and relevant United Nationsresolutions on the region. While The European Union has supported India's stand calling the fencing as *"improvement in technical means to control terrorists infiltration."* also pointing that the *Line of Control has been delineated in accordance with the 1972 Shimla agreement.*

2

LoC Tensions Cast Shadow on Indo-Pak Border

The tentative dates for the bi-annual talks have been finalised between August 30-September 4 even as the Union Home Ministry is vetting the contents of the meeting that will be discussed between the Directors General of the Border Security Force and Pakistan Rangers.

Sources said those involved in the proposed deliberations, however, kept their fingers crossed if the talks would happen on these dates or would be postponed as they have happened a few times earlier when tensions happened between the two countries along the LoC or the International Border in Jammu and Kashmir.

A host of issues like border fencing, confidence building measures for the benefit of border population on both sides, and construction of infrastructure is on the discussion table but the talks are going to be hogged by issues related to unprovoked firing, violation of ceasefire and firing from sniper weapons leading to fatal casualities of Indian troops, the sources said.

The delegation of both the forces will include the local commanders present on the frontier and the Indian side is confident of putting across on table the issue of unprovoked firing which vitiates the peace and tranquility of the border, they said.

The last DG level talks between the two forces were held in July last year in Delhi.

The other issues expected to be discussed during the forthcoming talks include subjects of trans-border crime, smuggling of fake Indian currency and sneaking of narcotics from across the border.

HOW PAKISTANIS AND INDIANS VIEW EACH OTHER

Pakistan's relations with its neighbor remain tense, and over the last five years Pakistani attitudes towards India have become more negative.

Currently, only 14% of Pakistanis see India in a positive light, while 75% give the country an unfavorable rating. A majority of Pakistanis consider India a more serious threat to their country than al Qaeda or the Taliban.

Likewise, Indian attitudes toward Pakistan are generally negative – 65% express an unfavorable opinion of Pakistan and a plurality considers Pakistan the greatest threat to their country.

Despite the tensions, Pakistanis and Indians agree that it is important to improve relations between the two nations. Publics in both countries are supportive of additional diplomatic talks and stronger trade ties across the border.

Views of India

Pakistanis have become increasingly critical of their traditional rival over the last five years. In 2006, one-third expressed a positive view of India, compared with just 14% in the current poll. Today, Pakistani attitudes toward India are nearly as negative as they were in the spring 2002 Pew Global Attitudes survey, conducted a few months after a standoff between the two countries following a December 2001 terrorist attack on the Indian parliament.

Pakistani views of India are considerably more negative than those in other Asian countries surveyed, although more than half (53%) of Chinese also have an unfavorable opinion of India. By comparison, India is much better regarded in Indonesia and Japan, where roughly six-in-ten (61% and 59%, respectively) have a favorable view of the country.

India's the Big Worry

Decades of military tensions between India and Pakistan continue to raise security concerns in the sub-continent, and today nearly three-in-four (74%) Pakistanis consider India a serious threat to their country, including 54% who say it is a *very* serious threat. Roughly half consider the Taliban (54%) and al Qaeda (49%) serious threats.

When asked to name the greatest threat to Pakistan – among India, the Taliban and al Qaeda – a majority of Pakistanis (57%) rate India as the greatest threat, while just 19% say the Taliban and only 5% think al Qaeda is the biggest threat.

Pakistanis are increasingly more likely to see India as the top threat; 48% said this was the case in 2009 and 53% named India in 2010. Fears about the Taliban have also declined; 19% name the Taliban as their country's biggest threat, compared with 23% a year ago and 32% in 2009.

The killing of Osama bin Laden has not significantly affected Pakistani views about the threat from al Qaeda or the Taliban. In the April 2011 survey conducted before the terrorist leader's death, 16% identified the Taliban as the greatest threat, while 4% said al Qaeda.

Pakistanis residing in the Punjab province are more likely to consider India the greatest threat than are residents of other provinces. Two-thirds in Punjab say that India poses the top threat, compared with 49% in Sindh and 44% among those residing in Khyber Pakhtunkhwa. PML-N supporters (69%) are also more likely than PPP supporters (51%) to name India as the leading threat.

Indian Views of Pakistan

Indian views of Pakistan are also overwhelmingly negative. Only 14% give Pakistan a favorable rating, while nearly two-thirds (65%) have a negative opinion.

By contrast, Pakistan is much better regarded in Indonesia, where roughly six-in-ten (62%) give the country a positive rating. However, in the other predominantly Muslim nations surveyed

– Lebanon, Egypt, Jordan, the Palestinian territories and Turkey – opinions about Pakistan are on balance negative. About half (51%) of Chinese and a 44%-plurality of Japanese respondents also have unfavorable views of Pakistan, as do 91% of Israelis.

Roughly three-in-four Indians (76%) consider Pakistan a serious threat to their country. More than six-in-ten also rate the Islamic extremist group Lashkar-e-Taiba (64%) and the communist extremist groups commonly known as Naxalites (62%) as serious threats. Half feel this way about China.

When asked to name the greatest threat to India – among Pakistan, Lashkar-e-Taiba, Naxalites and China – a plurality of Indians (45%) considers Pakistan the top threat. Nearly two-in-ten say this about Lashkar-e-Taiba (19%), while 16% rate Naxalites as the greatest threat and only 7% place China in this position.

PAKISTANIS AND INDIANS WANT IMPROVED RELATIONS

Even though tensions between Pakistan and India loom large, publics in both countries are supportive of greater diplomatic and economic ties across the border.

Large majorities of Pakistanis (70%) and Indians (74%) say it is important that relations between the two countries improve. Both publics also want more bilateral trade – nearly seven-in-ten (69%) Pakistanis see increasing trade with India as a good thing, while 67% of Indians also support this idea. In addition to trade ties, majorities in both countries are supportive of further diplomatic talks between the two nations.

At the crux of tensions between India and Pakistan lies the Kashmir dispute.

Nearly three-fourths (73%) of Pakistanis consider the Kashmir dispute a very big problem. Majorities in both countries think it is important to find a resolution to the Kashmir issue, but Pakistanis are more likely than Indians to give this issue high salience (80% vs. 66% very important). Majorities of Pakistanis across age, education and ethnic groups agree that resolving this issue is very important.

Many Say U.S. Tilts Toward India

Pakistanis are considerably less likely than Indians to see American policies in the region as fair toward both countries. Only 9% of Pakistanis see the U.S. approach in the sub-continent as fair, while more than half (52%) say U.S. policies favour India. Only 6% believe that U.S. policies favour Pakistan. Solid majorities of Punjab residents (63%) and PML-N supporters (69%) believe that American policies are biased in favour of India.

Indians are more divided on this issue. Nearly three-in-ten (27%) say that U.S. policies in the region are balanced, while a similar proportion (29%) believes that the U.S. favors India. Only 13% say that Pakistan garners greater favour.

Many in both countries think the India-U.S. relationship has grown stronger in recent years. A plurality of Indians (46%) says relations between their country and the U.S. have improved. An equal number (46%) of Pakistanis agree that India-U.S. relations have improved, up from 37% last year.

2011 INDIA–PAKISTAN BORDER SHOOTING

The 2011 India–Pakistan border shooting incident took place between 30 August (Tuesday) and 1 September 2011 (Thursday) across the Line of Control in Kupwara District/Neelam Valley resulting in one Indian soldier and three Pakistani soldiers being killed. Both countries gave different accounts of the incident, each accusing the other of initiating the hostilities.

Incident

Pakistani sources claimed that the fighting started when Indian border security forces opened fire on a Pakistani checkpoint based on the Line of Control in the Neelam Valley of Azad Kashmir, Pakistan. The Inter Services Public Relationsspokesman Major General Athar Abbas confirmed the incident had taken place while talking to BBC Urdu. Abbas dubbed the attack as unprovoked and said the attack had been protested with India during a border meeting. He claimed that three soldiers were moving from one post to another when they got lost during bad weather and after a 24-hour search, their bodies were recovered.

Lieutenant-Colonel J.S. Brar, spokesman for the Indian Army, claimed that the incident started when Pakistan made an infiltration bid in the Keran Sector of Kupwara District, Jammu and Kashmir on Tuesday (30 August 2011) which was foiled by Indian security forces. He claimed that on Wednesday (31 August 2011) night, at around 20:00 hours, an Indian border post was fired on by Pakistani troops. Following the first shots, both sides engaged in a firefight, with the Indians claiming that heavy mortars and machine guns were used, and that the shooting lasted for about 50 minutes. Accusing Pakistan of two ceasefire violations in the space of fifteen hours, India claimed that the exchange of fire continued at 1100 hours the following day after a brief lull.

Casualties

India confirmed the death of one soldier during the incident. He was identified as *Naib Subedar* Gurdayal Singh. Pakistan announced that three soldiers of the irregular Mujahid Battalion were also killed.

DIPLOMATIC DAMAGE FROM LATEST INDIA-PAKISTAN BORDER CLASHES

On 6 August 2013, five Indian soldiers were shot dead in an ambush in Indian-controlled Kashmir, near the India-Pakistan Line of Control (LoC). While it is unclear who was responsible for the attack, blame has been attributed to either militants backed by the Pakistan Army, or the Pakistani Special Forces themselves. Although Pakistan has denied any involvement and its Prime Minister, Nawaz Sharif, has sent his condolences over the killings, tensions have markedly increased. Intermittent exchanges of small arms fire across the LoC have occurred throughout the week, wounding several soldiers and civilians. The most recent incident occurred on 11 August, with both sides using machine guns.

Comment

While the incident on 6 August and the following border skirmishes are unlikely to escalate into more serious military actions, they are likely to damage the efforts of the Indian and Pakistani governments to improve relations between their countries. Both governments are showing restraint and a willingness to co-operate at the moment, but political pressure over a similar incident in January 2013, forced the Indian Prime Minister, Manmohan Singh, to suspend the official dialogue with Pakistan.

Talks between Indian and Pakistani bureaucrats over their territorial disputes were scheduled to restart this month, but that is now doubtful; many in India's opposition are stridently opposed to them taking place. The main Indian opposition party recently demanded that Singh's government cancel a planned meeting with Sharif in New York next month and even scale down relations with Pakistan by recalling the Indian High Commissioner to Islamabad.

With elections in India due next May, Singh's government is particularly susceptible to agitation from the Indian opposition and the notoriously jingoistic media, which could force it to take a harder stance against Pakistan. Although the current administration favours dialogue to reach a consensus with Pakistan, the public mood in India will make this politically difficult. Singh's government is frequently painted as being weak on border protection, owing to the incursions by Chinese and Pakistani forces at various times through the past year. Since the Indian Government is already contending with domestic anger over the rising cost of living, it is likely that it will heed calls to take some action to shore up its support, rather than just wait out the media storm before quietly restarting talks. While India's reaction is unlikely to be as extreme as the opposition and sections of the media are calling for, the government will almost certainly suspend the talks and make a diplomatic protest.

Perhaps a greater concern not just for relations in the sub-continent but for the region and beyond, is that this event highlights the Pakistani government's lack of control over at least some elements of its military forces and the militants aligned with Pakistan. The government of Prime Minister Sharif has been seeking to re-engage in dialogue with India for some time now, making it highly unlikely that it would have authorised such an attack. Consequently, although the efforts by Sharif to ease tensions and rebuild trust are widely seen as sincere, questions will again begin to rise about his government's ability to deliver on its peace agreements.

When India, or indeed any country, enters into security-based talks with Pakistan, the issue of how Pakistan can control its rogue elements and prevent them from tarnishing any deal, will need to be factored into the discussions. Given that Pakistan's democracy is newly established, it is unlikely to be able to give any reliable guarantees in this area. That alone may provide the Indian Government with a reasonable excuse for suspending the talks with Pakistan, now that it is politically expedient for them to do so.

INDO-PAKISTAN BORDER

India shares 3323 km long and complicated boundary with Pakistan. The India-Pakistan boundary is categorised under three different heads. The first is the international boundary also known as the 'Radcliff line'. It is 2308 km long and stretches from Gujarat to parts of Jammu district in Jammu and Kashmir. The second is the line of control (LoC), or the Cease Fire Line, which came into existence after the 1948 and 1971 wars between India and Pakistan. This line is 776 km long, and runs along the districts of Jammu (some parts), Rajouri, Poonch, Baramula, Kupwara, Kargil and some portions of Leh. And the third is the actual ground position line (AGPL), which is 110 km long and extends from NJ 9842 to Indira Col in the North. The LoC and the AGPL has been a scene of constant tensions with border skirmishes and firing between the armies and border guarding forces of both countries. The LoC has been vulnerable to constant infiltration by foreign terrorists, Kashmiri separatists and Pakistani army regulars for long.

Like the Bangladesh boundary, the India-Pakistan boundary also does not follow any geographical barrier. It runs through diverse terrain like deserts, marshes, plains, snow clad mountains, and winds its way through villages, houses and agricultural lands making it extremely porous. Porosity of this border has facilitated various illegal activities such as smuggling, drugs and arms trafficking, and infiltration. Heroin and fake Indian currency are the two predominant items of smuggling along this border. Other items include saffron, textile, mercury, which are smuggled from Pakistan. The villagers adjacent to the border are alleged to be involved in smuggling in a big way. Money laundering is also quite rampant along the border. A large scale hawala network is flourishing in Punjab, especially in Ludhiana. In addition, the border population has also been subjected to hostile propaganda by Pakistan designed to mislead and sway their loyalties. The Sir Creek area, due to its peculiar terrain, makes the movement of border guarding forces very difficult and thus, provides scope for illegal fishing in the creeks.

Future Options for Declaration of the Dispute

Over the past fifty years, besides the UN resolutions, observers and intellectuals have proposed various other options for resolving the Kashmir dispute time and again at the UN fora and at the bilateral India-Pakistan levels.

UN Resolutions: The Plebiscite Option

The UN Security Council resolutions of August 13, 1948 and January 5, 1949, proposed the plebiscite option for resolving the Kashmir dispute. However, it is important to note that the Government of India itself accepted *plebiscite* or *referendum* as a right of the Kashmiri people, when it filed the initial complaint against Pakistan before the United Nations on January 1, 1948, as pointed out in Part I of this paper. Beginning with Governor General Mountbatten, Indian leaders like Prime Minister Nehru also repeatedly made the commitment to 'the will of the Kashmiri people'.

After India filed its initial complaint, the UN Security Council passed the two important resolutions of August 13, 1948 and January 5, 1949. These resolutions laid down the principles and procedures for a free and impartial plebiscite under UN auspices. Broadly, the resolution of January 5, 1949, stated: '(a) the question of the accession of the State of Jammu and Kashmir to India and Pakistan, would be decided through the democratic method of a free and impartial plebiscite after the cease-fire and truce agreement provided for in the Resolution of August 13 had been carried out;

(b) the Secretary General of the UN would nominate a Plebiscite Administrator, who would be appointed by the government of Jammu and Kashmir and given powers which he considers necessary for holding a free and impartial plebiscite; (c) on implementation of the ceasefire and the truce agreement, the Commission and the Plebiscite Administrator would determine, in consultation with the Government of India, the final disposal of Indian and State Armed Forces, as well as the Forces in Azad Kashmir (in consultation with the local authorities); (d) persons who had entered the State since August 15, 1947 would be required to leave the State, and citizens of the State who had left the State on account of disturbances would be allowed to return.'

Both India and Pakistan accepted the above UN Resolutions. However, later, differences arose over the interpretation of various clauses of the resolutions, especially on the issues of demilitarisation and disbandment/disarming of the 'Azad Kashmir' forces.

India gave its own interpretation to the agreement and suggested that the Azad Kashmir forces be disbanded and the defence and administrative responsibility of the region be given to India and Indian Kashmiri authorities. Pakistan, on the other hand, was in favour of a complete and simultaneous withdrawal of armed forces personnel by both the countries.

On this issue, the President of the Security Council, General McNaughton, in his proposal of December 22, 1949, in para 2, clarified that the Resolutions of 1948 and 1949 called for demilitarisation of the whole State of Jammu and Kashmir and not merely Azad Kashmir: that 'demilitarisation should include the withdrawal from the State of Jammu and Kashmir of the regular forces of Pakistan; and the withdrawal of the regular forces of India not required for purposes of security or for the maintenance of local law and order.'

The UN Security Council passed Resolution 80 on March 14, 1950, which called upon the Governments of India and Pakistan 'to prepare and execute within a period of five months from the date of this resolution a programme of demilitarisation on the basis of the principles of paragraph 2 of General McNaughton's proposal, or of such modifications of those principles as may be mutually agreed.' Pakistan accepted that Resolution as well, but India maintained its position as regards the demilitarisation issue.

The UN Security Council passed Resolution 98, in December 1952. The UNSC Resolution, regarding demilitarisation issue clarified that: (Article 4) 'the Governments of India and Pakistan to enter into immediate negotiations under the auspices of the United Nations representative for India and Pakistan in order to reach agreement on the specific number of forces to remain on each side of the cease-fire line at the end of the period of demilitarisation, this number to be between 3,000 and 6,000 armed forces remaining on the Pakistan side of the cease-fire line and between 12,000 and 18,000 armed forces remaining on the India side of the cease-fire line.'

Though during the discussions Pakistan's representative to the UN, Mr. Zafrulla Khan, pointed out that the number of forces proposed was not fair, yet he said that Pakistan 'is prepared to go forward on the basis of this resolution.' The Indian representative, Mrs. Pandit, in her speech, however, categorically said, 'I should like to repeat that we reject the proposal in it and we are not prepared to enter into any talks on the basis suggested.'

Regarding the question of plebiscite, Pakistan was in favour of giving complete authority to the UN for holding, organising and supervising the plebiscite.

India, on the other hand, only wanted the non-binding advice of the UN. Various UN mediators were appointed to resolve this issue, but no one was successful in convincing India on a compromise.

Sir Owen Dixon, the UN mediator, in his report submitted in 1950, wrote: 'In the end I became convinced that India's agreement would never be obtained to demilitarisation in any such form, or to provisions governing the period of plebiscite of any such character, as would in my opinion, permit of the plebiscite being conducted in conditions sufficiently guarding against intimidation and other forms of influence and abuse by which the freedom and fairness of the plebiscite might be imperilled.' Dr. Frank P. Graham, appointed UN representative for India and Pakistan in 1951, submitted five reports, up to March 1953, but his efforts at mediation also proved to be unsuccessful as India would not agree on the size of the forces to be left on either side of the cease-fire line after demilitarisation. India, therefore, consistently refused to take recourse to all proposals of various statesmen and UN representatives for the holding of a plebiscite in Jammu and Kashmir. On the other hand, it is on record that Pakistan supported all such international mediation and UN efforts.

Defending the Indian position on plebiscite, Sisir Gupta, an Indian scholar, wrote: 'it became obvious even at the early stages of the Kashmir dispute that a plebiscite -an "ideal" solution according to some – because of the complexities in Kashmir was difficult to accomplish. Even as a democratic solution, it had loopholes. Kashmir, clearly, is not composed of one people: in religion, it has three major groups; in language, four. If there is a section which wants to secede from India, there are others who do not.' However, the fact of the matter is that, right from the beginning, India feared that if a plebiscite was held it would lose what it had already occupied. According to a Kashmiri activist, Prof. Mrs. Shamim Shawl, 'plebiscite is the most plausible solution of the problem. This has been accepted in the Resolutions of August 48 and January 1949. It is these resolutions, which confirm the disputed character of the problem and negate the Indian position that says Kashmir is an irrevocable part of India. India is in fact challenging the rightful and legal authenticity of the United Nations by delaying the implementation of UN resolutions.'

Keeping in view the basic genesis and nature of the dispute, the option incorporated in the then UN resolutions is still valid. The UN resolutions are not time-barred, as observed in 1956, by the UN Secretary General, Dag Hammarskjold, who clarified the important principle that 'the UN decision is valid until it has been invalidated by the organ which took it.'

The UN Trusteeship Option

Generally, this option proposes that Kashmir should be placed under UN Trusteeship and then plebiscite may be held for the final resolution of the dispute. It is argued that this will provide a face-saving for India, and will also give Kashmiris, on both sides of the Line of Control, enough time to come up with a joint option. The JKLF Chairman, Ammanullah Khan in December 1993, proposed: (1) complete, simultaneous withdrawal of Indian and Pakistani troops and civil administration, non-Kashmiri personnel from Jammu and Kashmir; (2) the reunification of Indian and Pakistani-controlled parts of Kashmir; (3) placement of the State under UN control for five to ten years; and (4) holding of a plebiscite. Well-known Pakistani economist, the late Dr. Mahbubul Haq, in an interview he gave to an Urdu Weekly *Hurmat*, in 1994, proposed that only the Kashmir Valley be placed under UN Trusteeship for ten years and then plebiscite be held in the Kashmir Valley.

As India regards Occupied Kashmir as its integral part, it is obvious that it will never voluntarily agree to the placing of the State, or the Kashmir Valley under UN trusteeship. *Secondly*, both the above trusteeship options support the plebiscite option under the UN auspices, an option that has been rejected by India even though in the early years of the dispute India committed itself to holding of the plebiscite.

As regards Pakistan and the Kashmiris, since the above proposals support a UN role and the option of plebiscite, in view of the already existing UN resolutions which provide the plebiscite option under UN auspices, the above proposal would mean unnecessarily prolonging the solution beyond five or ten years. Moreover, according to Article 76 of Chapter XII of the UN Charter one of the basic objectives of the trusteeship system is 'to promote the political, economic, social, and educational advancement of the inhabitants of the trust territories, and their progressive development towards self-government or independence, as may be appropriate to the particular circumstances of each territory and its peoples...' The case of Jammu and Kashmir does not require placement under UN trusteeship as the Kashmiris have, over the years, demonstrated their political will by waging an indigenous movement in Occupied Kashmir for their right of self-determination, underscoring the fact that their preferred option is self-determination.

The Partition Option

Regarding the option of the partition of Jammu and Kashmir, this has largely been an academic debate and various scholars have suggested different proposals. The *first* is a division-related option for Jammu and Kashmir, based on the holding of regional plebiscites.

This proposal was first given by UN Representative, Sir Owen Dixon, in his report of 1950-51. Called the 'Dixon Report', it proposed the idea of holding regional plebiscites, instead of a general plebiscite as proposed in the UN resolutions. The Owen Dixon Plan proposed the division of the State of Jammu and Kashmir into four main regions: Jammu, Ladakh, the Vale of Kashmir including Muzaffarabad, and Gilgit-Baltistan. According to his plan the district of Poonch was to remain with Pakistan. He proposed that of the four regions, Jammu and Ladakh should go uncontested to India and the Northern Areas to Pakistan. He concluded that in the Valley a plebiscite might be held to decide about its future. Pakistan, did not outrightly reject the proposal, but was in favour of a general plebiscite in the whole of Jammu and Kashmir. India on the other hand regarded Jammu and Kashmir as a unit of the Indian Federation and thus was not in favour of any regional plebiscite.

The second partition proposal is an option based on a 'Trieste-type' solution. The Trieste issue, between Italy and Yugoslavia, arose as a result of the two World Wars. After World War I, Trieste and the adjoining areas, including the whole valley of the Adige river and Istria, went to Italy, but in 1945 it was claimed by Yugoslavia on the grounds that Italy was guilty of aggression against Yugoslavia. However, Trieste and its environs and the Gorzia region to the northwest (Zone A) remained under Anglo-American control and the southern portion (Zone B) was under the control of the Yugoslav troops. Finally, in 1954, Italy and Yugoslavia agreed to a partition and Zone A (including Trieste) was given to Italy and Zone B to Yugoslavia. Italy agreed to maintain a free port at Trieste. Later, the agreement was given a *de jure* status by the 1975 Treaty of Osimo between Italy and Yugoslavia.

The 'Trieste'-type option for Jammu and Kashmir proposes that the Valley along with some adjoining parts of Jammu and the Pakistani side of Kashmir (Azad Kashmir), be made an autonomous units, under India and Pakistan, respectively. The LoC would be a soft border between the two autonomous units. The remaining areas on both sides of the LoC may be merged with India and Pakistan, respectively. India and Pakistan would be required to withdraw their forces under UN supervision. Again, this proposal lacks viability, as it does not address either the genesis of the dispute, nor the complexities that have accumulated since then to date. The struggle in Jammu and Kashmir is not for autonomy of any one region but for the right of self-determination to be expressed by the Kashmiris, as granted to them under UN resolutions. Also, India and Pakistan being parties to the dispute will continue to have a clash of interests in the proposed autonomous regions; therefore, this would certainly not result in any stability in the region. Moreover, the option implies that the existing Line of Control (LoC) may serve as the line of division. The LoC remains the UN-recognised ceasefire line (CFL) and was not drawn with any basis for serving as a permanent border, but with the intention of bringing about cessation of military hostilities.

The third partition proposal considers the conversion of the Line of Control (LoC) into an international border. This means maintenance of the prevailing *status quo*. This option is in principle supported by India. If it were accepted, India would take additional advantage by then propagating that it had conceded Indian territory to Pakistan and would try to emerge as a peacemaker in the region. As assessed by Robert Wirsing, 'by asserting the primacy of actual military *control* over punitive legal *entitlement*, it tacitly acknowledges India's dominant political standing in the region. By requiring Pakistan to relinquish its claim of the coveted Valley of Kashmir and the Kashmiri separatists their claim of independence, while at the same time entailing little or no detachment from India of territories now in its possession, it leaves existing political and economic arrangements essentially undisturbed. Thus, of the several conceivable forms of partition, it is clearly among the most generous to India.'

However, the 'the LoC as a border' option has to take into account the fact that the LoC is merely a ceasefire line, as well as take stock of the struggle for the right of self-determination that is going on in the Indian-held Kashmir. Moreover, Kashmiris do not recognise the LoC. Prof. Mrs. Shamim Shawl, a Kashmiri scholar from Srinagar, has argued that 'the proposal of division is in contravention of the basic principle that Jammu and Kashmir is an indivisible entity. It also violates the fundamental fact that the Kashmir problem is basically the problem of the people of Jammu and Kashmir. It is not a bilateral problem between India and Pakistan. Nor is it a territorial dispute.' Secondly, the present LoC is an altered ceasefire line, whereby India acquired territory through military aggression in 1971. Therefore, accepting LoC would mean legitimising Indian military aggression. Thirdly, the LoC as accepted by both Pakistan and India at Simla in 1972 does not exist anymore. Indian incursion into Siachen in 1984 has destroyed the sanctity of the ceasefire line.

Fourthly, some Western scholars have proposed the partition of Kashmir along ethnic/cultural, religious, and linguistic lines. For example the *Kashmir Study Group,* a US-based group comprising academics and diplomats from various countries as members, has made various proposals along these lines in its report entitled, *Kashmir: A Way Forward* (September 1999). The proposals suggested are as follows:

(a) Two hypothetical sovereign entities, self-governing in all aspects, established on both sides of the Line of Control on cultural and linguistic grounds. According to the study, 'On the Indian side of the LOC every tahsil in Kashmir proper and in Doda district in Jammu, and Gool Gulab Ghar tahsil in Udhampur district in Jammu would seek incorporation in the proposed state. All these areas are imbued with "Kashmiriyat" or interact with Kashmiri speaking people. On the Pakistani side it is conceivable that the whole of Azad Kashmir would opt to have a sovereign status. This is predominantly Punjabi-speaking, wholly Muslim area';

(b) A new sovereign state on the Indian side of LoC with no territorial exchange between India and Pakistan. The state would include 'within its maximum potential area the whole of Kashmir proper as well

as adjoining areas in which Kashmiri is either the majority language or that of a plurality of the population';

(c) Desirable territorial changes along and beyond the Line of Control in Jammu and Kashmir.

Viewing that 'LoC is dysfunctional and has been violated innumerable times', it proposes that a new state be created with territorial exchanges between India and Pakistan. However, it proposes that Pakistan gives almost twice as much area (7,366 sq. km) to India, than India ceding territory (4,501 sq. km) to Pakistan. The rationale given for such an exchange is ' overall, the territorial adjustments should not be excessively disruptive of the established order and yet should appear significant and be of such a nature as to allow all parties to claim a victory.'

The above proposals are again not viable solutions, as they tend to complicate the situation in Jammu and Kashmir and result in a further division of the region, rather than leading to a stable solution. Moreover, the 'Kashmir Study Group's' proposals make no provision for the right of self-determination of the people of Kashmir to which presently a military struggle is underway by the Kashmiris in Indian-occupied Kashmir.

The Independence Option

An option gradually evolved as a result of the impasse on the Kashmir issue is that of independence, generally known as the 'Third Option'. Under this option, the pre-Partition status of the Jammu and Kashmir State is to be restored and an independent state established.

The proposal is mainly advocated by the JKLF. Its Chairman, Amanullah Khan, in one of his articles says, 'the future independent Kashmir is to be neutral, like Switzerland, with friendly and trade relations with all its neighbours.'

According to Amanullah Khan's proposal, 'Independent Kashmir is to consist of five federating units: Kashmir Valley, Jammu province, Ladakh, Azad Kashmir and Gilgit-Baltistan, each enjoying considerable internal autonomy, having its own elected provincial government. At the centre there will be a bicameral parliament.' He further says, 'the re-unification and independence of the state can be brought about without making any drastic changes in the existing socio-economic, political and administrative structures of any of the present three units i.e. Indian occupied areas, Azad Kashmir and Gilgit-Baltistan.'

According to Indian scholars 'independence, either for part or all of J&K, is equally unrealistic.

They maintain that although an artificial product of war, the Line of Control does follow a rough and ready ethno-cultural divide in some measure.

Further, "self-determination" within the two parts of J&K could result in the Balkanisation of a mosaic put together by history, with every new 'self-determined' minority being assailed for a newly-created majoritarianism, which lesser minorities refuse to accept. Such an unravelling would be a recipe for strife, insecurity, and destabilisation of the region.'

The option for an independent Jammu and Kashmir state does not seem to be a viable solution, as the State would be land-locked and, therefore, permanently dependent on its neighbours. For India the proposition would be unacceptable because it could lead to a similar unravelling in other areas where separatist movements are going on in India.

As regards Pakistan, the 'third option' can be advantageous. An independent Jammu and Kashmir state would have a preference for good relations with a neighbour that has consistently extended its support to the principles of self-determination. Pakistan's position on the 'third option' has been that it should not confound the existent problems further, and, therefore, it stresses the need to address the issue in the light of the Security Council Resolutions, as a first step in the resolution of the dispute.

The Irish Model

Recently, various scholars have suggested the Irish model, based on the 'Good Friday Agreement' signed in April 1998 between the Governments of the United Kingdom of Great Britain and Northern Ireland and the Government of Ireland, as a possible option for resolving the Kashmir dispute between India and Pakistan.

The main features of the 'Good Friday Agreement' are: (a) it recognises the consent principle: that change in the status of Northern Ireland can only come about with the consent of the majority of its people. It acknowledges that while a substantial minority in the North and a majority on the island want a united Ireland, the majority in the North currently wishes to maintain the Union. However, it says that if that situation changes, there is a binding obligation on both governments to give effect to whatever wish the people of the North express; (b) it recognises 'the birthright of all the people of Northern Ireland' to identify themselves and be accepted as Irish, British or both; (c) it proposes concrete legislative and constitutional changes; such as, the Government of Ireland Act, claiming British jurisdiction over all of Ireland is to be replaced, future polls in the North on its status are to be held on the order of the Secretary of State for Northern Ireland. Such polls must be at least seven years apart; (d) it proposes a 108-member Assembly elected by proportional representation; (e) it establishes a North-South Ministerial Council under legislation at Westminister and the Oireachtas, to bring together ministers from the North and the Republic; (f) it establishes a British-Irish Council consisting of representatives of the British and Irish Governments, devolved in situations in Northern Ireland, Scotland and Wales, the Isle of Man and the Channel Islands; (g) it establishes a new British-Irish Conference; (h) reaffirms commitment to the total disarmament of all paramilitary organisations, and confirms intention to work constructively with the Independent Commission on Decommissioning; and, (i) establishes an independent commission to make recommendations for future policing arrangements in the North.

Based on the Irish model, some Indian scholars have made suggestions supporting autonomy for various regions of Jammu and Kashmir. For example, Amit A. Pandya, an Indian scholar, has proposed the following steps: (1) An India-Pakistan commission to discuss boundary issues in Jammu and Kashmir, and to engage in joint monitoring of the LOC; (2) Phased demilitarisation at the LOC, contingent first on substantial cessation of 'cross-border' terrorism; (3) Three-way (Indian, Pakistani, Kashmiri) commission on internal law and order. Kashmiris to be chosen from Pakistan-occupied Azad Kashmir and all Indian-occupied segments—Valley, Jammu and Ladakh. (4) Indian and Pakistani commitments to proceed with a scheme of local government reform and strengthening of local institutions and local autonomy in respective areas of Kashmir. (5) Issue-specific consultative bodies (water, power, tourism, finance) comprising such local units, and Indian Jammu & Kashmir State and Azad Kashmir governments. (6) Regularly scheduled and publicity-free consultative mechanism for Indian government's talks with all parties, and with non-party civil society institutions, within Indian Kashmir on political issues. (7) Corresponding mechanism for Azad Kashmir. (8) Consultative mechanism for talks among all parties on ethnic and religious minority protections. (9) Consultative mechanism for dialogue between these processes on the Indian and Pakistani side of the LOC. (10) Indian commitment to allow free access, consistent with security requirements, to independent and credible Indian human rights monitoring organizations, and to Indian, and Pakistani press. Corresponding commitment by Pakistan for Azad Kashmir.

Another Indian scholar, Professor Sumantra Bose, basing his suggestions on the Irish model proposes three dimensions. *Dimension one: the New Delhi-Islamabad axis,* involving the 'establishment of a permanent India-Pakistan Intergovernmental Conference to promote the harmonious and mutually beneficial development of the totality of relationships between the two countries.' As suggested by Professor Bose, this body is to be chaired by the respective prime ministers, and its twice-yearly meetings to be rotated between Indian and Pakistani cities. *Dimension two: the New Delhi-Srinagar and Islamabad-Muzaffarabad axis,* here the 'objective in Kashmir would be the gradual, incremental normalisation of politics within Kashmir in both Indian-and Pakistani-controlled zones, and the devising and implementation of political frameworks which can foster a working degree of internal accommodation and cooperation between the representatives of communities holding radically different basic political allegiances.' *Dimension three: the Srinagar-Muzaffarabad axis,* proposes 'along with the progressive normalisation of the overall framework of India-Pakistan relations and the gradual normalisation of life and politics in both sides of the Kashmir border', that there is greater need to make the border porous. He further suggests 'the establishment of a cross-border Jammu and Kashmir Council for Cooperation, with representatives from inclusive, elected and autonomous governments from both sides of the line of control.'

These Indian proposals, selectively use the Irish model, but basically support autonomy for the regions of Jammu and Kashmir under the supervision of India and Pakistan. The central aspects focusing on self-determination and total disarmament after implementation of the agreement are ignored. The Indian proposals are similar to the idea of a condominium with dominant Indian influence. Also, the LoC has been proposed as the dividing line and a soft border. This is against the genesis of the Kashmir dispute, which is not for greater autonomy or 'self-government', as proposed, but for the right of self-determination to be expressed by the Kashmiris. However, as Dr. Mazari has suggested, it is the central aspects of the Irish model, which are relevant in case of the Kashmir dispute and could be used as guiding principles for a resolution of the conflict. For instance the underlying principle is *recognition of the right of the people as of Northern Ireland* to choose their political future through a referendum. Also, the principle of deweaponisation is linked to it, as following the implementation of the Agreement.

3

Radcliffe Line

The Radcliffe Line was announced on 16 August 1947 as a boundary demarcation line between India and Pakistan upon the Partition of India. The Radcliffe Line was named after its architect, Sir Cyril Radcliffe, who as chairman of the Border Commissions was charged with equitably dividing 175,000 square miles (450,000 km^2) of territory with 88 million people.

BACKGROUND

On 15 July 1947, the Indian Independence Act 1947 of the Parliament of the United Kingdom stipulated that British rule in India would come to an end just one month later, on 15 August 1947. The Act also stipulated the partition of the Provinces of British India into two new sovereign dominions: the Union of India and the Dominion of Pakistan.

Before partition, some 40% of the area of India was covered by princely states. These states were in subsidiary allianceswith the British, who were responsible for their external affairs, but they were not British possessions and did not form part of British India. Thus, the British could not grant them independence, nor partition them. The Indian Independence Act abandoned the suzerainty of the British Crown over the princely states and dissolved the Indian Empire, so that the rulers of the states found themselves fully independent and were free to decide for themselves whether to accede to one of the new dominions or to remain independent. In the event, almost all decided quickly to join India or Pakistan. A small number did not. Pakistan was intended as a Muslim homeland, while the new India was secular with a Hindu majority.

Muslim-majority British provinces in the north were to become the foundation of Pakistan. The provinces of Baluchistan (91.8% Muslim before partition) and Sindh (72.7%) were granted entirely to Pakistan.

However, two provinces did not have an overwhelming majority — Bengal in the north-east (54.4% Muslim) and the Punjab in the north-west (55.7% Muslim). The western part of the Punjab became part of West Pakistan and the eastern part became the Indian state of East Punjab, which was later divided between a smaller Punjab State and two other states. Bengal was also partitioned, into East Bengal (in Pakistan) and West Bengal (in India). Following independence, the North-West Frontier Province (whose borders with Afghanistan had earlier been demarcated by the Durand Line) voted by a narrow margin in a controversial referendum to accede to Pakistan, despite a boycott by the most popular Pukhtun movement in the province at that time.

The Punjab's population distribution was such that there was no line that could neatly divide Hindus, Muslims, and Sikhs. Likewise, no line could appease the Muslim League, headed by Jinnah, and the Indian National Congress led by Jawaharlal Nehru and Vallabhbhai Patel, and by the British.

Moreover, any division based on religious communities was sure to entail "cutting through road and rail communications, irrigation schemes, electric power systems and even individual landholdings." However, a well-drawn line could minimize the separation of farmers from their fields, and also minimize the numbers of people who might feel forced to relocate.

As it turned out, on "the sub-continent as a whole, some 14 million people left their homes and set out by every means possible — by air, train, and road, in cars and lorries, in buses and bullock carts, but most of all on foot — to seek refuge with their own kind." Many of them were slaughtered by an opposing side, some starved or died of exhaustion, while others were afflicted with "cholera, dysentery, and all those other diseases that afflict undernourished refugees everywhere". Estimates of the number of people who died range between 200,000 (official British estimate at the time) and two million, with the consensus being around one million dead.

Process and Key People

A crude border had already been drawn up by Lord Wavell, the Viceroy of India prior to his replacement as Viceroy, in February 1947, by Lord Louis Mountbatten. In order to determine exactly which territories to assign to each country, in June 1947, Britain appointed Sir Cyril Radcliffe to chair two Boundary Commissions—one for Bengal and one for Punjab.

The Commission was instructed to "demarcate the boundaries of the two parts of the Punjab on the basis of ascertaining the contiguous majority areas of Muslims and non-Muslims. In doing so, it will also take into account other factors."

Other factors were undefined, giving Radcliffe leeway, but included decisions regarding "natural boundaries, communications, watercourses and irrigation systems", as well as socio-political consideration. Each commission also had 4 representatives—2 from the Indian National Congress and 2 from the Muslim League. Given the deadlock between the interests of the two sides and their rancorous relationship, the final decision was essentially Radcliffe's.

After arriving in India on 8 July 1947, Radcliffe was given just 5 weeks to decide on a border. He soon met with his fellow college alumnus Mountbatten and travelled to Lahore and Calcutta to meet with commission members, chiefly Nehru from the Congress and Jinnah, president of the Muslim League. He objected to the short time frame, but all parties were insistent that the line be finished by the 15 August British withdrawal from India. Mountbatten had accepted the post as Viceroy on the condition of an early deadline. The decision was completed just a couple of days before the withdrawal, but due to political manoeuvring, not published until 17 August 1947, two days after the grant of independence to India and Pakistan.

Problems in the Process

Boundary-making Procedures

All lawyers by trade, Radcliffe and the other commissioners had all of the polish and none of the specialized knowledge needed for the task. They had no advisers to inform them of the well-established procedures and information needed to draw a boundary. Nor was there time to gather the survey and regional information. The absence of some experts and advisers, such as the United Nations, was deliberate, to avoid delay. Britain's new Labour government "deep in wartime debt, simply couldn't afford to hold on to its increasingly unstable empire." "The absence of outside participants—for example, from the United Nations—also satisfied the British Government's urgent desire to save face by avoiding the appearance that it required outside help to govern—or stop governing—its own empire."

Political Representation

The equal representation given to politicians from Indian National Congress and the Muslim League appeared to provide balance, but instead created deadlock. The relationships were so tendentious that the judges "could hardly bear to speak to each other", and the agendas so at odds that there seemed to be little point anyway. Even worse, "the wife and two children of the Sikh judge in Lahore had been murdered by Muslims in Rawalpindi a few weeks earlier." In fact, minimizing the numbers of Hindus and Muslims on the wrong side of the line was not the only concern to balance. The Punjab Border Commission was to draw a border through the middle of an area home to the Sikh community. Lord Islay was rueful for the British not to give more consideration to the community who, in his words, had "provided many thousands of splendid recruits for the Indian Army" in its service for the crown in World War I. However, the Sikhs were militant in their opposition to any solution which would put their community in a Muslim ruled state. Moreover, many insisted on their own sovereign state, something no-one else would agree to.

Last of all, were the communities without any representation. The Bengal Border Commission representatives were chiefly concerned with the question of who would get Calcutta. The Buddhist tribes in the Chittigong Hill Tracts in Bengal had no official representation and were left totally without information to prepare for their situation until two days after the partition.

Perceiving the situation as intractable and urgent, Radcliffe went on to make all the difficult decisions himself. This was impossible from inception, but Radcliffe seems to have had no doubt in himself and raised no official complaint or proposal to change the circumstances.

Local Knowledge

Before his appointment, Radcliffe had never visited India and knew no one there. To the British and the feuding politicians alike, this liability was looked upon as an asset; he was considered to be unbiased toward any of the parties, except of course Britain. Only his private secretary, Christopher Beaumont, was familiar with the administration and life in the Punjab. Wanting to preserve the appearance of impartiality, Radcliffe also kept his distance from Viceroy Mountbatten.

No amount of knowledge could produce a line that would completely avoid conflict; already, "sectarian riots in Punjab and Bengal dimmed hopes for a quick and dignified British withdrawal". "Many of the seeds of postcolonial disorder in South Asia were sown much earlier, in two centuries of direct and indirect British rule, but, as book after book has demonstrated, nothing in the complex tragedy of partition was inevitable."

Haste and Indifference

Had the Commission been more careful, gaffes in the division could have been avoided. For example, there were instances where the border was drawn leaving some parts of a village in India and some in Pakistan. Since he had just a month, Radcliffe saw little point in being careful to skirt villages. His border was drawn right through thickly populated areas instead of between them. There were even instances where the dividing line passed through a single house with some rooms in one country and others in the other.

Radcliffe justified such casual division with the truism that no matter what he did, people would suffer. The thinking behind this justification may never be known since Radcliffe "destroyed all his papers before he left India".

He departed on Independence Day itself, before even the boundary awards were distributed. By his own admission, Radcliffe was heavily influenced by his lack of fitness for the Indian climate and his eagerness to depart India.

The implementation was no less hasty than the process of drawing the border. On 16 August 1947 at 5:00pm, the Indian and Pakistani representatives were given two hours to study copies, before the Radcliffe award was published on the 17th.

Secrecy

To avoid disputes and delays, the division was done in secret. The final Awards were ready on 9 August and 12 August, but not published until two days after the partition.

According to Read, there is some circumstantial evidence that Nehru and Patel were secretly informed of the Punjab Award's contents on August 9 or 10, either through Mountbatten or Radcliffe's Indian assistant secretary.

Regardless of how it transpired, the award was changed to put a salient east of the Sutlej canal within India's domain instead of Pakistan's. This area consisted of two Muslim-majority tehsils with a combined population of over half a million. There were two apparent reasons for the switch: (1) the area housed an army arms depot and (2) contained the headwaters of a canal which irrigated the princely state of Bikaner, which would accede to India.

Likewise, it is not known how Radcliffe was persuaded to award the Chittagong Hill Tracts to Pakistan. This came as a shock to Patel and Nehru who had assumed the areas would be awarded to India since they were 98% non-Muslim.

Similarly, the decision to award India the Muslim-majority districts of Murshidabad and Malda in Bengal was kept so secret that the inhabitants hoisted the Pakistani flag there till the award was made public on 17 August 1947.

The truth of how these decisions were made may never be known, since Radcliffe destroyed all of his records and Mountbatten expressly denied any special-knowledge or favouritism.

Implementation

After the partition, the fledgling governments of India and Pakistan were left with all responsibility to implement the border. After visiting Lahore in August, Viceroy Mountbatten hastily arranged a Punjab Boundary Force to keep the peace around Lahore, but 50,000 men was not enough to prevent thousands of killings, 77% of which were in the rural areas.

Given the size of the territory, the force amounted to less than 1 soldier per square mile. This was not enough to protect the cities much less the caravans of the hundreds of thousands of refugees who were fleeing their homes in what would become Pakistan.

Both India and Pakistan were loath to violate the agreement by supporting the rebellions of villages drawn on the wrong side of the border, as this could prompt a loss of face on the international stage and require the British or the UN to intervene.

(This did not prevent them from getting into immediate conflict over the former princely state of Kashmir, as this territory was not a part of the Radcliffe agreement.)

Border conflicts led to three wars, in 1947, 1965, and 1971, as well as the May 1998 dual tests of nuclear weapons and the Kargil conflict of 1999.

Disputes along the Radcliffe Line

There were two major disputes regarding the Radcliffe Line, the Chittagong Hill Tracts and the Gurdaspur District. Minor disputes evolved around the districts of Malda, Khulna, and Murshidabad of Bengal and the sub-division of Karimganj of Assam.

Chittagong Hill Tracts

Chittagong Hill Tracts had a majority non-Muslim population of 97% (most of them Buddhists), but was given to Pakistan. The Chittagong Hill Tracts People's Association (CHTPA) petitioned the Bengal Boundary Commission that, since the CHTs were inhabited largely by non-Muslims, they should remain within India. Since they had no official representation, there was no official discussion on the matter, and many on the Indian side assumed the CHT would be awarded to India.

On 15 August 1947, many of the tribes did not know to which side of the border they belonged. On 17 August, the publication of the Radcliffe Award put the CHTs in Pakistan. The rationale of giving the Chittagong Hill Tracts to Pakistan was that they were inaccessible to India and to provide a substantial rural buffer to support Chittagong (now in Bangladesh), a major city and port; advocates for Pakistan forcefully argued to the Bengal Boundary Commission that the only approach was through Chittagong.

Two days later, the CHTPA resolved not to abide by the award and hoisted the Indian flag. The Pakistani army dealt with the protest but its polemic somewhat remains with some of its non-Muslim majority arguing for its cessation.

Gurdaspur District

Under British rule, the Gurdaspur district was the northernmost district of the Punjab Province of British India. The district itself was administratively subdivided into four tehsils: Shakargarh, Gurdaspur, Batala, and Pathankot. Of the four, only Shakargarh Tehsil, which was separated from the rest of the district by the Ravi river, was awarded to Pakistan and became part of Sialkot District within the West Punjab province of Pakistan.

The rest of the district, retaining the name Gurdaspur, became part of India's East Punjab state. The division of the district was followed by a population transfer between the two nations, with Muslims leaving for Pakistan and Hindus and Sikhs leaving for India.

The entire district of Gurdaspur had a plurality of Muslims, which was a majority when counting the Ahmadiyya community as Muslim. Ahmadiyya were counted as Muslim even though they had been declared non-Muslim by Muslim clergy.

The district was home to a large concentration of Ahmadiyyas, their cultural centres, and their spiritual centre Qadian. In the

1901 census, the population of Gurdaspur district was 49% Muslim, 40% Hindu, and 10% Sikh. At the time of partition, the census showed the following distribution of Muslims and non-Muslims:

Part of district	*Majority*	*% Muslim (including Ahmadiyya)*
Shakargarh tehsil	Muslim	51%
Gurdaspur tehsil	Muslim	51%
Batala tehsil	Muslim	53%
Pathankot tehsil	non-Muslim	33%
Entire District (all four tehsils)	Muslim	50.6%
Area awarded to India	non-Muslim	less than 50%

It has been speculated that the following arguments were made before the boundary commission by Lord Mountbatten and others in favour of awarding much of Gurdaspur to India:

1. The territory would allow the kingdom of Kashmir to be contiguously accessible to India, so that its ruler could opt to integrate with the Indian Union.
2. Pathankot tehsil contained a direct railway link with the adjoining Hoshiarpur and Kangra districts of East Punjab.
3. Batala and Gurdaspur tehsils would provide a buffer to the Sikh holy city of Amritsar, whose district would otherwise be surrounded by Pakistani territories on three of its four sides.
4. If the area east of the Ravi river was considered as one block, it would have a slight non-Muslim majority. This block would consist of Amritsar and most of Gurdaspur district (excluding Shakargarh).
5. Also, by doing this, the majority of the Sikh population (58%) would fall into East Punjab; by doing the opposite, a slight majority would be left in Pakistan and this would increase the number of Sikh refugees.
6. This could help pacify the Sikh population who lost major tracts of lands in West Punjab.

Firozpur District

To counterbalance the relatively small share of Gurdaspur district awarded to Pakistan, Radcliffe attempted to instead transfer Firozpurand Zira tehsils in Firozpur district to Pakistan. This was opposed by the Maharaja of Bikaner because Harike headworks on the confluence of the Satluj and Beas rivers, from where a canal originated, the only source of water for his desert state was in Ferozepore.

It was only after he threatened Mountbatten, that he would accede his state to Pakistan if Firozpur was awarded to West Punjab, that the award was changed at the last minute and all of Firozpur district was awarded to India. ,

Malda District

Another disputed decision made by Radcliffe was division of the Malda district of Bengal. The district overall had a slight Muslim majority, but was divided and most of it, including Malda town, went to India.

The district remained under East Pakistan administration for 3–4 days after 15 August 1947. It was only when the award was made public that the Pakistani flag was replaced by the Indian flag in Malda.

Khulna and Murshidabad Districts

The entire Khulna District with a slight Hindu majority of 52% was also given to East Pakistan in lieu of the much smaller Murshidabad district with a 70% Muslim majority, which went to India.

Karimganj

Sylhet district of Assam joined Pakistan in accordance with a plebiscite. However, the Karimganj sub-division with a Muslim majority was severed from Sylhet and given to India. As of the 2001 Indian Census, Karimganj still has a Muslim majority of 52.3%.

4

New Facets in India-Pakistan Relations

The terrorist attacks of September 11, 2001 in New York and Washington have had profound implications on developments in India-Pakistan relations. The American led offensive against the Taliban resulted in an end to Taliban rule and the installation of a democratically elected Government headed by President Hamid Karzai in Afghanistan.

But, the Taliban, the Al Qaeda and their allies affiliated to the "International Islamic Front" formed by Osama bin Laden in February 1998, retreated into safe havens across the Afghanistan-Pakistan border. They set up base in Baluchistan and the tribal areas (North and South Waziristan) of Pakistan's Northwest Frontier Province. While Pakistan assisted the US and its western allies in tracking down some Al Qaeda leaders, the Taliban leadership was not touched.

It has now regrouped and commenced attacking American led NATO forces in Afghanistan's Southern and Eastern Provinces, adjacent to Afghanistan's borders with Pakistan. One major impact of the removal of the Taliban from power and the passage of UN Security Council Resolution 1363 was the decision by western powers to ban all those organizations affiliated with Osama bin Laden's "International Islamic Front".

The organizations that were thus banned included four extremist Islamist groups backed by Pakistan's Inter Services

Intelligence (ISI) that were playing a leading role in terrorist violence in Jammu and Kashmir (J&K) The terrorist organizations banned internationally included the *Lashkar e taiba*, the *Harkat ul Mujahidee* n, the *Harkat ul Jihad ul Islami* and the *Jaish e Mohammed*. While these organizations continue to operate under new names, the Pakistan Government came to realize that mere resort to terrorist violence in an attempt to force India out of J&K was proving counterproductive and that political initiatives had to be undertaken, if the international community was to be persuaded of Pakistan's commitment to ending terrorist violence and normalizing relations with India.

These developments have resulted in a sustained dialogue between India and Pakistan over the past three years, to enhance cooperation and promote confidence. An agreement has been signed on prior notification of missile tests and measures to avoid incidents at sea between the two navies are being finalized.

New border routes have been opened for travel between the two countries and travel between the two sides of Jammu and Kashmir between Srinagar and Muzzafarabad has resumed after lapse of nearly half a century. It has been agreed for the first time to promote trade across the LOC in J&K. Similar travel arrangements are envisaged between Poonch in the Jammu Region and Rawalkot across the LOC. India has proposed further easing of restrictions for travel between the two sides of Jammu and Kashmir by opening bus routes between Kargil and Skardu in the isolated "Northern Areas" of the State. Most importantly, a cease fire across the Line of Control has been observed by both sides since November 2003.

It was in this background that President Musharraf stated that progress could be made in resolving the issue of J&K only if both sides explore mutually acceptable proposals. He has proposed that J&K should be divided into seven different regions, followed by the "demilitarization" of identified regions. He has specifically demanded that Indian forces should be withdrawn from the urban centres of Baramulla, Kupwara and Srinagar. President Musharraf has also advocated "self governance" in J&K without clarifying whether such "self governance" would be equally applicable to areas under Pakistan's control. Finally, he has proposed that there should be a system of "Joint Management" of Jammu and Kashmir by India and Pakistan. While welcoming "new ideas" from President Musharraf, India's Prime Minister Dr. Manmohan Singh has proposed that while borders cannot be changed they can be made "irrelevant" or just "mere lines on a map".

He has said that people of both sides of the Line of Control (LOC) in J&K should be allowed to move and trade freely across the LOC. Responding to General Musharraf's proposal of "Joint Management", Dr. Manmohan Singh has suggested that India and Pakistan should devise "cooperative and consultative mechanisms" to promote cooperation across Jammu and Kashmir. Discussions between India and Pakistan on these proposals have been taking place in recent months. Measures to resolve the issue of J&K figured prominently for the first time when the Foreign Secretaries of India and Pakistan met in New Delhi in November 2006. New Delhi appears to be ready to discuss General Musharraf's proposal for "selfgovernance" and would be quite prepared to discuss greater devolution of powers and autonomy in a manner under which there is harmonization in the nature and extent of self-governance and devolution of powers on both sides of the LOC in J&K. At the present moment, the State of J&K under Indian Administration enjoys far greater autonomy than the regions of "Azad Kashmir" and the "Northern Areas" under Pakistan's control. Both "Azad Kashmir" and the "Northern Areas" are directly administered by governing "Councils" presided over by the Prime Minister of Pakistan who wields his authority through the Federal Ministry of Kashmir Affairs. Local representatives of these areas have virtually no powers, even in the appointment of Government functionaries.

Given Pakistan's continuing assistance to armed terrorist groups functioning out of Muzzafarabad in "Azad Kashmir" under the banner of a "United Jihad Council" India cannot obviously agree to any proposal for the "demilitarization" of areas it presently governs in J&K. Moreover, J&K lies on the vital lines of communications to India's western borders with China. Free movement and deployment of India's forces in J&K is, therefore, essential for the security of its frontiers with China. But, should Pakistan effectively ban and disarm groups waging *"Jihad"* in Jammu and Kashmir from territory under its control, India could consider redeployment and reduction of its forces in J&K, provided Pakistan takes corresponding measures on its side of the LOC, both in "Azad Kashmir" and the "Northern Areas'.

These are issues that appear to have figured in both formal and informal discussions between India and Pakistan in recent months. While these "new ideas" for resolving Jammu and Kashmir have figured prominently in discussions and have been the focus of extensive media attention, one has to inject a sense of caution and realism on the path ahead. President Karzai has made no secret of his conviction that the Musharraf Government is actively aiding, arming, training and providing safe haven for the Taliban on Pakistani territory. There are, similarly, strong sentiments in India that the Pakistan Government continues to use terrorism as an instrument of State policy to promote its interests and territorial ambitions. The revival of the Taliban has encouraged Pakistan based terrorist groups like the *Lashkar e Taiba* that the climate is ripe to promote *Jihad* not merely in Jammu and Kashmir, but in other parts of India also.

Further, if borders are indeed to be made "irrelevant" as proposed by Dr. Manmohan Singh then Pakistan will have to remove existing trade and economic restrictions on relations with India and join with other South Asian countries in SAARC to make South Asia and Economic Community for the free movement of goods, services and investment within the next fifteen years. Pakistan appears to be totally averse to moving in this direction. There is thus a climate of continuing uncertainty about the directions Pakistan's policies will take in coming months. Much will depend on political developments within Pakistan in coming months. Both India and Afghanistan will have to wait and see whether the post-election political scenario in 2007 in Pakistan results in moderate elements opposed to religious extremism taking over the reins of Government, or whether the Islamist elements in the army and in the political set up will retain their hold over the conduct of Pakistan's policies.

PAKISTAN'S POLICY IN THE CHANGING SCENARIO

The events of 9/11, the attack on the Indian parliament, and the following war-like situation between India and Pakistan not only greatly impacted the Kashmiri resistance movement but also compelled Islamabad to change its track on Kashmir. Moreover, the unfriendly international environment and Pakistan's deep involvement in Afghanistan forced Islamabad to rethink its relations with India and its Kashmir policy. The decision of General Pervez Musharraf to join the US-led War on Terror was also a factor in changing Islamabad's strategic position on Kashmir, particularly in terms of its ideological foundation. The economic condition of the country, unrest in the tribal areas, and — allegedly externally sponsored — violence in some parts of Balochistan, and the growing engagement along the Afghan border also played an instrumental role in bringing about a paradigm shift in Islamabad's thinking towards India. It is also said that Pakistan's trusted friends, like China and Saudi Arabia, advised it to seek an unconventional way out for a lasting deal with India over the Kashmir issue and bilateral relations; besides, constant persuasion from the United States also continued.

Pakistan's capacity to protract the low cost conflict in Kashmir is beyond any doubt. Although the likely spillover effects of this on Pakistan's polity are obvious, they will be, to a great degree, manageable. On the other hand, despite its conventional military superiority and strong diplomatic backing from the world, India could not subdue the resolve of Pakistan to support Kashmir's right to self-determination and its demand for sovereign equality with India. Pakistan's ties with the United States, and its role as an ally of the West, are considered advantageous for seeking a settlement of the Kashmir issue. As the country's former Foreign Secretary Shamshad Ahmad observed:

> We cannot deny the post-9/11 reality that our "friends," the Americans, now have deeper than ever stakes in India-Pakistan rapprochement as a factor of stability for regional and global peace.

The 'covert' US engagement with Islamabad, Delhi and Kashmiris is no longer a secret. Washington has expressed its desire at a number of times to help settle the Kashmir issue within the existing territorial parameters but with minor realignment. It views India as a potential rival to China, not only in the region but also in global affairs. Siddharth Srivastava, a New Delhi-based journalist, observes:

The US is striving to build India as a strategic counterweight to China, along with Japan and Australia.

Termed as naïve by critics, Pakistan's calculations of the ground realities are optimistic, being based on the belief that India will never be able to bring normalcy into Kashmir because Kashmiris are highly skeptical towards it, and that India will need Pakistan's support and will ultimately make tangible transformations in its current stance over Kashmir. The majority of Kashmiris do not trust the Indian government and, ever since the eruption of the resistance, their aspiration for the right of self-determination has multiplied manifold and now cuts across even the hardcore pro-India circles in the Kashmir Valley. India's carrot and stick tactics and the brutalities of its forces have alienated the local population and invoked armed resistance, which may not die down easily. It is this assessment of the situation that emboldened Islamabad to make tangible concessions on Kashmir and bring India to the table for talks. Some also believe that the personal ambition of the President Musharraf — his wish to be regarded in history as a statesman who settled one of the world's most complicated disputes — is a driving factor that has brought essential changes in Islamabad's policies.

Besides various other factors that caused India and Pakistan to change their policies on the Kashmir issue, back channel diplomacy led by the US played a major role in alleviating the crisis and creating a viable atmosphere for initiatives towards a comprehensive normalization process.

Change in India's Approach

For a long time, India's approach for dealing with Pakistan had revolved mainly around zero tolerance in any concerns related to India's security or political ideology. However, its inability to 'punish' Pakistan and to break its back economically (by creating a war-like environment in the region) had a sobering impact on the Indian mindset and led New Delhi to conclude that its conventional policies vis-à-vis Pakistan and Kashmir were getting nowhere. In the past, New Delhi had publicly pronounced several times that it would take punitive action and destroy what it alleged were militant training camps inside Azad Jammu and Kashmir (AJK) by air strikes. However, its hostile attitude did not yield the desired results and Islamabad did not succumb to its pressure.

At the same time, economic tycoons and multinational companies were pressuring the Indian government to normalize relations with Islamabad as hostile relations between the two neighbors and the constant fear of war had a negative impact on business activity and international investment. New Delhi needed peace in the region and internal stability to continue its current annual growth rate of 8-10 percent and obtain further foreign investment. As one researcher on the peace process put it:

Improved relations would lead to improved trade: there was money to be made, and this had become a strategic objective for both Islamabad and New Delhi.

India realized that its successful economic journey would cease if it did not settle disputes with Pakistan. It had to think about the immense potential in bilateral trade and in trade with landlocked Afghanistan and Central Asia via Pakistan. Besides, India aspires for a permanent seat in the UN Security Council for which it had to ensure friendly relations with neighbors and settle the Kashmir issue in the context of which India is regarded among those countries that did not comply with the UNSC resolutions. Moreover, the Kashmir resistance poses a huge financial burden on the Indian treasury. It is also acknowledged that the Indian security forces do not have the capacity to fix the problem; rather, they invite anger by frequently committing severe human rights violations that aggravate the already complex situation.

After the withdrawal of Indian forces from the Pakistani borders, Pakistan made a chain of unilateral concessions pronounced by President General Musharraf himself. It began with a unilateral ceasefire on LoC announced by Prime Minister Zaffarullah Khan Jamali in November 2003. In the following month, speaking to *Reuters*, General Musharraf said he had "left aside" the 55-year-old demand for a UN mandated plebiscite on Kashmir and wished to meet India "halfway" in a bid for peace in the subcontinent.

These multiple pulls created a sense of obligation among the Indian ruling elite to at least take some measures to show that they were serious about settling the problems. Eventually, the Indian Prime Minister Atal Behari Vajpayee went to Kupwara in the south of the Kashmir Valley and offered a hand of friendship to Pakistan in April 2004. This was regarded a departure from the conventional Indian thinking on Kashmir and Pakistan, and paved the way for further initiatives on Kashmir. It also created a palatable environment for Vajpayee to visit Islamabad to attend the South Asian Association for Regional Cooperation (SAARC) summit.

Musharraf's 'Out of the Box' Thinking

Islamabad has consistently said that it supports the resistance in IHK diplomatically and politically, and has nothing to do with the armed struggle. It has also invariably linked talks with India with progress on the Kashmir settlement. But it relinquished both of these stands in the quest to find a compromised solution. Pakistan accepted the responsibility to rein in militants operating from areas under its control. It also pledged to stop all kinds of cross-border activities from Azad Kashmir. Pakistan had never acknowledged the armed resistance in IHK as terrorism, but astonishingly, it ceded even this stance and conceded to the Indian interpretation of the movement. As a retired former Ambassador aptly commented:

This amounted to an admission of its guilt and was unprecedented in that Pakistan unilaterally took on a responsibility that was not only almost impossible to honor, but even more importantly, it was given without any reciprocal obligation by the other side.

To further the shift in policy, the Pakistani President articulated his ideas on Kashmir for the first time while speaking to journalists during an *iftar*dinner held in Islamabad in October 2004. Although he said these were "off the cuff" ideas, the nature of the proposals on the Kashmir settlement that he forwarded suggests that he had in mind a well-conceived and thought-out plan, on which he was gauging feedback. The crux of the proposals is outlined below:

- Identify seven regions, demilitarize them, and change their status before looking for possible options to resolve the dispute.
- The status quo in Kashmir is unacceptable and the LoC cannot be a solution to the lingering dispute.
- As a starting point for a step-by-step approach on the option of demilitarization, the regions on both sides of the LoC need to be analyzed for local culture and demographic composition. After identifying these regions, there could be gradual demilitarization, following which the two sides could discuss who should control these areas.
- Pakistan and India could also have joint control of these areas or the United Nations could be asked to play a role.

Later, Musharraf dilated upon his ideas with the *CNBC* anchorperson, Karan Thapar, on January 8, 2006. He suggested the concept of self-governance and joint management of the entire Kashmir area. In his words, "self-governance is more than autonomy but less than independence. In other words, both India and Pakistan will keep the parts of Kashmir they control but under their joint management. Self-governance is devolved to the Kashmiris, independence being firmly ruled out."

The interviewer, Karan Thapar, afterwards elaborated this concept in his article, saying, "...The self-governance would apply to the full state of Jammu and Kashmir as it existed in 1947. This means it would be implemented in Northern Areas (Gilgit Baltistan). Additionally, the border within old Kashmir state would be open and thus irrelevant."

Subsequently, Musharraf had a comprehensive discussion on his proposals with the noted Indian lawyer and journalist, A. G. Noorani, who published it in the Indian magazine *Frontline* on August 12-25, 2006. Later on, President Musharraf also spoke to *NDTV* on similar ideas, going further to clearly articulate his position as follows:

- Kashmir will have the same borders but people will be allowed to move freely back and forth in the region;
- The region will have self-governance or autonomy, but not independence;
- Troops will be withdrawn from the region in a phased manner
- A joint supervision mechanism will be set up with India, Pakistan and Kashmir represented in it.

The proposals offered by Musharraf sent clear signals that: a) Islamabad was ready to compromise its traditional stance that the people of Kashmir will decide their destiny through free and fair plebiscite; b) Indian and Pakistani sovereignty would remain as it currently was at the end of the day; c) The LoC would be irrelevant, except as a line on a map to demarcate both parts of the state; d) Self-governance or self rule would be granted to both parts of Kashmir and joint management established.

Pakistan's proposals paved the way to move forward on a slightly faster track as India did not view them as being against its strategic or political interests. Previously, Pakistan had banked on the UNSC resolutions that guaranteed the right of self-determination to the Kashmiris, besides recognizing Pakistan as a principal party to the dispute. Musharraf relinquished these positions unilaterally without seeking any quid pro quo. In other words, he came close to almost acknowledging the Indian claim that Kashmir could not be receded from the Union. India also tactfully rephrased its traditional stance that "J&K is its integral part" in more acceptable language, now asserting that "Borders cannot be redrawn but any kind of solution could be acceptable to India." Musharraf agreed to this proposition while rejecting the status quo and showed willingness to embrace some kind of joint management of the state.

Moreover, Pakistan accepted the pro-Indian Kashmiri leadership's role in the future dispensation and changed its position that only the All Parties Hurriyat Conference (APHC) should be the representative of Kashmiri people in the negotiation process. President Musharraf said that the President of the National Conference, Omer Abdullah, and Mahbooba Mufti had a role to play in the Kashmir political landscape. This gesture comforted the Indian establishment as Pakistan's demands were in line with their own views and interests.

These major departures from the traditional stance made Musharraf a good bet for India to deal with Pakistan on Kashmir and settle other issues broadly allied to Pak-India trade and access to markets in Central Asia and Afghanistan.

A Review of the Composite Dialogue

The dialogue process between Islamabad and New Delhi is slowly progressing despite several ups and downs. It is often said that the continuation of the process is in itself a success because, in the past, the two countries have been unable to remain engaged in a sustainable dialogue. However, the substance of the process and prospects of its success need to be analyzed.

Until February 1994, India and Pakistan were engaged in sporadic dialogues that always ended with zero progress. This is why both countries formally suspended dialogue in 1994. Islamabad's approach was to settle the Kashmir issue first, after which the other problems would get settled almost automatically, whereas India was interested in dilating first on other issues, such as trade and travel. Eventually, to bridge the gap between the two positions, both governments agreed to address all political and territorial issues simultaneously, including Jammu and Kashmir. Consequently, the foreign secretaries of the two countries met in Islamabad and resumed the stalled dialogue process in June 1997. They institutionalized the process by identifying eight areas to deliberate upon and established working groups to make progress on each issue separately but simultaneously.

This entire process was called off when the Kargil confrontation occurred. As discussed earlier, post-9/11 events also contributed in the stalemate between the two countries. Later, in 2004, India and Pakistan launched a renewed peace process aimed at resolving all their longstanding disputes. However, the Kashmir dispute still dominates over other issues. Even after voicing his new approaches, President Musharraf said that if progress on Kashmir could not make headway, the entire process would be back to square one. Recently, Prime Minister Shaukat Aziz has underscored the settlement of Kashmir as a precondition for further progress on other related disputes as well as for offering trade and business opportunities to India.

Since January 2004, both neighbors have been engaged on two different levels. The first is the official level, at which concerned officials from both sides meet periodically and report their progress to foreign secretaries, who meet to review the outcome and discuss the Kashmir, peace and security issues, before, finally, the foreign ministers meet to take stock of developments and set the rules for further dialogue. The second level of engagement is back-channel diplomacy. Pakistan's National Security Secretary, Tariq Aziz, who is known to be a close aide of President Musharraf, and India's S. K. Lamba, former High Commissioner to Pakistan, are engaged in a serious dialogue. However, it has been said that only five people in Pakistan are truly in the loop on the actual state of bilateral negotiations. Therefore, no one can really assess the behind-the-curtains activities or predict the contours of solutions.

So far, at the official level, both countries have completed four rounds of a composite dialogue. This process received a dent when the Mumbai train blasts on July 11, 2006 caused a postponement in the foreign secretary-level talks. India blamed elements from Pakistan for their involvement in the blasts but no evidence was provided by the Indian government to Pakistan. This decision was in violation of the joint statement, issued on April 18, 2005, by the leaders of Pakistan and India, which states that, "Terrorist acts would not be allowed to derail the peace process." Eventually, sanity prevailed and the stalled process was resumed in November 2006. Likewise, in February, the Lahore-bound Samjhauta Express became a target of bomb blasts that killed 68 passengers, most of whom were Pakistani. Islamabad reacted with caution and did not allow the peace process to derail, despite the immense loss of its citizens' lives. The question does arise how New Delhi would have reacted had Indian citizens been the victims.

The fourth round of composite dialogue was held in Islamabad on March 13-14, 2007, with a focus on the Jammu and Kashmir dispute and peace and security. In the context of peace and security, the two sides discussed a wide range of issues relating to their conventional and nuclear military capabilities and reviewed the entire process. The Pakistani team sought India's response to President Musharraf's "ideas" on the resolution of the Kashmir issue and emphasized the need for forward movement on Jammu and Kashmir, saying it was time to move from confidence-building measures to dispute resolution.

Among related issues, Pakistan pushed for early finalization of the agreements on speedy return of inadvertent line crossers; quarterly flag meetings of the sector commanders at the LoC; and liberalization of the visa regime. Pakistan also proposed some new cross-LoC confidence building measures, including allowing sports activities and launch of helicopter and postal services between Srinagar and Muzaffarabad.

In addition, Pakistan tabled a new proposal on anti-ballistic missiles. Siachen, Sir Creek and economic cooperation were among the other issues discussed.

Following are the significant consensus points of the fourth round of foreign secretary-level talks:

- After years of reluctance, Pakistan agreed to the Indian proposal of launching a bus service between Kargil and Skardu in the Northern Areas.
- It was agreed that a truck service between Srinagar and Muzaffarabad would be launched in a few months;
- It was agreed that the Joint Committee of Retired Judges, set up to look into the prisoners issue, would begin its work soon and suggest ways to ensure the humane treatment of Indian prisoners in Pakistani jails and Pakistani prisoners in Indian jails;
- The two countries agreed to conclude an agreement on "No Development of New Posts and Defense Works" along the LoC and proposed drafts for new border control guidelines along the International Border;
- The two sides agreed to work on finalizing a liberalized visa regime, including a proposal for group tourism.

Although the meeting could not settle the problem of demilitarizing Siachen, it was able to narrow down differences on some elements. The political leadership of both countries appears optimistic about resolving this issue in the days ahead.

Likewise, the formation of a Joint Counter-Terrorism Mechanism is also a significant development. India has long blamed Pakistan for any terrorist activities occurring on its territory. The Mechanism offers an opportunity for thorough investigation of incidents prior to the pronouncements of conclusions. However, it was reported in sections of the Pakistani and Indian press that Islamabad seeks to keep the armed resistance in J&K out of the ambit of the Joint Anti-Terrorism Mechanism. At a joint press conference with the Indian Foreign Secretary Shivshankar Menon, his Pakistani counterpart, Riaz Mohammad Khan, said that Jammu and Kashmir was "disputed" and should not be "mixed" with the initiatives that are between India and Pakistan only. The visible achievement of the four rounds of foreign sectaries' level dialogue is the initiation of a Srinagar-Muzaffarabad bus service and, of late, the opening of entry points along the LoC for civilian crossing. Although the 42-month dialogue process has not yielded the desired results, both the governments seem to be closer to agreements on a number of issues.

Besides, the two countries have also exchanged some proposals through the back channel on the settlement of the Jammu and Kashmir dispute. However, very few people of the two governments are fully aware of what is going on behind the scene. Concerned citizens and the general public on both sides know virtually nothing. This makes the back channel process vulnerable: nobody knows how stakeholders and the public will react when the solution is finally made public.

India's Mixed Response

Initially, the Indian leadership was quick to turn down President Musharraf's proposals on Kashmir, making it clear that sharing the sovereignty of Jammu and Kashmir with Pakistan was out of the question. However, due to the host of factors outlined above, it eventfully realized that it had to reciprocate and take the proposals into serious consideration.

The Indian Prime Minister made some reconciliatory remarks that encouraged pro-settlement forces in Kashmir and Pakistan. India resumed the negotiation process with APHC's Mirwaiz faction and also held meeting with Sajjad Ghani Lone, Chairman of the People's Conference and to the leader of Jammu & Kashmir Liberation Front (JKLF), Yasin Malk. The Indian Prime Minster held three Kashmir-related roundtables with the pro-India leadership of IHK and formed five working groups to seek recommendations on various issues.

The pro-independence leadership was also invited but it did not participate, demanding that a separate meeting be held with it instead of a joint sitting with pro-India politicians. Notably, President Musharraf personally encouraged the pro-independence APHC leadership to join talks with India and Pakistan separately, as this would be a step in the direction of trilateral talks. There is a feeling in a large section of the Indian establishment and public opinion that Pakistan has narrowed down its position and come closer to that of India's, despite its use of different jargon and nuances.

It is interesting to note that, in the last two years, Indian Prime Minister Manmohan Singh has spoken on his vision of how to settle the Kashmir issue several times. On March 24, 2006, in Amritsar, he argued for a step-by-step approach and commencement of dialogue with the people "in their areas of control" to improve the quality of governance. Regarding the future status of the LoC, he said that it might eventually become a mere line on a map, and that people might be able to visit and trade freely. He made a departure from his government's earlier stated position by acknowledging that the "the two parts of Jammu and Kashmir can, with the active encouragement of the governments of India and Pakistan, work out cooperative consultative mechanisms so as to maximize the gains of cooperation." He also offered a treaty of friendship between India and Pakistan.

Subsequently, at the Second Round Table Conference held in Srinagar in May 2006, the Indian Prime Minister indicated that he might take some institutional arrangements to bring people from both sides of the LoC closer to each other. While meeting with a APHC Conference delegation in New Delhi, he said India might create an environment in which a person could live in Srinagar or Muzaffarabad without any legal restriction. He reiterated that India was willing to move beyond its stated position, and expressed his openness to any ideas that might contribute to the ongoing thought process.

Finally, speaking to a meeting of Indian businessmen in New Delhi, Prime Minister Manmohan Singh repeated his hope for a treaty of peace and friendship with Pakistan and emphasized the need for linkage among South Asian states for economic development. This was the second time he had spoken of such a treaty in the period of about a month.

Just one month earlier, he had initiated his idea of a treaty of peace and friendship at a public rally in Amritsar. Echoing the same line a few days earlier, the Indian External Affairs Minster Paranab Mukarjee had said that India had to be prepared for some give and take in the border talks with China and Pakistan and should be prepared to shun rigid claims of national sovereignty if the talks were to be meaningful.

These pronouncements indicate that the Indian leadership is willing to have a phased-out formula for the resolution of the Kashmir issues. Nevertheless, it is neither relinquishing Indian sovereignty over Jammu and Kashmir, nor ready to trade off territory. At the end of the day, the people of Jammu and Kashmir may have de facto reunification of the state, which will give them psychological satisfaction. Apart from Monmohan Singh's reconciliatory remarks, a number of other key political stakeholders, such as Mufti Muhammad Sayyed's People's Democratic Party (PDP), National Conference, and APHC's Mirwaiz faction all support the Islamabad approach on Kashmir with slightly varied interpretations.

In this context, the Indian government has adopted a policy of engaging both Kashmiris and Pakistan in the dialogue process, separately but simultaneously. It suggests that New Delhi has attached huge expectations to an internal agreement with the people of Kashmir, giving relatively less importance to the external factor. However, it recognises the significance of people-to-people contacts across the LoC and, therefore, agreed to initiate the Srinagar-Muzaffarabad bus service and allowed Kashmiri leaders to travel on it to Muzaffarabad in July 2005. It has also given relatively better political space to the Mirwaiz faction of APHC and frequently facilitated its travel outside the country.

On the other hand, a number of Indian officials and commentators are restlessly following the beaten track of bitterness, continuing to hurl accusations at Pakistan with no regard for the emerging environment. Officials in India's top echelons quite frequently use isolated events to accuse Pakistan of terrorism without offering any substantial evidence. At times, Islamabad's sincerity is questioned. For instance, according to Satish Chandra, former Deputy National Security Advisor to the Indian government:

Is the military in Pakistan sincere in wanting good relations with India? Pakistan's engagement in the current dialogue process is due to compulsion of external pressures and military exigencies which have tied up substantial Pakistani forces on the West.

In April 2005, when Musharraf visited New Delhi, both the gov-ernments made announcements that the peace process was irreversible and no incident would be permitted to derail it. But immediately after the Mumbai bomb blasts, New Delhi called off the dialogue process and stalled the foreign secretary-level talks for almost three months. Indeed, New Delhi left no stone unturned to prove that Pakistan was a haven for terrorists and was involved in promoting terrorist networks inside India, particularly in the occupied Jammu and Kashmir. Satish Chandra observed:

Pakistan's involvement in terrorism is well-known. It is not limited to Jammu and Kashmir, but extends to several parts of India, including the northeast. One of my major concerns was that in many parts of India, including New Delhi, we are a hair's breadth away from a major terrorist attack.

In view of such contradictions, it may be assumed that either opinion within the Indian establishment is divided on the future course of action, or New Delhi has a well-defined, official double-edged policy of conducting talks with Islamabad and, at the same time, continuing its blame game to keep the latter under pressure. It is possible that New Delhi wishes to maintain tactical ambiguity to keep both pro- and anti-peace process forces confused with mixed signals. Such an approach also allows the Indian government to drag its feet on the peace process whenever it desires.

It appears that India does not care if its stance sends negative signals to the people of Pakistan, or if it reinforces the argument before them that Delhi is not responding to Musharraf's flexibility, even in diluted form. On the other hand, Musharraf has consistently applauded Vajpayee and Manmohan Singh, calling them statesmen, but the Indian leadership has never reciprocated the gesture. Musharraf has earned a lot of appreciation across the world for his efforts to solve the Kashmir problem but this too has made little impression on the Indian establishment.

Some leading Indian opinion makers believe that Pakistan had no option but to comply with Indian demands. This view has been echoed by former Indian Prime Minister Inder Kumar Gujral in the following words:

What options does he [Musharraf] have? His country faces innumerable problems. He also finds India growing taller and taller. His friends, the Americans, have told him not to rock the boat.

Thus, the process of reconciliation and the blame game are continuing simultaneously, indicating that the Indian establishment has yet to enter true reconciliation mode. Naturally, several questions arise about this complex Indian attitude. The answer primarily lies in the changed ground realities; for instance, back and forth movement across LoC has admittedly gone down, while militants are no longer a major threat to the security forces. Moreover, with the tacit approval of Islamabad, the fencing of the LoC has been completed without any real hassle. The unfaltering commitment on the part of Pakistan to respect the ceasefire along the LoC is a further encouraging factor. Inside Kashmir, the APHC stands divided into two factions and one of them, headed by Mirwaiz Omer Farooq, is in touch with Indian interlocutors, seeking a compromised settlement of the issue within the Indian Union.

New Stakeholders

Recently, Kashmiri domestic politics took a dramatic turn when the President of the pro-India National Conference, Omar Abdullah, made a striking demand. He said that no solution for Kashmir was possible without the involvement of Hizbul Mujahideen (HM) in the dialogue process. He urged India and Pakistan to hold talks with the United Jihad Council and HM's chief, Syed Salauddin.

Besides Omer Abdullah, the PDP chief Mehbooba Mufti has also consistently advised New Delhi to bring HM on board. JKLF leader Yasin Malik, known as the pioneer of militancy, also sets dialogue with HM as a precondition to a peaceful resolution of the Kashmir dispute. Moreover, a number of intra-Kashmir dialogue conferences organized by the Centre for Dialogue and Reconciliation, Delhi, have persistently been arguing for a seat for militants in the ongoing process.

HM has welcomed the suggestion for the first time in its 17-year armed resistance. Its inclusion in the dialogue has become a bipartisan demand of the Kashmiri stakeholders, cutting across the political divide. However, several questions arise regarding HM's future course of action. It is a fact that HM has played an instrumental role in highlighting the Kashmir issue by rendering huge sacrifices. It commands immense respect and credibility among the masses. Its chief, Syed Salauddin, is a household name in Kashmir and is regarded as one of the most trusted leaders of the state.

CBMs: A Blank Cheque for HR Violations

Despite a number of Confidence Building Measures (CBMs), the articulation of positive statements in the top echelons of the two countries, and several rounds of high level tête-à-tête between Indian and Pakistani officials, there has not been even a slight decline in the level of human rights violation in Indian-held Kashmir. Fake encounters and disappearances are still staged. The violations are so high that even the pro-Indian mainstream, along with the "separatist parties" — as India calls them — are up in arms against the government and security forces on this issue.

In the context of the ongoing peace process, it was not a misplaced expectation that, at least to improve its democratic image, the Indian government would take special measures to ensure respect for human rights and stop indiscriminate killings of civilians in the state. It was also necessary to get public support for the ongoing dialogue process. But events show that human rights abuses have actually doubled and random killings continue as a routine matter in IHK. It is quite surprising that the world community does not let a single opportunity slip to condemn human rights violations by resistance outfits but is silent on the acts of barbarism committed by the forces.

The Indian brutalities fuel feelings of vengeance among Kashmiris and invite more violence, which helps in providing fresh blood to the dissidents. It should be borne in mind that, in the initial years, the character of the resistance movement was not violent or communalized as it later became. However, even peaceful protests were dispersed with gunfire. The Indian forces imprisoned all renowned political figures and ceased all avenues for the peaceful and non-violent components of the struggle. Eventually, not only the youth but also professionals and the political leadership were dragged into armed struggle. These views were echoed in the editorial comments of the Jammu-based *Kashmir Times* on January 5, 2005:

The poor track record of Indian forces on human rights front, which includes not just physical torture but also the mental trauma and agony of being looked upon with suspicion and subjected to every day humiliation in one's own home by a man in uniform who is for all practical purposes an outsider, thus becomes a major source of spread of militancy in its fanatic form, as is evident today.

Given, Kashmiri leaders often say that the current Indian strategy is aimed at crushing the Kashmiri struggle for self-determination under the disguise of parlays with Pakistan. This is why Indian forces are vigorously pursuing their military operations in the state. Secondly, as long as the two sides remain engaged in talks, the international community and human rights organizations will not voice any concerns lest it derail the dialogue process and spoil the atmosphere. Besides, Pakistan is consciously avoiding making human rights a point in the talks, fearing that it might annoy India to the extent that it backs out of the negotiations. India is taking undue advantage of this deliberate silence. On the other hand, it has practically given India a soft opportunity to suppress all the significant voices in the state.

It is also a known fact that the Indian armed forces have developed stakes in the J&K conflict. Over a period of time, they have developed a huge infrastructure and extract immense benefits from the festering wounds of Kashmir. They are entrusted with several draconian powers and prerogatives to conduct arbitrary operations and commit custodial killings. It is a proven fact that the security forces take money from local people through intimidation and threats.

Therefore, the huge military set-up in J&K has itself become a bottleneck in the peace process. Several Kashmir watchers believe that it was the military and intelligence establishment that compelled the Congress-led government to not budge from the Indian stated position on the issue. The ruling class in Delhi today also believes that Islamabad is on the receiving end and its game plan has been exhausted. So, eventually, the Indian writ on Kashmir shall be fully reestablished.

Dissident voices

Syed Ali Gilani, Chairman of his own faction of APHC, has emerged as a leading critic of the current peace process. He believes that the process is going to bury the Kashmir issue rather than settling it according to the people's wishes. His views have a strong following of politically aware lawyers, intellectuals, youth and women inside Kashmir. Apart from his political and religious ideology, he commands respect from all segments of Kashmiri society because of his firm stand on resolution of Kashmir according to the wishes of its people. Militant outfits, too, regard him as a source of aspiration. Hizbul Mujahideen, the largest indigenous militant outfit, has been especially under his influence since its inception. Armed groups, such as Lashkar and Jaish, have also expressed great respect for him. Because of his position within these outfits, he has emerged as one of the key influential leaders of the Valley. It is often said that he holds the key to the peaceful settlement of Kashmir.

On January 17, 2007 a strike was observed in the Valley to mark a protest against the visit of Mirwaiz Omer Farooq and his colleagues to Islamabad. Interestingly, however, public response to his recent strike call had been overwhelming, with the calling it a near to complete strike. This signifies the failure of the moderate APHC factions to take people into confidence. Mirwaiz visited Islamabad in January 19-27, 2007. He had meetings with President Pervez Musharraf twice and other government functionaries, besides sitting with a large number of political entities and Kashmiri parties. However, he could not get in touch with Syed Salahudin, the Hizbul Mujahideen commander-in-chief, as he declined to meet him. Likewise, in Azad Kashmir, apart from the ruling Muslim Conference, no other political party or civil society group supported the current formulation of the Kashmir settlement. Evidently, within Kashmiri opinion, the current moves do not enjoy reasonable support, which makes the entire process vulnerable and weak.

CURRENT SITUATION WITH PAKISTAN

The ongoing standoff with India is referred to as crisis instability which may flare-up every now and then. The CBMs are still unstable after 2002 standoff and will remain until a process in initiated. The Islamists in Pakistan do not want a 'flash in the pan' peace initiative with India but a comprehensive one where they are projected as the dominant side dictating the peace. Pakistan needs a 'win' against the non-Muslim India so that the Pakistan state and ashrafs gain as the sole winning political center of the subcontinent. This is supposed to create a tide towards Islam in the sub-continent and topple the Indian union. Since the defeat in Kargil some ex generals have even advocated stalemated defeat of India in such a way that a spin would be given to the Pakistan 'win'. With that event the honor and dignity of the Pakistan nation and its ideology is going to be restored and become dominant against non-Muslim ideology in the sub-continent. The dominance of the Islamic political center and its Pakistan ideology in the sub-continent is the long term goal of the ashrafs and its supporters for uniting with Bangladesh and Muslims of India. With the ideology of Pakistan still in dispute the future of Pakistan in the long term as a single political unit is in doubt.

Since the fourteenth century madaris have been the seats of learning, of interpretation of religious texts and the source of dialectical discourses about Islam. At their height they produced great scientists, mathematicians and scholars. Resistance to British rule, and subsequent anti-west attitudes, date from the division of religious and secular education in India when madaris took on the role of defending the Islamic educational tradition against the British formal education system of schools and colleges. They became the seat of Muslim resistance to British rule.

Pakistan- What kind of a state?

Since 1947 Pakistan had 13 Commanders-in-Chief/Chiefs of Army Staff.

1. Gen. Sir Frank Messervy (1947-1948) - A British

2. Gen. Sir Douglas David Gracey (1948-1951) A British

3. Gen. Muhammad Ayub Khan (1965 War Field Marshal) A Pathan

4. Gen. Muhammad Musa (1958-1966) A Baluch

5. Gen. Muhammad Yahya Khan (1966-1971) A Pathan

6. Lt. Gen. Gul Hassan Khan (1971-1972) A Punjabi

7. Gen. Tikka Khan (1972-1976) A Punjabi

8. Gen. Zia-ul-Haq (1976-1988) A Muhajir (Julundar)/Pathan (by domicile)

9. Gen. Mirza Aslam Beg (1988-1991) A Muhajir

10. Gen. Asif Nawaz Janjua (1991-1993) A Punjabi

11. Gen. Abdul Waheed Kakar (1993-1996) A Baluch

12. Gen. Jehangir Karamat (1996-1998) A Punjabi

13. Gen. Pervaiz Musharraf (1998-Present) A Muhajir

In the days of General Zia-ul-Haq the senior civil and military officers often made a public display of their religiousness to build their image and career.

Chairman of the Joint Chiefs of Staff Committee office was created on a permanent basis on March 1, 1976 with General Mohammad Sharif as the first incumbent (March 1976-October 1978). The chairman is designated as the senior-most military officer but has no operation control of the troops. Out of the 11 chairmen so far, nine came from the Army, one from the Navy (Admiral Sirohi) and one from the Air Force (Air Chief Marshal Farooq Feroze Khan). Two Army Chiefs (Jahangir Karamat and Pervez Musharraf) concurrently held the office. In the first week of October 1999, Admiral Fasih Bokhari resigned as the Naval Chief after the permanent appointment of Chief of Army Staff General Pervez Musharraf to the office of chairman by the then government of Nawaz Sharif. Admiral Bokhari was then the senior-most service chief. He decided to quit on account of a junior service chief's elevation as chairman.

The office of the Vice Chief of Army Staff does not exist on a permanent basis. When General Zia-ul-Haq combined the presidency with the command of the army, he appointed four Vice Chiefs of Army Staff. They were: Sawar Khan (April 1980-March 1984), KM Arif (March 1984-March 1987) and Mirza Aslam Beg (March 1987-August 1988). After his death in an air crash on August 17, 1988, General Aslam Beg was appointed as the Chief of Army Staff. It may be mentioned that Lt General (later General) Muhammad Iqbal Khan served as Deputy Chief of the Army Staff (July 1978-April 1980). He was made Chairman of Joint Chiefs of Staff Committee in April 1980.

General Pervez Musharraf who similarly combines presidency with the command of the army has appointed General Muhammad Yousuf (October 2001-October 2004) and now General Ahsan Saleem Hayat as the Vice Chiefs. The seniority is not the only criterion for appointment to the top slots in the military. Those making the decision also take into account an assessment of professional merit. This involves objective as well as subjective considerations. The officer's acceptability to the appointing authority is crucial to the appointment. In the present context, General Pervez Musharraf is the service chief as well as the head of state. He initiated the appointment procedure as the army chief and made the appointments as the president. The decision to bypass some officers rested with him.

On several occasions in the past, senior officers were bypassed for appointment of the army chief. Some of the well-known appointments of army chiefs that fall into this category include elevation of Generals Muhammad Musa (appointed in October 1958), Yahya Khan (appointed in September 1966), Gul Hassan (appointed in December 1971), Zia-ul-Haq (appointed in March 1976), Abdul Waheed Kaker (January 1993) and Pervez Musharraf (appointed in October 1998). There are also instances of appointment of the senior-most officers to the position. The most recent examples include Generals Aslam Beg (appointed in August 1988), Asif Nawaz Janjua (appointed in August 1991) and Jahangir Karamat (appointed in January 1996).

If you look at the list of past Army Chiefs the Muhajir(refugee) Army Chiefs have been the most aggressive against India and continue to be. Pakistan after 55 years of independence has seen a strong milady influence in the destiny of the country. It has emerged as a religious state and hardly as a nation state. Even though it has centrifugal forces and sub nationalism it has a strong political force which has held the nation together. It is a torn country and not a welfare state with the institution of the army being the most powerful influence sustained inside the country. In the beginning of the new century, its political life is splintered and enveloped in multiple crises. The existence of the national feelings is being challenged and economy is in shambles and poverty is soaring. Confronted with intense political divide, increasing economic problem, increasing social violence, terrorism and sectarianism, Pakistans sense of insecurity has deepened more than ever before.

Pakistan change of leadership has been closely connected to Indian political stability and perception. India was supposed to not survive as one country at the time of independence. But after 1957 election India stabilized as a democracy and Pakistan changed its strategy by making Ayub Khan as the administrator in 1958. The Pakistani elite figured out that India would be stable and only a strong military rule in Pakistan would prevent India from absorbing Pakistan. Also under Ayub the 1965 war was fought which disconnected Pakistan from India emotionally. This was the aim of most of the war between India and Pakistan. In 1977 India went through a change of government with Janata Dal coming over. This government was also stable enough that Pakistani elite figured out that an army rule in Pakistan would stabilize it. Zia took over the government with a coup against Bhutto in 1977. In 1999 after the Kargil war defeat the Pakistani elite and army sensed that the country seemed very unstable. Also the Indian government of Hindu right took power in India and was more stable. This made Musharraf and his army group to take over the government in a coup.

In 1971, Pakistan lost East Pakistan, which eventually became the independent state of Bangladesh. This might have happened regardless of India's attitude or actions because of the internal strains and the difficulty of maintaining a physically divided state. When India interfered, nevertheless, and claimed credit for the establishment of Bangladesh, it forced Pakistan into the realm of loss not only in terms of geostrategic factors, but also in terms of power and prestige. Pakistan reacted to this loss, first of all in 1972, by launching a military nuclear program. After India exploded a test nuclear device in 1974, Pakistan's sense of loss, or impending loss, became more acute, and it devoted significantly greater resources to its covert nuclear weapons program.

P.N. Dhar, in his memoirs, Indira Gandhi, the Emergency and Indian Democracy, explained what "final settlement" meant. After the breakdown of the formal Shimla talks, Indira Gandhi and Zulfiqar Ali Bhutto had decided to meet one last time. It was at this one-to-one meeting that the Shimla Agreement was born. In that meeting, Bhutto had apparently agreed verbally to change the nomenclature of the "cease-fire line" of 1948 into the "line of control" and promised that this would gradually acquire the "characteristics of an international border". This was to be the "final settlement". By 1976, Bhutto had reneged on his promise and was openly claiming that Kashmir was a dispute. In India, Emergency had been declared by then and Indira Gandhi was bogged down in domestic politics.

The second way that Pakistan pursued the return to its reference point of power and prestige after 1971 disgrace was to agitate for the removal of Kashmir from Indian control. Pakistan took significant risks for this policy even though Kashmir was never under its control, but Kashmir became a surrogate arena where Pakistan could fight to reestablish its sense of power in its relationship with India. These risks become even more frightening as the two states move closer to fully developed and open military nuclear programs. While the presence of nuclear weapons in the region frightens many, it might also act to decrease violent conflict in the region. Nevertheless, the number of crises in South Asia seems to have increased along with the movement of India and Pakistan towards nuclear weapons, and there were real war scares in 1987 and 1990.

Since the late 1970s, the Pakistan army has maintained a mutually profitable relationship with Islamic elements in the country. The Islam cists have offered two critical inputs to the military: they have provided armed manpower for the military's security agendas in the neighborhood, as in Afghanistan since 1979 and in India since 1989. And they have been ever ready to join hands with the military to undermine popularly elected and mainstream civilian governments inimical to the military's corporate view of Pakistan's interests in one way or another. Examples of the latter assistance proliferate. In 1977, the Nizam i Mustafa movement that shook Z A Bhutto's government and set the stage for the seizure of power by the military; in 1990 the Islami Jamhoori Ittehad came to the rescue of the military by thwarting Benazir Bhutto's bid to return to power after she had been sacked by President Ishaq Khan at the behest of General Aslam Beg; in 1999 during Nawaz Sharif's summit with Atal Bihari Vajpayee in Lahore, the mullahs rampaged on the streets of Lahore after the military determined that Mr. Vajpayee's "peace offerings" were not in Pakistan's interest. Kargil was the straw that broke the civilian government's back.

But that relatively stable equation was seriously jolted by what happened on and subsequent events in the region and beyond. Pakistan's military establishment was compelled by the United

States to abandon its Islamists friends or allies in and out of government in Afghanistan. This led to much heartache and even resentment among Pakistan's jihadi circles and their Al Qaeda friends who had taken refuge with them. The resentment was transformed into resistance when the military was compelled by the US to start targeting Al Qaeda elements and their supporters and sympathizers in Pakistan. The resistance then came to be focused on the person of General Musharraf who seemed to symbolize the gradual pro-West about-turn that Pakistan was taking under his leadership. Eventually a consensus solidified among all armed and unarmed Islam cists in Pakistan that General Musharraf was trying to make a permanent strategic virtue out of what had originally seemed to be temporary tactical vice. Certainly, by stressing the need for a moderate and enlightened Islam at peace with itself and with the rest of the world, including live and let policies with India, and insisting that the threat to Pakistan was internal rather than external, economic rather than political, General Musharraf seemed to be getting ready to cross the Rubicon. This "Islamists" consensus in the country was henceforth articulated at two levels: the insistence by the MMA that General Musharraf should be stripped off his army uniform forthwith; and renewed attempts by armed "Islamic" terrorists to assassinate him. How should General Musharraf respond to this threat?

One way of addressing this question is to ask what might happen to Pakistan in the event that General Musharraf is eliminated from the scene violently and unexpectedly. Clearly, the army could either reclaim all power under a new chief unilaterally "elected" by itself and go on to suspend or abrogate the constitution, prime minister and parliament. In the event, it could press ahead with General Musharraf's reformist agenda by cutting the "Islam cists" down for good in and out of state and government, thereby ensuring international support for the economy and keeping the country afloat; or the army could go the other way, strengthen its "Islamists" credentials by allying with the mullahs and jihadis, restore a state of hostility in the region and incur the wrath of the international community as a dangerous foe rather than uncertain friend. The latter option would obviously be disastrous from Pakistan's point of view. In the other post-Musharraf option, the army could retreat to the barracks and decide to exert covert power (as it decided to do in 1988 after General Zia's sudden exit) while enabling the MMA and PMLQ to join hands, thereby further enlarging the ideological and religious space available to the most reactionary elements in the country. This would be a most unstable arrangement and one that would eventually accentuate Pakistan's problems at home and abroad, a sort of slow rather than sudden death.

Dr Akbar Ahmed, Ibn Khaldun professor of Islamic studies at the American University, said religiously motivated acts, including the assassinations of sectarian rivals while they were praying in mosques were indicative of the "troublesome state of Islam" in Pakistan today. He said to understand this violence, fundamental questions about the role of Islam in Pakistan must be addressed. The answer to the question as to who is defining Islam in this way mirrors a historical cause-and-effect relationship that explains the reasons behind the radical view of the religion throughout Pakistan's domestic scene.

Dr Ahmed said Pakistan's prominence in the Muslim world stems from its large population, its nuclear status, its post- role in association with the United States, but most importantly from the perception held by most of its people since the country's creation that it is an Islamic state. Pakistan's creation, he added, was the result of a movement based on a clear Islamic vision and so the people of Pakistan continue to feel responsible for defining, guiding and shaping Islam. The fundamental question, nevertheless, for Pakistanis has been what version of Islam is real Islam. Each group has its own definition of Islam and there is no consensus on the "final version."

Going back into history, he said that Islam was first brought to Southeast Asia in the 8th century by Arabs who employed the doctrine of Ijtihad to reapply and *adapt the religion's fundamental principles to other cultures*. The inherent values of empathy and compassion in Ijtihad allowed for these civilizations to coexist, each respecting the other's culture and traditions. Citing the example of Aurangzeb and Dara Shikoh, he pointed out that while one espoused an exclusivist interpretation of Islam, the other advocated a mystical synthesis of the religion with the Hinduism. "This story represents a much larger clash within Islam," he added.

Dr Ahmed said the "exclusivist" approach to Islam emerges when the Pakistani society faces a threat and is put on the defensive. The same tension, he stressed, was reflected in the Pakistan movement. The Quaid-e-Azam, the father of Pakistan, favored the enlightened "Aligarh approach" but adopted a more exclusivist one as the movement struggled for success. He said the exclusivist model that had prevailed throughout Pakistani history, including today. The prevailing view in Pakistan that Islam is under siege is crystallized by the country's tense relationship with India, its non-Muslim neighbor. The "inclusionist" model of Islam has almost entirely faded in terms of state and official interpretation. This exclusivist model is marked by intolerance and strong anti-Westernism. He warned that Pakistani society would become more and more radicalized because the population believes that Islam is under siege. There is a belief in Pakistan amongst extremist elements that they should continue to hate and despise India, and that strengthens the ideological foundations.

Pakistan's core problem in the past three decades has been an elusive quest for a stable political order, in which relations amongst the political parties and between the armed forces and the political parties are governed by certain "rules of the game". It is the absence of these "rules of the game" that has resulted in internecine political warfare among Pakistani politicians and parties, with a "zero sum game" approach and a "winner takes all" outcome. As a consequence, the 1969, 1977 and 1999 military coups in Pakistan had the support of a large section of politicians, who viewed military take-over as an easy short cut to the removal of their rivals and paving their path to power.

Today's Pakistan is a military pretending its sponsor is a functioning state. The government shows little sense of responsibility for the welfare of the man on the street or the woman in the field. Pakistani identity succumbs when tribal, family, ethnic or regional rivalries come into play. The adjective "lawless" often is used to describe the vast Northwest Frontier Province adjoining Afghanistan. Yet that territory may be the strictest rule-of-law portion of the country — although the law is not one of ratified constitutions, but of Pukhtunwali, of the tribe, based upon religion and cultural traditions immune to modernity. Any foreign businessman can attest that the "lawless" parts of Pakistan are those most evidently under control of the government.

After, Gen. Musharraf's best chance was to recognize that Islamabad's Afghan policy had failed dangerously and to turn his back resolutely on those who had designed it. He and his supporters needed to purge the extremist elements that had crowded into the Inter Services Intelligence agency and, to a lesser extent, the military. Instead, Gen. Musharraf played musical chairs at the top, while leaving the radicalized field structures largely intact. *He now heads an internally divided government, in which some elements cooperate impressively with American counterparts, while others work to protect violent extremists and preserve terrorist networks.*

Despite his indefatigable sense of duty, the demands of his position have been too much for Gen. Musharraf. Meanwhile, the military, the ISI, and the rest of the government are torn between the very human anxiety to back the ultimate winner and loyalties to the state, to the institutional military, to self-perpetuating bureaucracies, to friends and allies hunted by America, to family and tribe, and to competing visions of Islam.

Could the Pakistani government do more in the war against terror? Certainly. But the military is terrified of breaking the long-standing patterns of doing business that have allowed the pretences of a state to continue. The military could move forcefully into the Northwest Frontier Province and Baluchistan, but it does not see the risk of casualties and bloody rebellion as worth taking just to please America's passing fancy. Pakistanis remember all too well that the U.S. walked away from them before.

East of the Indus, the government is willing to pursue known terrorists — particularly if they are not Pakistani nationals. But it has been unwilling to take a stand against the organized domestic extremists whose avowed goal is to remake Pakistan as a strict Islamic state and who sponsor violence to achieve their ends. All the while the mirage of a "liberated" Kashmir blinds Pakistan's leadership to the country's rational self-interest. At present,

Washington has no choice but to work — carefully — with Gen. Musharraf, a head of state who insists on a sovereignty he cannot enforce over territory that continues to harbor both international terrorists and Afghan renegades. There are no better options available to Washington than continuing to pressure the Pakistani government behind closed doors, while avoiding any public humiliation of a leader who, nevertheless imperfect, remains preferable to any known alternatives. On the crucial issue of the hot pursuit of terrorists across the Afghan border into Pakistan, the U.S. must not be deterred, but must go to all possible lengths to maintain public deniability.

Perhaps the best for which we can hope is that Pakistan will continue to muddle through, never quite collapsing. Incremental progress against Pakistan-based terrorists may be the best level of cooperation we realistically can expect, given the indecisive nature of the Musharraf regime. Increasingly, Pakistan looks like a problem that can only be contained, not solved. Finally, Washington and New Delhi must plan for various scenarios were the current government in Islamabad to fall, if Gen. Musharraf were to be assassinated, or, the worst case, if hostilities were to break out between India and Pakistan.

The Islamists Pakistan that nurtured, trained and armed Al Qaida is the logical outcome of partition. Once a state was created on the basis of religion with concomitant ethnic cleansing, further Islamization was needed. Otherwise, as General Zia said, if not Islamization, then Pakistan "might as well rejoin mother India".

Winston Churchill, on hearing of partition and the creation of Pakistan said

"So we have had the last laugh after all"

The Legacy of Muslim Rule in India:

It took five hundred years for Muslim rule establishment (712-1206) and one hundred and fifty years for its decline and fall (1707-1857). The benchmarks of its establishment are C.E. 712 when Muhammad bin Qasim invaded Sind, 1000 when Mohamed of Ghazni embarked upon a series of expeditions against Hindustan, 1192-1206 when Prithvi Raj Chauhan lost to Muhammad Ghauri and Qutbuddin Aibak set up the Turki Sultanate at Delhi, and 1296 when Alauddin Khalji pushed into the Deccan. The stages of its downfall are 1707 when Aurangzeb died, 1739 when a trembling Mughal Emperor stood as a suppliant before the Persian invader Nadir Shah, 1803 when Delhi was captured by the British, and 1858 when the last Mughal ruler was sent to Rangoon as a prisoner of the "Raj".

For five centuries-thirteenth to seventeenth-nevertheless, most parts of India were under Muslim rule, though with varying degrees of effectiveness in different regions of the country. But at no single point of time was the whole country ruled exclusively by the Muslims. On the other hand the five hundred year long Muslim rule did not fail to influence Indian political and cultural life in all its facets. Muslim rule apart, Muslim contact with India can be counted from the seventh century itself.

Strategic thinking of Pakistan and its leadership

A window into the strategic thinking of leadership in the last 60 years is shown in the following article by Khalid Hasan.

Geopolitics of the British Raj was based on the concept of external and internal buffers. As the western border becomes active, Pakistan needs to take the writ of the state to this internal buffer region. It may be shocked to discover after fifty years that the region is not committed to the security of Pakistan and has its own separate or separatist economic and security perceptions

It is time to change from the geopolitics of a warrior state to that of a trading nation. (Very significant paradigm shift in thinking only time will tell) We think we can normalize relations with India after creating a nuclear deterrence with it and encourage it to trade in the goods of our western neighbors through us. This will be a true paradigm shift. Ironically, Pakistan's security will now hinge on the well-being of India's economy very Pakistani somehow knows that his country is geopolitically important. If you ask him to elaborate he will probably say that it is well placed to communicate with the Muslim states of Central Asia and the Middle East. But geopolitically, Pakistan must facilitate communication between two regions to become strategically important.(This is a direct result of the pressure of the Indo-Iran tie up and transportation corridor) That is perhaps not so clear in the Pakistani mind because it is not a trader's mind. Its geopolitical sense is warlike, imagining benefit from breaking possible communication between two regions for 'security'. Pakistan is important because it is a part of South Asia abutting on Central Asia and the Gulf states. Yet, at one point in its recent history Pakistan actually forswore its geopolitical significance by declaring that it was a Middle Eastern state.

More often, Pakistan has felt endangered by its geographic location. This fear is the legacy of British Raj. It saw Pakistan as a kind of buffer territory between itself and the 19th-20th century Tsarist-Soviet advance in Central and High Asia, Afghanistan and Iran.

The British Raj perception of geopolitics was retained by Pakistan after 1947 and during the cold war. Pacts were entered into on the basis of the theory of a Soviet pursuit of 'warm waters'. A will of Peter The Great was taken out of the archives, dusted and applied to the expansion of Afghan-Soviet relations. Pakistan's other 'geographic' obsession on its eastern border, namely India, prevented it from supplying military muscle to the 'warm waters' theory. It shaped its foreign policy in such a way that its Western borders were secured through cold war international alliances. It turned eastward and safely fought wars with India without endangering the western front. (A weak strategy)

Neighbors as geography: Geographic determinism is not such an effective yardstick with which to analyze strategy and foreign policy. Nations can negate the permanent determinants by creating other 'imaginative' elements of policy. One important aspect of geography is 'neighbors'; and strategies get formulated on the basis of how nations relate to their neighbors. In history, the idea of the nation-state has created hostile neighbors. Nationalisms got formed on the basis of 'the other' and it usually turned out to be a neighbor. It negated such emotive factors as transnational religious feeling. In its various phases, Pakistan has felt hostile towards India, Afghanistan and Iran. (Because the state was created out of violence and by negating itself from the larger civilizational state)

Geography is among the 'tangibles' of strategic thinking. Size, location, climate, etc, can be factors of advantage or disadvantage, to be exploited or overcome. Geographic factors relating to other states too can impose permanent parameters of policy. Whether the state is insular, landlocked or littoral is supposed to determine how it will behave.

'Spatial organization', nevertheless, worked more decisively during an earlier phase of human civilization. Iranians did not become seafaring in contrast to Arabs because the Gulf was deep on their coast which was studded with mountains. In modern times geography has been conquered by technology. That is why the application of the theory of 'warm waters' to the Soviet Union was so primitive; the theory that Americans seek to spy on China by grabbing Kashmir for themselves is equally primitive. Geography can become intensely important in a transient phase, as in the case of post- Pakistan, but will subside if the state ignores its imperatives. The post- advantage against India is equally transient.

Theory of geopolitics: Pakistani-Canadian scholar and former ambassador Muhammad Yunus in his excellent textbook Foreign Policy: A Theoretical Introduction (OUP, 2003) has discussed geopolitics and traced its origin as theory to Sir Halford Mackinder who thought of the globe as 'world island' with a 'heartland'. Yunus discusses the geopolitical theory under the rubric of 'neighbors' and finds it more useful as a factor in geopolitical determinism. ('You can't choose your neighbors.') A state will subordinate all interest to its reaction to the policies of a neighbor. While giving a more useful gloss to the geographic dimension, it takes away its permanence. A state can change its geopolitical vision by changing the tenor of its relations with its neighbors. There is no such thing as 'geographic destiny' or fate. A lower-riparian state should not think of conquering the upper-riparian state to secure its rivers; it can offset the disadvantage of the upper riparian by offering a countervailing advantage. The geopolitical aspect of the jihad ('grab the rivers') in Kashmir therefore is untenable in modern times. (Here is the true reason for the jihad and chenab plan)

Pakistan inherited its geostrategic vision from British Raj. This vision was embedded in the way its territory was organized under what is today called the theory of The Great Game. As British India struggled against what it saw as the southward expansion of the Tsarist empire, it erected buffers to avoid getting into direct conflict. These buffers were of two kinds: the external buffer, which comprised a neighboring state rendered partially un-sovereign; and the internal buffer as territory which was partially administered. India saw an entire swathe of its western and north-western territory as a kind of 'first area of engagement' with an advancing power. The populations in these partially administered regions were obliged to fight as an irregular vanguard in return for their autonomy from the central administration.

The whole of Baluchistan and the seven federally administered tribal areas (FATA) played the role of such 'marches' and obtained in return a measure of independence from Indian sovereignty. Today, Pakistan is confronted with problems in this 'buffer' region because its new but partially realised geostrategic reality requires it to be completely settled within the ambit of Pakistan's sovereignty. As the western border becomes active, Pakistan needs to take the writ of the state to this buffer region. It may be shocked to discover after fifty years that the buffer is not committed to the security of Pakistan and has its own separate/separatist economic and security perceptions. (Significant perception and the weakest point of the state.)

Military's special relationship with geopolitics: Geopolitical thinking is most useful in military strategy-making. It bestows permanence and makes training easy. It is because of the static nature of military thinking that its separation from political thinking is not advisable. If military thinking is made permanent through ideology or any other means of militarization of the state, the stasis of military thinking endangers the very existence of the state. It is important that civilian statesmen ring changes in the country's understanding of geopolitics periodically and allow the military to absorb it and reformulate its strategy.

It is in this sense of its negative permanence that Ambassador Yunus is reluctant to accord great importance to geography as the ultimate determinant of strategy. The idea of the 'internal buffer' has been misused by Pakistan by allowing the Baluchistan-FATA semi-administered area to continue beyond 1947 and by using the concept in other related areas. For instance, jihad and its territory of low-intensity conflict was employed as a kind of confliction 'buffer' with India much the same way as the British Raj used the warlike tribes of the northwest. There is some evidence that warlike Sipah Sahaba, with its early funding from the Arabs in Rahimyar Khan, was sought to be used as a confliction buffer against India along the Rajasthan border.

Pakistan's geopolitical straitjacket: By being Indo-centric, Pakistan's foreign policy has acquired a fixed geopolitical identity. (The monkey trap) Pakistani nationalism has prevented this geopolitical compulsion from changing.

This nationalism has made certain that Pakistan's army remain a crucial part of geopolitical thinking; in turn, the Pakistan army has contributed profoundly to the composition of the Pakistani worldview.

It was a gradual militarization of the civilian mind in Pakistan that kept the country's geopolitics intact. Because of lack of timely change, the policy collapsed in the mid-1900s. Failures of policy are usually reflected in the global and regional isolation of the state. Isolation as punishment is built into the post Second World War collective security system requiring that nations unwilling to accept punishment avoid isolation. That in essence is also the nature of international law as evolved in the UN Security Council.

In the post cold war period Pakistan was most challenged to alter its geopolitical perceptions. The western regions of Pakistan took on a new significance which Pakistan ignored.

The 'internal buffer' which depended so much on the cold war support from the western bloc underwent a change in its identity without the strategic elite in Islamabad taking any notice of it. In 1991, after the break-up of the Soviet Union, Pakistan woke up partially and fitfully to the economic significance of the region of Central Asia. One must take note of Islamabad's effort to perceive Pakistan's interest in economic terms in the shape of the agreements it reached with the newly independent states of Central Asia in the early 1990s. It dreamed of gas pipelines running across Afghanistan and across the 'internal buffer' territories inside Pakistan.

But pipelines to where? The geopolitics of Pakistan's India policy overcame this brief period of fantasy. Geopolitics was used to start a low-intensity conflict in Kashmir which depended even more on 'exemption' from the writ of the state awarded to the 'non-state actors' of jihad.

What was awarded to the 'internal buffers' of FATA and Baluchistan in the past was now given to virtually all cities where the jihadi outfits formed their jihad hinterlands. A new geopolitical realization had also dawned: that Pakistan's location was not so much of economic benefit as of military advantage. Militias were used not only to engage in low-intensity conflict with India but also to destabilize neighboring states where Pakistan sought influence in competition with India and, for some time, Iran.

A difficult paradigm shift: It is the failure of military geopolitical thinking that the UN Security Council resolution 1373 was imposed on Pakistan under Chapter Seven of the UN Charter in the aftermath of. In other words, it is the failure of the permanently imposed Indo-centric policy that has brought us to the juncture of considering a paradigm shift. We are now poised to seek a different kind of 'strategic depth' to the west of the country.

We have revived the early-1900s dream of being a transit state that would play an ancillary role to India's large regional economy and survive under an increasingly Darwinist global economic order. We think we can normalize relations with India after creating a nuclear deterrence with it and encourage it to trade in the goods of our western neighbors through us. Ironically, Pakistan's security will now hinge on the well-being of India's economy. (Because the masters want it to)

The irony is nevertheless that the paradigm shift in our geopolitical thinking has come more conclusively while an army general is in control in Pakistan. A Pakistani still thinks that his country is geopolitically important but he is being called upon to embrace the concept to trade instead of war. This is an unfamiliar formulation and makes him angry. The political system, nurtured on fifty years of Indo-centric nationalism, rejects the idea of selling Pakistani electricity to India, or seeking rent from an Iranian gas pipeline going to India, after putting the Kashmir issue on the backburner.

One wonders how far the military itself is delinked from its old geopolitics to allow projections of conflict to be replaced by projections of economic profit. The general has thought aloud about his 'alternative dream' and gone ahead with the construction of Gwadar deep-sea port. Ironically he is being pulled back by the burden of the old geopolitics and its ancillary nationalism inculcated by the paramountcy of the army in Pakistan. (Euphemism for Baloch nationalism and separatist violence)

5

The Pakistan/India Conflict: Familiar Faces and Nuclear

HOLOCAUST

The ongoing tensions between Pakistan and India over the disputed border of Kashmir encapsulate the most volatile geopolitical sector of the world, dwarfing even the Israel-Palestine conflict in terms of potential explosiveness. Both India and Pakistan are nuclear armed.

By late 2002 it was generally considered that disquiet between the two countries had dramatically calmed, a naïve misconception when in hindsight, the same consensus prevailed at the end of 2001.

It was at that point that terrorists stormed the Indian parliament in Delhi, killing twelve people and catapulting India and Pakistan to the brink of nuclear war. One single act of large-scale terrorism will re-fuel the possibility of imminent conflict. As I will document, the likelihood of that happening is immense.

Is there a hidden hand that seeks to bring nuclear war to the region and if so for what purpose? How does this relate to the New World Order and can the conflict be classified as another example of the Hegelian dialectic, the order out of chaos scenario? Who benefits and where is the evidence?

Before we answer these questions let's take a brief look at the history of the region.

A LEGACY OF INSTABILITY

The mountainous region of Kashmir has been a flashpoint between India and Pakistan for more than 50 years. The territory has witnessed a number of violent incidents recently against the background of continuing tension between India and Pakistan. Forces from both countries deployed along the frontline are regularly shelling each other, causing deaths and injuries to civilians in the area. There are fears that even a minor incident along the border could trigger a conflagration between the two nuclear-capable powers, and both President Musharraf and Prime Minister Vajpayee are under considerable domestic pressure not to back down.

The territory of Kashmir was hotly contested even before India and Pakistan won their independence from Britain in August 1947. Under the partition plan provided by the Indian Independence Act of 1947, Kashmir was free to accede to India or Pakistan. The Maharaja, Hari Singh, wanted to stay independent but eventually decided to accede to India, signing over key powers to the Indian Government - in return for military aid and a promised referendum. Since then, the territory has been the flashpoint for two of the three India-Pakistan wars: the first in 1947-8, the second in 1965.

In 1999, India fought a brief but bitter conflict with Pakistani-backed forces who had infiltrated Indian-controlled territory in the Kargil area.

In addition to the rival claims of Delhi and Islamabad to the territory, there has been a growing and often violent separatist movement fighting against Indian rule in Kashmir since 1989. Islamabad says Kashmir should have become part of Pakistan in 1947, because Muslims are in the majority in the region. Pakistan also argues that Kashmiris should be allowed to vote in a referendum on their future, following numerous UN resolutions on the issue. Delhi, however, does not want international debate on the issue, arguing that the *Simla Agreement of 1972* provided for a resolution through bilateral talks. India points to the Instrument of Accession signed in October 1947 by the Maharaja, Hari Singh.

Both India and Pakistan reject the so-called "third option" of Kashmiri independence.

A demarcation line was originally established in January 1949 as a ceasefire line, following the end of the first Kashmir war. In July 1972, after a second conflict, the Line of Control (LoC) was re-established under the terms of the Simla Agreement, with minor variations on the earlier boundary. The LoC passes through a mountainous region about 5,000 meters high. The conditions are so extreme that the bitter cold claims more lives than the sporadic military skirmishes. North of the LoC, the rival forces have been entrenched on the Siachen glacier (more than 6,000 meters high) since 1984 - the highest battlefield on earth.

The LoC divides Kashmir on an almost two-to-one basis: Indian-administered Kashmir to the east and south (population about nine million), which falls into the Indian state of Jammu and Kashmir; and Pakistani-administered Kashmir to the north and west (population about three million), which is labeled by Pakistan as "Azad" (Free) Kashmir. China also controls a small portion of Kashmir.

Religion is an important aspect of the dispute. Partition in 1947 gave India's Muslims a state of their own: Pakistan. So a common faith underpins Pakistan's claims to Kashmir, where many areas are Muslim-dominated. The population of the Indian state of Jammu and Kashmir is over 60% Muslim, making it the only state within India where Muslims are in the majority.

There are several groups pursuing the rival claims to Kashmir. Not all are armed, but since Muslim insurgency began in 1989, the number of armed separatists has grown from hundreds to thousands. The most prominent are the pro-Pakistani Hizbul Mujahideen. Islamabad denies providing them and others with logistical and material support. The Jammu and Kashmir Liberation Front (JKLF) was the largest pro-independence group, but its influence is thought to have waned. Other groups have joined under the umbrella of the All-Party Hurriyat (Freedom) Conference, which campaigns peacefully for an end to India's presence in Kashmir.

Indian forces announced a unilateral ceasefire against militant groups in November 2000, but violence continued. Attempts to get talks going between the government and the separatist parties have foundered over separatist demands that Pakistan should be included in any dialogue. India says there can be no discussion involving Pakistan because it sponsors violence in Kashmir.

India and Pakistan failed to narrow their differences over Kashmir at a summit in the Indian city of Agra in July 2001. Since then, they have continued to trade accusations and outside attempts to get them to resolve their differences have made no headway.

Running parallel to this regional history is the disturbing evidence of how and why Globalist New World Order interests have instituted a specific program of fomenting this conflict and how this links in to the war on terrorism.

ENTER THE HIDDEN HAND

It's common knowledge in intelligence circles that the Inter Services Intelligence Agency (Pakistan's secret service) runs the entire country in the shadow of dictator General Pervez Musharraf. In turn, the CIA co-ordinate the activities of the ISI. This alliance gave birth to Osama bin Laden, Al-Qaeda and the current war on terrorism. Osama bin Laden left Saudi Arabia in 1979 to fight the invading Soviets in Afghanistan. By 1984 he was running the front organization known as MAK, (Maktab al-Khidamar) which eventually mutated into Al-Qaeda, consisting of the more extreme members of the former group. During the war MAK was nurtured by Pakistan's Inter-services Intelligence Agency, ISI.

The ISI was the CIA's covert ally and conduit against Moscow's occupation. Via the ISI the kindergarten Al-Qaeda were trained, armed, funded and empowered by the CIA.

The new covert U.S. assistance began with a dramatic increase in arms supplies - a steady rise to 65,000 tons annually by 1987, as well as a "ceaseless stream" of CIA and Pentagon specialists who traveled to the secret headquarters of Pakistan's ISI on the main road near Rawalpindi, Pakistan. There the CIA specialists met with Pakistani intelligence officers to help plan operations for the Afghan rebels, bin Laden included. The Central Intelligence Agency, using Pakistan's ISI, played a key role in training the Mujahideen.

The BBC reported that the ISI aided bin Laden's escape from Afghanistan at the end of 2001, Afghan interior minister Younis Qanooni has accused the Pakistani secret service of helping al-Qaeda leader Osama Bin Laden flee Afghanistan.

Speaking in an interview with Iranian television, Mr Qanooni said the Pakistani ISI (Inter Services Intelligence) was at odds over Bin Laden with the Pakistani Government, which has supported the American-led war against terror An Afghan defence ministry spokesman suggested last week that Bin Laden had crossed from the Tora Bora region into Pakistan the week before. Since the CIA are basically the administrative masters of the ISI, they mandated and approved bin Laden's escape.

As we touched upon earlier, in October 2001, reports surfaced in numerous outlets from the Times of India to CNN, detailing how ISI director-general Lt-Gen Mahmud Ahmad was forced to retire after it emerged that he had hotwired $100,000 to the 9/11 lead hijacker, Mohammed Atta, While the Pakistani Inter Services Public Relations claimed that former ISI director-general Lt-Gen Mahmud Ahmad sought retirement after being superseded on Monday, the truth is more shocking.

Top sources confirmed here on Tuesday, that the general lost his job because of the "evidence" India produced to show his links to one of the suicide bombers that wrecked the World Trade Centre. The US authorities sought his removal after confirming the fact that $100,000 was wired to WTC hijacker Mohammed Atta from Pakistan by Ahmad Umar Sheikh at the instance of Gen Mahumd. Senior government sources have confirmed that India contributed significantly to establishing the link between the money transfer and the role played by the dismissed ISI chief.

While they did not provide details, they said that Indian inputs, including Sheikh's mobile phone number, helped the FBI in tracing and establishing the link. Pakistan's direct links to Al-Qaeda and other terrorist organizations are obviously extremely disturbing in light of the fact that everything the ISI does has to be approved by the CIA.

Furthermore, by direct order of President Bush, an estimated 8,000 members of Al-Qaeda and the Taliban were rescued via cargo planes as Kunduz fell to the Northern Alliance in November 2001. Bush had ordered the United States Central Command to set up a special air corridor to help insure the safety of the Pakistani rescue flights from Kunduz to the northwest corner of Pakistan, about two hundred miles away. This left both the Delta Force and Northern Alliance indignant. Northern Alliance soldier Mahmud Shah was bewildered at the events stating, "We had decided to kill all of them, and we are not happy with America for letting the planes come."

A senior U.S. defense advisor told the London Times, "Everyone brought their friends with them. You're not going to leave them behind to get their throats cut."

There were two official explanations for the airlift. One was that rescuing 8,000 known Al-Qaeda and Taliban was 'an accident.'

The other, and only slightly more plausible reason was that Pakistani dictator General Pervez Musharraf had a huge geopolitical weight on his shoulders in endorsing US military operations in Afghanistan.

The cost was the threat of internal insurgency and the overthrow of his regime. Musharraf bargained with Bush. If these Pakistani Army officers, intelligence advisers and volunteers could just be spared, his political survival would be almost ensured. Musharraf's message to the Americans had been that he didn't want to see body bags coming back to Pakistan. Bush agreed to protect the Pakistani leader, providing the rescued Taliban elements would be accessible to American intelligence.

This was not the case because after the airlift the Al-Qaeda and Taliban leaders went AWOL.

To emphasize, these 8,000 rescued individuals were high-level Taliban and al-Qaeda operatives fighting against the United States. These secret airlifts gave these terrorists refuge primarily in Kashmir, the disputed border.

The first incident that could have led to a nuclear war between India and Pakistan occurred when, on December 13th 2001, a suicide squad of five heavily armed Muslim terrorists drove past a barrier at the Indian Parliament, in New Delhi, and rushed the main building. At one point, the terrorists were only a few feet from the steps to the office of India's Vice-President, Krishan Kant.

Nine people were killed in the shoot-out, in addition to the terrorists, and many others were injured. Indian intelligence quickly concluded that the attack had been organized by operatives from two long-standing Kashmiri terrorist organizations that were believed to be heavily supported by the ISI. Was this operation, which would have lead to full-scale war between the two powers had there been more casualties, a consequence of the planning of elite Pakistani and Taliban officials who were rescued on order of the U.S. 21 days earlier?

Here we see the grand chessboard in action, previously discussed by such *luminaries* of the global elite as Zbygniew Brzezinsky.

Let's use the analogy of one person playing a sole game of chess, moving the pieces on both sides of the board, black and white. Al-Qaeda and similar terrorist organizations are the pawns on the global chessboard. Many believe they are operating of their own free will when in reality an unseen hand is dictating their every movement. They can be sacrificed at any time for the greater good. The end justifies the means. If they reach the other side of the board, as in the game of chess, they may well be promoted to a higher authority, but still they are under control of the same influence.

In the movement of the Al-Qaeda pawns from Afghanistan to Kashmir by the Bush administration and its Globalist controllers, we witness an orchestrated shift in emphasis from the war on terrorism to the Pakistan-India conflict and the Muslim bomb. This is the next stage in the New World Order out of chaos game plan - the blue touch-paper for world war three.

On June 3rd, the Hindustan Times confirmed that dozens of surviving Al-Qaeda operatives had infiltrated into Pakistan after yet another incident where they were allowed to leave unharmed when they could have been apprehended. The event took place in Peshawar, where top Taliban and Al-Qaeda leadership, including some of Osama bin Laden's chief protectors such as the Taliban's deputy foreign minister Abdul Rahman Zaid and top defense ministry official Jalil Yousafzai, attended the funeral of a former anti-Soviet guerrilla fighter. The ISI monitored them but still amazingly allowed them to leave without arrest.

Again, the CIA controlled Pakistani authorities are protecting known terrorists, offering them safe passage to Kashmir where a single suicide bomb or political assassination could inflame the entire region and throw it into the abyss of a nuclear war that would have worldwide implications.

RED DRAGON RISING

China is an ally of Pakistan. Since the two countries do not share a common history, language, culture or religion and have followed diametrically opposite models of economic and political development, it is clear that China is using Pakistan as a long-term geopolitical tool. Many prolific authors and geopolitical analysts such as Gordon Thomas have highlighted and documented the twofaced behavior of Jiang Zemin's communist superpower.

A long-term agenda to bring America to its knees by means of a surprise attack is the ultimate goal. We should be reminded, in this context, of an August 1998 document from the Chinese Central Military Commission that was sent to all corps commanders of the Peoples Liberation Army. The leaked document details how the United States is increasingly vulnerable and could not withstand even a limited nuclear strike from China. Despite its military prominence, America remains unwilling to sacrifice cities in a tit-for-tat war, whereas the Chinese are fully prepared to do so. Therefore, Beijing could hold off Washington if hostilities erupted over Taiwan.

While publicly offering meek support of the war on terrorism, voluminous evidence suggests that China have actually been supporting the Taliban and Osama bin Laden all along.

Furthermore, the Bush administration have deliberately ignored the China threat and continue to transfer sensitive computer technology to the Communists, the only practical purpose of which is to design nuclear weapons.

On the morning of September 11th 2001, terrorists linked to the Al-Qaeda network that was being protected by the Taliban in Afghanistan slammed three planes into the World trade Centre and the Pentagon. At the same time a Chinese delegation was in Kabul putting pen to paper on a lucrative economic support package with the Taliban. This was by no means the beginning of friendly China-Taliban relations.

As far back as 1998 the Iranian official press said there was a secret defense agreement between China and the Taliban. In 2000, two Chinese telecommunications firms, Huawei Technologies and ZTE, signed contracts to provide limited phone service for Kabul and Kandahar, with a specific focus on equipping Osama bin Laden, who was based there at the time. I n early 2001, a Taliban delegation visited Beijing to continue to foster good relations. China's ambassador to Pakistan has also made at least one recent trip to Kabul and met with Taliban officials in Pakistan's capital Islamabad.

China continued to support bin Laden and the Taliban as the war broke out in Afghanistan in October of 2001. Debka File intelligence reported that, on October 5th, two days before American air strikes began, a convoy of 15,000 Chinese Muslims were sent to reinforce the Taliban. In a later report, Debka also disclosed that large quantities of Chinese-manufactured ammunition were discovered in the Tora Bora cave hideouts of Osama bin Laden. The arms cache included mortar shells, anti-tank rockets and ammunition for various types of automatic rifles and machine guns of Chinese manufacture, abandoned by fleeing Al-Qaeda men.

In early December 2001 U.S. Undersecretary of State John Bolton met with Chinese Vice Foreign Minister Wang Guangya, urging him to renew a demand that the Chinese curb missile cooperation with Pakistan that was encouraging the likelihood of terrorism and nuclear conflict with India in the region of Kashmir.

The sanctions were imposed on the China Metallurgical Equipment Corp. for allegedly transferring ballistic missile technology to Pakistan in violation of a November 2000 agreement with the United States.

This technology was in danger of falling into the hands of extremists who could use nuclear, biological and chemical weapons to attack India. Taking the perspective of historical precedent, China continued to provide Syria, North Korea and possibly Libya with high-tech weaponry despite U.S. warnings, it is unlikely that the meeting had any success and China persists to foment anxiety that could lead to a nuclear exchange between Pakistan and India.

China continued to goad both Pakistan and India into conflict right up to late 2001.

The *Hindustan Times* reported,

The hostile actions by the Chinese in Arunachal Pradesh and Sikkim is, according to strategic experts, part of a well-thought-out move to corner India on two fronts. China has also beefed up its presence in Myanmar's Coco Islands on the Bay of Bengal and plans to move in two aircraft carriers that are under construction now to the area. "India cannot concentrate exclusively on the western theatre with Pakistan if China undertakes these measures along Arunachal and Sikkim. And it could well be that it is goading Pakistan to anti-Indian actions in Rajasthan, Punjab and Kashmir. A distracted India is a weaker India and China stands to gain the most from it," pointed out a senior army officer.

We have established that the highest levels of U.S. intelligence and the Bush administration directly fomented hostility in Kashmir, via a conduit in the war on terrorism. China have also played a role in escalating tension in the region by covertly supporting Taliban and Al-Qaeda leaders who would later infiltrate Kashmir. China has also armed Pakistan.

PROFITS OF DEATH

A minimum of three million people would be killed and 1.5 million seriously injured if even a "limited" nuclear war broke out between India and Pakistan. The estimates are comprised of the immediate casualty list from blast, fire and radiation if only a tenth of both countries' nuclear weapons were exploded above 10 of their largest cities. It does not take account of the inevitable suffering that would result from the loss of homes, hospitals, water and energy supplies, or the cancers that could develop in future years.

Both world wars were caused by lesser events. Who is responsible for this holocaust scenario? Who is arming both Pakistan and India, heightening the possibility of war, and for what reason? Once again, familiar names emerge. Firstly, the Times of India reported in August of 2001 that the San Rafael California-based Berkeley Nucleonics Corporation supplied at least five nuclear pulse generators to India from 1998 onwards.

Three of the devices were exported to the Bhabha Atomic Research Centre and two to the Nuclear Power Corporation. Pulse generators are devices that can be used to calibrate instruments that measure atomic reactions. Berkeley Nucleonics, which was founded in 1963, is a highly regarded manufacturer of electronics instrumentation, especially for nuclear research industries. Representatives of the company were actually indicted for this illegal transfer. However, the most interesting aspect of this transfer was that the president of the company claimed he was "cajoled" by unnamed government agents into making the shipment.

Who were these secret operatives and why were they so desperate for India to receive these nuclear materials? From this perspective we can see that the pieces on the global chessboard were being assembled well in advance of the re-emergence of India-Pakistan tensions in December 2001.

In January of 2002, the Moscow Times reported that British Prime Minister Tony Blair made a visit to India and Pakistan in an attempt to calm ethnic tensions between the two. In reality he was pushing the sale of a lucrative deal with arms merchant BAE Systems for 60 new jet fighters. The Russian newspaper stated, Blair's minions are putting the squeeze on India to accept a $1.4 billion deal with arms merchant BAE Systems for 60 new jet fighters.

This will no doubt have a very "calming influence" on the balance of power as the subcontinent teeters on the brink of nuclear war—the same kind of calming influence gasoline has on fire. Of course, if Blair can get those billion warbucks into BAE's coffers, *Master Georgie* will be very pleased. For one of BAE's business partners is—God, this is almost too easy! — our old friends the Carlyle Group. Faithful readers know that Daddy Bush—the former peddler of poison gas to Iraq—has long been feeding at the Carlyle trough, working his contacts with Saudi royalty, the bin Laden family, Asian dictators, South American junta honchos and other respectable characters to cement sweetheart deals for the Reagan-Bush retreads who skim the cream off Carlyle's $13 billion nest egg.

The BBC reported these BAE-India negotiations back in August 2001, stating, BAE Systems has insisted it is confident of securing a £1bn Hawk jets deal with India despite reports the sale faces collapse. The company is in discussions with the Indian Government over the purchase of 66 advanced trainer jets. Reports in the media suggested that the air force is now poised to pull out of the plan and buy Russian MiG jets instead. But management and unions at BAE Systems say they are confident an agreement will be struck.

The Carlyle Group is one of the biggest Aerospace & Defense contractors in the world today. They manage approximately $14 billion in assets, without actually manufacturing anything. This is by no means their only sector of interest but it's certainly their primary focus of attention. The group is staffed by some of the most powerful individuals on the planet, including former U.S. President George Herbert Walker Bush and former British Prime Minister John Major.

Obviously, since September 11th the explosion of the arms market has seen their profits smash through the roof. However, Carlyle state, "We're not too keen on discussing anything related to the political nature of the people at Carlyle." There's a very good reason for this. Until October 2001, the bin Laden family had a stake in Carlyle. President Bush's father met with the bin Laden family two months before the September 11 attacks. The Wall

Street Journal went so far as call outright for George Herbert Walker Bush to resign from the group.

The bin Laden family, publicly at least, withdrew from Carlyle. No doubt they received a healthy severance pay.

UNITED STATES' ROLE AND INFLUENCE ON THE INDIA-PAKISTAN CONFLICT

Although the Soviet Union played a critical role in formally ending the second India-Pakistan war in 1965—through the Tashkent Declaration—its close military and security relationships with Delhi during much of the Cold War years decreased its influence over Islamabad, which became increasingly linked to the United States for the supply of arms. China's discreet missile and nuclear linkages with Islamabad, along with memories of the India-China border war of 1962, precluded Beijing's influence over the India-Pakistan dispute. Despite an apparent shift in Beijing's position since 1996 (especially during the Kargil conflict in 1999 when it refrained from publicly supporting Pakistan, and due to its concerns over Islamist extremists in Xinjiang province), elements of future India-China competition make it difficult for Beijing to influence Delhi. While French, European Union or Japanese influence appear limited, a potential British role exists only alongside the United States, with the latter doing much of the 'heavy lifting'. Notwithstanding Washington's unprecedented and simultaneous influence over both Delhi and Islamabad, the nature and extent of its future engagement in the India-Pakistan conflict remains unclear.

Kashmir Dispute

In view of India's asymmetrical relationship with Pakistan—population, size, economic strength and relative military power—Delhi has invariably resisted the role of a third party or the United Nations in its conflict with Pakistan; it is precisely for these reasons that Islamabad has favoured such a role, with the hope that 'internationalization' would provide a favourable resolution of the Kashmir dispute. India's disillusionment with the international community over Kashmir began soon after Independence, when

Prime Minister Jawaharlal Nehru took Pakistan's aggression against India in Kashmir to the United Nations on 1 January 1948.

Instead of being seen as the aggrieved party, losing Indian territory to an armed attack by Pakistan—following the signing of the Instrument of Accession by the Hindu ruler of the predominantly Muslim province of Jammu and Kashmir on 26 October 1947— India became a party to the dispute.

Subsequent UN Security Council resolutions advocating the future of Kashmir on the basis of a UN-mandated plebiscite—after the withdrawal of armed forces by both countries from divided Kashmir—were ignored by Delhi, as was the United Nations force, the UN Military Observer Group in India and Pakistan (UNMOGIP). Since the UN-sponsored ceasefire to the first India-Pakistan war over Kashmir on 1 January 1949, UNMOGIP has been deployed to monitor the ceasefire line—currently, the Line of Control (LoC) (the *de facto* border dividing Indianand Pakistan-administered Kashmir).

For Islamabad, however, the UN Security Council resolutions on Kashmir boosted its position on Kashmir, and justified its stance that it was a territorial dispute between the two sides. This contradicted Delhi's view that Kashmir was 'not a disputed territory', with the only point of contention being Pakistan's 'illegal occupation of a portion of the state', fortified by a Parliamentary resolution to this effect in the early 1990s. Even though it was clear that neither Pakistan nor India were inclined to withdraw forces from divided Kashmir, Islamabad was not averse to using UN Security Council resolutions on a plebiscite in Kashmir for political purposes.

However, Indian and Pakistani positions on a plebiscite and the status of Kashmir appeared to change in December 2003-January 2004. In an interview with Reuters in mid-December 2003, Pakistan's President Musharraf, in a bold move, publicly offered to drop Pakistan's traditional demand for a UN plebiscite in Kashmir, and meet India 'half-way' in a bid to resolve the Kashmir dispute. Musharraf reportedly stated, '... we are for the United Nations Security Council resolutions whatever it stands for. However, now we have left that aside'. Although this was subsequently denied by Pakistani officials, it was clear that this was simply a recognition that a UN plebiscite could never have been implemented, in view of Indian and Pakistani intransigence. Yet, it had been a major irritant to Delhi, which welcomed Musharraf's statement. Subsequently, in the joint press statement of 6 January 2004, following the meeting between Indian Prime Minister Vajpayee and Musharraf, on the sidelines of the twelfth South Asian Association for Regional Cooperation (SAARC) Summit in Islamabad, Delhi implicitly agreed that Kashmir was disputed territory, by explicitly agreeing that Kashmir was to be settled 'to the satisfaction of both sides'.

'Third Party' Involvement in War

Notwithstanding India's aversion to a 'third party' (including UN) role in its dispute over Kashmir, this did not apply to assistance in formally ending wars, or in the 1990s, preventing the outbreak of full-fledged conventional war. The second India-Pakistan war in 1965, for example, ended with a UN Security Council-sponsored ceasefire on 23 September 1965. Three months later, Indian Prime Minister Lal Bahadur Shastri and Pakistani President Mohammed Ayub Khan met in Tashkent and signed an agreement to formalize the end of the war and the withdrawal of their armed forces to positions held prior to 5 August 1965. The erstwhile Soviet-brokered 'Tashkent Agreement' of 10 January 1966 also pledged continued negotiations and the observation of ceasefire terms on the ceasefire line.

During this period, American policy towards South Asia remained fairly ambivalent, although an attempt at engagement on the Kashmir dispute had been made during the Eisenhower Administration in the 1950s. Although the Kennedy Administration was able to initiate direct negotiations between India and Pakistan—in the aftermath of the 1962 India-China war, the talks failed; by the mid-1960s the United States had virtually given up on Kashmir. During the 1971 India-Pakistan war, the United States 'tilt' towards Pakistan—through the deployment of an aircraft carrier task force in the Bay of Bengal in the midst of the war—whatever its intent or purpose—made it difficult for India, among other reasons, to develop a satisfactory 'comfort level' with the United States on security issues. Despite American economic and military sanctions on Pakistan in 1979 in an attempt to stem its covert nuclearweapons programme, Pakistan's role as a front-line state against the Soviet occupation of Afghanistan in the 1980s alleviated this situation. The demise of the former Soviet Union, along with India's economic liberalization in the aftermath of the 1991 economic crisis, began to lead to more favourable Indo-American relations.

In the late 1990s, high publicity American engagement with South Asia took place on nuclear issues, sparked off by multiple Indian and Pakistani nuclear tests in May 1998. On 11 and 13 May 1998, India carried out a series of five underground nuclear tests, twenty-four years after its first 'peaceful nuclear explosion' on 18 May 1974. This was promptly followed by six Pakistani nuclear tests on 28 and 30 May 1998. Although the immediate American reaction was to impose economic and military-related sanctions on both India and Pakistan, their respective importance in United States foreign policy soon generated less coercive measures to counter proliferation. In a significant development, within the Lahore Memorandum of Understanding (MoU), both countries agreed to develop confidence-building measures (CBMs) in the nuclear and conventional fields aimed at the avoidance of conflict within nine months of the nuclear tests. The Lahore documents—signed at the Summit between Vajpayee and Pakistani Prime Minister Nawaz Sharif in Lahore—appeared to provide the momentum towards enhanced and formalized nuclear stability in South Asia.

American Facilitation in the Kargil Conflict, 1999

Unfortunately, the Lahore framework remains unimplemented, with the single exception of advanced notification of ballistic missile flight tests on a unilateral basis—in the 'spirit' of the Lahore MoU—although this has generated its own share of controversy over the years. Pakistan's military intrusion across the LoC, allegedly at the time of the Lahore Summit, effectively ended all moves towards regional nuclear stability. Instead, India and Pakistan were involved in an armed conflict with each other for the first time after their nuclear tests; the Kargil conflict of May-July 1999 formally ended with United States facilitation.

In early 1999, Pakistan's regular and irregular forces crossed the LoC and occupied positions in the Kargil sector of Indian-administered Jammu and Kashmir, for reasons that are as yet unclear. When this was detected in early May 1999, Delhi's response was swift and comprehensive, involving the use of land and air forces to evict the intruders from the Indian side of the LoC.

After several weeks of increasingly bloody conflict, Indian forces captured the key heights of Tololing (14 June) and Tiger Hill (early morning on 4 July). With Pakistani forces suffering critical defeats, it was expected to be only a matter of time before they were pushed back across the LoC; but, undoubtedly this would have raised Indian casualties further.

Meanwhile, the United States was urging Pakistan to respect the LoC and withdraw its forces across the LoC, while at the same time, urging India to restrain itself from crossing the LoC to open another front in the conflict. Notwithstanding Delhi's public statements on not using force across the LoC, the potential for escalation into a full-scale conventional war raised fears in the international community of the risk of inadvertent nuclear escalation.

In early July, the Pakistani Prime Minister flew to Washington, concerned over Pakistan's increasing international isolation. At a hastily organized meeting with President Clinton on 4 July, Sharif requested American intervention to stop the fighting and resolve the Kashmir issue. But Clinton came down heavily on Sharif, and told him that a clear Pakistani withdrawal to the LoC was essential. Clinton also told Sharif that Pakistan was preparing its nuclear arsenal for possible deployment at the instructions of the Army Chief, General Musharraf, which was apparently taking place without Sharif's knowledge.

Amidst considerable American pressure, Sharif finally agreed 'to take concrete and immediate steps for the restoration of the LoC', which was accepted by Vajpayee when it was conveyed to him prior to its publicization. In effect, the United States facilitated a formal end to the Kargil conflict, which shortly afterwards saw the withdrawal of all Pakistani forces to its own side of the LoC without many additional Indian casualties. American facilitation on the Kargil conflict—in Delhi's favour— came as quite an unexpected surprise to many in India's Ministries of External Affairs and Defence. This was, in effect, the first time in fifty years that the United States had sided with India against Pakistan 'openly and firmly'. This soon led to a greater 'comfort level' with the United States, followed by Clinton's successful visit to India in March 2000, followed by Vajpayee's visit to the United States in the final days of the Clinton Administration.

American Facilitation in the India-Pakistan Border Confrontation, 2001–2002

Even though the United States became involved in resolving the Kargil conflict, it is the Americanled war on terror in South Asia and the subsequent India-Pakistan border confrontation that has brought about a significant change in American engagement in South Asia. Following the American attack against Afghanistan in October 2001—targeting the terrorist Al-Qaeda leadership responsible for the attacks on the United States and their Taliban hosts—Pakistan became a frontline state for American logistics support and intelligence facilities in Afghanistan. A number of American military personnel and equipment also remain deployed in Pakistani military bases in support of the ongoing war on terror in Afghanistan.

However, the attack on the Indian Parliament on 13 December 2001—allegedly by Pakistanbased Jaish-e-Mohammed terrorists—threatened to disrupt the ongoing American-led military campaign in Afghanistan. As part of its 'coercive diplomacy' against Pakistan, Delhi launched 'Operation Parakram' ('valour') on 19 December 2001, which constituted the largest mobilization of the Indian armed forces. This was a deliberate move, taking place amidst the war on terror, to threaten military action against Pakistan if its demands to end alleged Pakistan-sponsored cross-border terrorism were not met. This included the deployment of India's three strike corps (comprising armoured and mechanized formations) at forward positions on the international border with Pakistan. With Pakistan's countermobilization, nearly one million armed personnel were deployed across the India-Pakistan borders. In view of the nuclear-armed status of both states, there appeared to be considerable risk of nuclear escalation—by misperception or miscalculation—following the break-out of a conventional war. On 20 March 2002, the Director of the Central Intelligence Agency (CIA), George Tenet, warned the United States Senate Armed Services Committee that the chances of a war in the region were the highest since 1971.

Having repeatedly stressed the sanctity of the LoC during the Kargil war, India's prospective actions—threatening the use of force across the LoC—set off alarm bells in Washington and London. Meanwhile, Pakistan appeared equally determined to counter an Indian military attack with conventional and nuclear forces. With the deliberate disruption of normal diplomatic communication, Delhi and Islamabad were communicating with each other on nuclear and conventional matters on a public basis during much of the ten months of the 2001–2002 border confrontation. These nuclear signals were multiple in nature, carried out at multiple levels, and addressed to multiple constituencies—internal, regional and international. For both India and Pakistan, the most important constituencies were the domestic public, each other and the United States, which had the most influence in the region. For Delhi, the United States could help put pressure on Pakistan to cease cross-border infiltration of militants into Indian-administered Kashmir; for Islamabad, the United States could restrain Delhi from military action.

With tensions heightening following the terrorist attack on an Indian Army residential camp in Kaluchak, Jammu, on 14 May 2002, and Delhi's subsequent nuclear signalling, a flurry of high-level American and British choreographed visits took place to Delhi and Islamabad. The contours of a possible easing of India-Pakistan tensions began to emerge from Jack Straw's visit at the end of May. On 28 May, Straw visited Islamabad, where he urged Musharraf to take action on the ground to counter cross-border 'terrorism' in Indian-administered Kashmir. In Delhi the next day, Straw urged India to exercise restraint and prevent its armed forces from using force across the LoC. He also told Delhi that Musharraf had promised to curb infiltration into India and to close down 'terrorist' camps in Pakistan-administered Kashmir by the time of Armitage's visit to the region in early June. On his return to London on 31 May, Straw publicly expressed his concern over the 'dangerous situation' in the region, 'when you have one million men under arms on either side of the LoC, all in a high state of alert and readiness, both countries have nuclear weapons, and one of them—Pakistan— has said they reserve the right to use them first'. This essentially signalled the issue of travel advisories on 1 June by the Governments of the United States, the United Kingdom, Canada, France, Japan, Australia, New Zealand and others, urging their citizens to leave India and Pakistan immediately, and warned others from travelling to either country. The travel advisories led to an exodus of business visitors, tourists, diplomatic personnel and their dependants, largely from India, as they had already pulled out from Pakistan earlier. Ostensibly ordered for fear of an outbreak of war, this unprecedented step caused much annoyance in Delhi, which perceived it as an attempt to pressure it against launching an attack across the LoC.

On 31 May, United States Secretary of State Colin Powell publicly criticized Pakistan for the 'continuing' infiltration across the LoC, despite Musharraf's assurances that it would be ended. The following day, in an interview with the BBC, Musharraf indicated that 'instructions' had been given by Pakistan to cease such activity. Although it was still too early to say that it had stopped, Powell emphasised that '... when, and if, it does stop, it must also stop permanently'. On 6 June, United States Deputy Secretary of State Richard Armitage arrived in Islamabad to build on Straw's visit, and hammer out a deal between India and Pakistan. After a tough meeting, Musharraf gave Armitage a commitment that he would end cross-border infiltration 'permanently'. This was a considerable improvement on his pledge to Straw a week earlier to curb infiltration into India. While Delhi formally welcomed this development, it expressed caution in terms of implementation. Consequently, Armitage described India-Pakistan tensions as 'a bit down on both sides'. Within days of Armitage's departure from Delhi, the thaw in India-Pakistan tensions was evident. In effect, American facilitation successfully eased India-Pakistan tensions, and ended the ten-month border confrontation—

the longest period of military mobilization between the two countries.

India-Pakistan Joint Press Statement, 6 January 2004

In a dramatic development on the sidelines of the twelfth SAARC Summit in Islamabad in January 2004, India and Pakistan agreed to resume an official-level dialogue after a three-year hiatus. The Joint Statement of 6 January 2004 also noted that Delhi agreed to settle Kashmir 'to the satisfaction of both sides', and that Islamabad would not permit 'any territory under Pakistan's control to be used to support terrorism in any manner'. On 18 February 2004, after three days of official-level 'talks on talks' in Islamabad, India and Pakistan agreed to resume their bilateral 'composite dialogue' in May–June 2004, soon after the Indian general elections. This is to take the form of a 'composite dialogue' on eight issues, including two—on 'peace and security, including CBMs' and 'Jammu and Kashmir'— at the Foreign Secretary-level. The two foreign ministers are to meet in August 2004 to review progress. Both Delhi and Islamabad had strong motivations to reach an accord during the SAARC Summit. For Vajpayee, a personal desire for a stable bilateral relationship with Pakistan—his third and final peace effort—had been initiated with his 'hand of friendship' speech in Srinagar in April 2003, and buttressed by approaching general elections in April 2004; for Musharraf, two assassination attempts within eleven days in December 2003 had led to a renewed vigour to fight terrorism of all kinds, along with the increasing radicalization of domestic politics. Vajpayee's rising popularity, seen by the results of the Indian assembly elections in November 2003, also boosted Islamabad's view that it would be advisable to deal with Vajpayee himself.

In addition, American pressure on Islamabad to end cross-border infiltration into Indianadministered Kashmir, and to a lesser extent on India—to begin an official-level dialogue with Pakistan—may also have played a part in the success of bilateral diplomacy on the sidelines of the multilateral summit. Even if the United States had facilitated such a dialogue, it would have been advisable to have maintained this in a low-key manner, for fear of undermining the fledgling peace process.

INDIA DISCOVERS INFILTRATION AND MOBILIZES

Initially, these incursions were not detected for a number of reasons: Indian patrols were not sent into some of the areas infiltrated by the Pakistani forces and heavy artillery fire by Pakistan in some areas provided cover for the infiltrators. But by the second week of May, the ambushing of an Indian patrol team led by Capt Saurabh Kalia, who acted on a tip-off by a local shepherd in the Batalik sector, led to the exposure of the infiltration. Initially, with little knowledge of the nature or extent of the infiltration, the Indian troops in the area assumed that the infiltrators were jihadis and claimed that they would evict them within a few days. Subsequent discovery of infiltration elsewhere along the LOC, and the difference in tactics employed by the infiltrators, caused the Indian army to realize that the plan of attack was on a much bigger scale. The total area seized by the ingress is generally accepted to between 130 km^2 – 200 km^2;

The Government of India responded with Operation Vijay, a mobilisation of 200,000 Indian troops. However, because of the nature of the terrain, division and corps operations could not be mounted; subsequent fighting was conducted mostly at the regimental or battalion level. In effect, two divisions of the Indian Army, numbering 20,000, plus several thousand from theParamilitary forces of India and the air force were deployed in the conflict zone. The total number of Indian soldiers that were involved in the military operation on the Kargil-Drass sector was thus close to 30,000. The number of infiltrators, including those providing logistical backup, has been put at approximately 5,000 at the height of the conflict. This figure includes troops fromPakistan-administered Kashmir who provided additional artillery support.

The Indian Air Force launched Operation Safed Sagar in support of the mobilization of Indian land forces, but its effectiveness during the war was limited by the high altitude and weather conditions, which in turn limited bomb loads and the number of airstrips that could be used.

The Indian Navy also prepared to blockade the Pakistani ports (primarily Karachi port) to cut off supply routes. Later, the then-

Prime Minister of Pakistan Nawaz Sharif disclosed that Pakistan was left with just six days of fuel to sustain itself if a full-fledged war had broken out.

India attacks Pakistani Positions

The terrain of Kashmir is mountainous and at high altitudes; even the best roads, such as National Highway 1D from Leh to Srinagar, are only two lanes. The rough terrain and narrow roads slowed traffic, and the high altitude, which affected the ability of aircraft to carry loads, made control of NH 1D (the actual stretch of the highway which was under Pakistani fire) a priority for India. From their observation posts, the Pakistani forces had a clear line-of-sight to lay down indirect artillery fire on NH 1D, inflicting heavy casualties on the Indians. This was a serious problem for the Indian Army as the highway was its main logistical and supply route. The Pakistani shelling of the arterial road posed the threat of Leh being cut off, though an alternative (and longer) road to Leh existed via Himachal Pradesh.

The infiltrators, apart from being equipped with small arms and grenade launchers, were also armed with mortars, artillery and anti-aircraft guns. Many posts were also heavily mined, with India later stating to having recovered more than 8,000 anti-personnel mines according to an ICBL report. Pakistan's reconnaissance was done through unmanned aerial vehicles and AN/TPQ-36 Firefinder radars supplied by the US. The initial Indian attacks were aimed at controlling the hills overlooking NH 1D, with high priority being given to the stretches of the highway near the town of Kargil. The majority of posts along the Line of Control were adjacent to the highway, and therefore the recapture of nearly every infiltrated post increased both the territorial gains and the security of the highway. The protection of this route and the recapture of the forward posts were thus *ongoing objectives* throughout the war.

The Indian Army's first priority was to recapture peaks that were in the immediate vicinity of NH 1D. This resulted in Indian troops first targeting the Tiger Hill and Tololing complex in Dras, which dominated the Srinagar-Leh route. This was soon followed by the Batalik-Turtok sub-sector which provided access to Siachen Glacier. Some of the peaks that were of vital strategic importance to the Pakistani defensive troops were Point 4590 and Point 5353. While 4590 was the nearest point that had a view of NH 1D, point 5353 was the highest feature in the Dras sector, allowing the Pakistani troops to observe NH 1D. The recapture of Point 4590 by Indian troops on June 14 was significant, notwithstanding the fact that it resulted in the Indian Army suffering the most casualties in a single battle during the conflict. Though most of the posts in the vicinity of the highway were cleared by mid-June, some parts of the highway near Drass witnessed sporadic shelling until the end of the war.

Once India regained control of the hills overlooking NH 1D, the Indian Army turned to driving the invading force back across the Line of Control. TheBattle of Tololing, among other assaults, slowly tilted the combat in India's favor. The Pakistani troops at Tololing were aided by Pakistani fighters from Kashmir. Some of the posts put up a stiff resistance, including Tiger Hill (Point 5140) that fell only later in the war. Indian troops found well-entrenched Pakistani soldiers at Tiger Hill, and both sides suffered heavy casualties. After a final assault on the peak in which 10 Pakistani soldiers and 5 Indian soldiers were killed, Tiger Hill finally fell. A few of the assaults occurred atop hitherto unheard of peaks – most of them unnamed with only Point numbers to differentiate them – which witnessed fierce hand to hand combat.

As the operation was fully underway, about 250 artillery guns were brought in to clear the infiltrators in the posts that were in the line-of-sight. The BoforsFH-77B field howitzer played a vital role, with Indian gunners making maximum use of the terrain that assisted such an attack. However, its success was limited elsewhere due to the lack of space and depth to deploy the Bofors gun.

It was in this type of terrain that aerial attacks were used with limited effectiveness. French made Mirage 2000H of the IAF were tasked to drop laser-guided bombs to destroy well-entrenched positions of the Pakistani forces. However, The IAF lost a MiG-27 strike aircraft which it attributed to anengine failure as well as a MiG-21 fighter which was shot down by Pakistan; initially

Pakistan said it shot down both jets after they crossed into its territory. One Mi-8 helicopter was also lost, due to Stinger SAMs.

On May 27, 1999, Flt. Lt. Nachiketa developed engine trouble in the Batalik sector and bailed out of his craft. Sqn Ldr Ajay Ahuja went out of his way to locate his comrade but was shot down by a shoulder-fired Stinger missile. According to reports, he had bailed out of his stricken plane safely but was apparently killed by his captors as his body was returned riddled with bullet wounds.

In many vital points, neither artillery nor air power could dislodge the outposts manned by the Pakistani soldiers, who were out of visible range. The Indian Army mounted some direct frontal ground assaults which were slow and took a heavy toll given the steep ascent that had to be made on peaks as high as 18,000 feet (5,500 m). Since any daylight attack would be suicidal, all the advances had to be made under the cover of darkness, escalating the risk of freezing. Accounting for the wind chill factor, the temperatures were often as low as "15 °C to "11 °C (12 °F to 5 °F) near the mountain tops. Based on military tactics, much of the costly frontal assaults by the Indians could have been avoided if the Indian Military had chosen to blockade the supply route of the opposing force, virtually creating a siege. Such a move would have involved the Indian troops crossing the LoC as well as initiating aerial attacks on Pakistan soil, a manoeuvre India was not willing to exercise fearing an expansion of the theatre of war and reducing international support for its cause.

Two months into the conflict, Indian troops had slowly retaken most of the ridges that were encroached by the infiltrators; according to official count, an estimated 75%–80% of the intruded area and nearly all high ground was back under Indian control.

Withdrawal and Final Battles

The outbreak of armed fighting, Pakistan sought American help in de-escalating the conflict. Bruce Riedel, aide to then President Bill Clinton reported that the US intelligence had imaged Pakistani movements of nuclear weapons to forward deployments for fear of the Kargil hostilities escalating into a wider conflict between the two countries. However, President Clinton refused to intervene until Pakistan had removed all forces from the Indian side of the Line of Control. Following the Washington accord on July 4, where Sharif agreed to withdraw Pakistani troops, most of the fighting came to a gradual halt, but some Pakistani forces remained in positions on the Indian side of the LOC. In addition, the United Jihad Council (an umbrella for extremist groups) rejected Pakistan's plan for a climb-down, instead deciding to fight on.

The Indian army launched its final attacks in the last week of July; as soon as the Drass subsector had been cleared of Pakistani forces, the fighting ceased on July 26. The day has since been marked as *Kargil Vijay Diwas* (Kargil Victory Day) in India. By the end of the war, India had resumed control of all territory south and east of the Line of Control, as was established in July 1972 as per the Simla Agreement.

World Opinion

Pakistan was criticised by other countries for instigating the war, as its paramilitary forces and insurgents crossed the Line of Control. Pakistan's primary diplomatic response, one of plausible deniability linking the incursion to what it officially termed as "Kashmiri freedom fighters", was in the end not successful. Veteran analysts argued that the battle was fought at heights where only seasoned troops could survive, so poorly equipped "freedom fighters" would neither have the ability nor the wherewithal to seize land and defend it.

Moreover, while the army had initially denied the involvement of its troops in the intrusion, two soldiers were awarded the Nishan-E-Haider (Pakistan's highest military honour). Another 90 soldiers were also given gallantry awards, most of them posthumously, confirming Pakistan's role in the episode. India also released taped phone conversations between the Army Chief and a senior Pakistani general where the latter is recorded saying: "the scruff of [the militants] necks is in our hands," although Pakistan dismissed it as a "total fabrication". Concurrently, Pakistan made several contradicting statements, confirming its role in Kargil, when it defended the incursions saying that the LOC itself was disputed. Pakistan also attempted to internationalize the Kashmir issue, by linking the crisis in Kargil to the largerKashmir conflict but, such a diplomatic stance found few backers on the world stage.

As the Indian counter-attacks picked up momentum, Pakistani prime minister Nawaz Sharif flew to meet U.S. President Bill Clinton on July 4 to obtain support from the United States. Clinton rebuked Sharif, however, and asked him to use his contacts to rein in the militants and withdraw Pakistani soldiers from Indian territory. Clinton would later reveal in his autobiography that "Sharif's moves were perplexing" since the Indian Prime Minister had travelled to Lahore to promote bilateral talks aimed at resolving the Kashmir problem and "by crossing the Line of Control, Pakistan had wrecked the [bilateral] talks." On the other hand, he applauded Indian restraint for not crossing the LoC and escalating the conflict into an all-out war.

G8 nations supported India and condemned the Pakistani violation of the LOC at the Cologne summit. The European Union also opposed Pakistan's violation of the LOC. China, a long-time ally of Pakistan, insisted on a pullout of forces to the pre-conflict positions along the LoC and settling border issues peacefully. Other organizations like the ASEAN Regional Forum too supported India's stand on the inviolability of the LOC.

Faced with growing international pressure, Sharif managed to pull back the remaining soldiers from Indian territory. The joint statement issued by Clinton and Sharif conveyed the need to respect the Line of Control and resume bilateral talks as the best forum to resolve all disputes.

Gallantry Awards

A number of Indian soldiers earned awards for gallantry during the campaign.

- Grenadier Yogendra Singh Yadav, 18 Grenadiers, Param Vir Chakra
- Lieutenant Manoj Kumar Pandey, 1/11 Gorkha Rifles, Param Vir Chakra, Posthumous
- Captain Vikram Batra, 13 JAK Rifles, Param Vir Chakra, Posthumous

- Captain Anuj Nayyar,17 JAT Regiment, Maha Vir Chakra, Posthumous
- Major Saravanan, 1 Bihar, Vir Chakra, Posthumous
- Squadron Leader Ajay Ahuja, Indian Air Force, Vir Chakra, Posthumous
- Rifleman Sanjay Kumar, 13 JAK Rifles, Param Vir Chakra
- Major Rajesh Singh Adhikari, 18 Grenadiers, Maha Vir Chakra, Posthumous

Two Pakistani soldiers received the Nishan-e-Haider.

- Captain Karnal Sher Khan, Nishan-e-Haider, Posthumous
- Havaldaar Lalak Jan, Northern Light Infantry, Nishan-e-Haider, Posthumous

Impact and Influence of Media

The Kargil War was significant for the impact and influence of the mass media on public opinion in both nations. Coming at a time of exploding growth in electronic journalism in India, the Kargil news stories and war footage were often telecast live on TV, and many websites provided in-depth analysis of the war. The conflict became the first "live" war in South Asia; it was given such detailed media coverage that one effect was the drumming up of jingoistic feelings.

The conflict soon turned into a news propaganda war, in which press briefings given by government officials of each nation produced conflicting claims and counterclaims. The Indian government placed a temporary news embargo on information from Pakistan, banning the telecast of the state-run Pakistani channel PTV and blocking access to online editions of the *Dawn* newspaper. The Pakistani media criticized this apparent curbing of freedom of the press in India, while India media claimed it was in the interest of national security. The Indian government ran advertisements in foreign publications including *The Times* and *The Washington Post* detailing Pakistan's role in supporting extremists in Kashmir in an attempt to garner political support for its position.

As the war progressed, media coverage of the conflict was more intense in India than in Pakistan. Many Indian channels showed images from the battle zone in a style reminiscent of CNN's coverage of the Gulf War (one of the shells fired by Pakistan troops even hit a Doordarshan transmission centre in Kargil while coverage continued). Reasons for India's increased coverage included the greater number of privately owned electronic media in India compared to Pakistan and relatively greater transparency in the Indian media. At a seminar in Karachi, Pakistani journalists agreed that while the Indian government had taken the press and the people into its confidence, Pakistan had not.

The print media in India and abroad was largely sympathetic to the Indian cause, with editorials in newspapers based in the west and other neutral countries observing that Pakistan was largely responsible for the conflict. Some analysts believe that Indian media, which was both larger in number and more credible, may have acted as a force multiplier for the Indian military operation in Kargil and served as a morale booster. As the fighting intensified, the Pakistani version of events found little backing on the world stage. This helped India gain valuable diplomatic recognition for its position.

WMDs and the Nuclear Factor

Since Pakistan and India each had weapons of mass destruction, many in the international community were concerned that if the Kargil conflict intensified, it could lead to nuclear war. Both countries had tested their nuclear capability in 1998 (India conducted its first test in 1974 while it was Pakistan's first-ever nuclear test). Many pundits believed the tests to be an indication of the escalating stakes in the scenario in South Asia. When the Kargil conflict started just a year after the nuclear tests, many nations desired to end it before it intensified.

International concerns increased when Pakistani foreign secretary Shamshad Ahmad made a statement on May 31 warning that an escalation of the limited conflict could lead Pakistan to use "any weapon" in its arsenal. This was immediately interpreted as a threat of nuclear retaliation by Pakistan in the event of an extended war, and the belief was reinforced when the leader ofPakistan's senate noted, "The purpose of developing weapons becomes meaningless if they are not used when they are needed." Many such ambiguous statements from officials of both countries were viewed as warnings of an impending nuclear crisis where the combatants would consider use of their limited nuclear arsenals in 'tactical' nuclear warfare in the belief that it would not have ended in mutual assured destruction, as could have occurred in a nuclear conflict between the United States and the USSR. Some experts believe that following nuclear tests in 1998, the Pakistani military was emboldened by its nuclear deterrent to markedly increase coercion against India.

The nature of the India-Pakistan conflict took a more sinister turn when the U.S. received intelligence that Pakistani nuclear warheads were being moved towards the border. Bill Clinton tried to dissuade Pakistan prime minister Nawaz Sharif from nuclear brinkmanship, even threatening Pakistan of dire consequences. According to a White House official, Sharif seemed to be genuinely surprised by this supposed missile movement and responded that India was probably planning the same. In an article in May 2000 Dr Sanjay Badri-Maharaj claimed that India too had readied at least five nuclear-tipped ballistic missiles, but could not back up this claim with any official proof.

Sensing a deteriorating military scenario, diplomatic isolation, and the risks of a larger conventional and nuclear war, Sharif ordered the Pakistani army to vacate the Kargil heights. He later claimed in his official biography that General Pervez Musharraf had moved nuclear warheads without informing him. Recently however, Pervez Musharraf revealed in his memoirs that Pakistan's nuclear delivery system was not operational during the Kargil war; something that would have put Pakistan under serious disadvantage if the conflict went nuclear.

The threat of WMD included chemical and even biological weapons. Pakistan accused India of using chemical weapons and incendiary weapons such as napalm against the Kashmiri fighters. India, on the other hand, showcased a cache of gas masks as proof that Pakistan may have been prepared to use non-conventional weapons. US official and the Organisation for the Prohibition of Chemical Weapons determined that Pakistani allegations of India using banned chemicals in its bombs were unfounded.

AFTERMATH

India

From the end of the war until February 2000, the Indian stock market rose by over 30%. The next Indian national budget included major increases in military spending.

There was a surge in patriotism, with many celebrities expressing their support for the Kargil cause. Indians were angered by media reports of the death of pilot Ajay Ahuja, especially after Indian authorities reported that Ahuja had been murdered and his body mutilated by Pakistani troops. The war had produced higher than expected fatalities for the Indian military, with a sizeable percentage of them including newly commissioned officers. One month after conclusion of the Kargil war, the Atlantique Incident – where a Pakistan Navy plane was shot down by India – briefly reignited fears of a conflict between the two countries.

After the war, the Indian government severed ties with Pakistan and increased defence preparedness. India increased its defence budget as it sought to acquire more state of the art equipment. Media reported about military procurement irregularities and criticism of intelligence agencies like Research and Analysis Wing, which failed to predict the intrusions or the identity/number of infiltrators during the war. An internal assessment report by the armed forces, published in an Indian magazine, showed several other failings, including "a sense of complacency" and being "unprepared for a conventional war" on the presumption that nuclearism would sustain peace. It also highlighted the lapses in command and control, the insufficient troop levels and the dearth of large-calibre guns like the Bofors. In 2006, retired Air Chief Marshal, A.Y. Tipnis, alleged that the Indian Army did not fully inform the government about the intrusions, adding that the army chief Ved Prakash Malik, was initially reluctant to use the full strike capability of the Indian Air Force, instead requesting only helicopter gunship support. Soon after the conflict, India also decided to complete the project – previously stalled by Pakistan – to fence the entire LOC.

The end of the Kargil conflict was followed by the 13th Indian General Elections to the Lok Sabha, which gave a decisive mandate to the National Democratic Alliance (NDA) government. It was re-elected to power in September–October 1999 with a majority of 303 seats out of 545 in the Lok Sabha. On the diplomatic front, Indo-U.S. relations improved, as the United States appreciated Indian attempts to restrict the conflict to a limited geographic area. Relations with Israel – which had discreetly aided India with ordnance supply and matériel such as unmanned aerial vehicles and laser-guided bombs, as well as satellite imagery – also were bolstered.

Kargil Review Committee

Soon after the war the Atal Bihari Vajpayee government set up an inquiry into its causes and to analyze perceived Indian intelligence failures. The high-powered committee was chaired by eminent strategic affairs analyst K. Subrahmanyam and given powers to interview anyone with current or past associations with Indian security, including former Prime Ministers. The committee's final report (also referred to as the 'Subrahmanyam Report') led to a large-scale restructuring of Indian Intelligence. It, however, came in for heavy criticism in the Indian media for its perceived avoidance of assigning specific responsibility for failures over detecting the Kargil intrusions. The Committee was also embroiled in controversy for indicting Brigadier Surinder Singh of the Indian Army for his failure to report enemy intrusions in time, and for his subsequent conduct. Many press reports questioned or contradicted this finding and claimed that Singh had in fact issued early warnings that were ignored by senior Indian Army commanders and, ultimately, higher government functionaries.

In a departure from the norm the final report was published and made publicly available. Some chapters and all annexures, however, were deemed to contain classified information by the government and not released. K. Subrahmanyam later wrote that the annexures contained information on the development of India's nuclear weapons program and the roles played by Prime Ministers Rajiv Gandhi, P. V. Narasimha Rao and V P Singh.

Pakistan

Faced with the possibility of international isolation, the already fragile Pakistan economy was weakened further. The morale of Pakistan forces after the withdrawal declined as many units of the Northern Light Infantry suffered heavy casualties. The government refused to accept the dead bodies of many officers, an issue that provoked outrage and protests in the Northern Areas. Pakistan initially did not acknowledge many of its casualties, but Sharif later said that over 4,000 Pakistani troops were killed in the operation. Responding to this, Pakistan President Pervez Musharraf said, "It hurts me when an ex-premier undermines his own forces," and claimed that Indian casualties were more than that of Pakistan. The legacy of Kargil war still continues to debated on Pakistan's news channels and television political correspondents, which Musharraf repeatedly appeared to justified the causes and preludes of the Kargil war.

Many in Pakistan had expected a victory over the Indian military based on Pakistani official reports on the war, but were dismayed by the turn of events and questioned the eventual retreat. The military leadership is believed to have felt let down by the prime minister's decision to withdraw the remaining fighters. However, some authors, including Musharraf's close friend and former American CENTCOM Commander General Anthony Zinni, and former Prime minister Nawaz Sharif, state that it was General Musharraf who requested Sharif to withdraw the Pakistani troops. In 2012, Musharraf's senior officer and retired major-general Abdul Majeed Malik maintained that Kargil was a "total disaster" and gave bitter criticism to General Musharraf. Pointing out to the fact that Pakistan was in no position to fight India in that area; it was the Nawaz Sharif government that initiated the diplomatic process by involving the US President Bill Clinton and got Pakistan out of the difficult scenario. Malik maintained that soldiers were not "Mujaheddin" but an active-duty serving officers and soldiers of Pakistan Army.

In a national security meeting with Prime minister Nawaz Sharif at the Joint Headquarters, General Musharraf became heavily involved with serious altercations with Chief of Naval Staff Admiral

Fasih Bokhari who ultimately called for a court-martial against General Musharraf. Taking participation in the arguments, Chief of Air Staff Air Chief Marshal PQ Mehdi quoted that "any intervention by the Navy and the PAF into disputed land of Indian-controlled Kashmir would be perceived as an escalation to all-out declared war". After witnessing Musharraf's criticism given to his fellow officers, ACM PQ Mehdi decided to give Musharraf a favor after issuing orders to PAF's F-16s for the patrolling missions near the Skardu Valley. The Pakistan Navy largely remains camouflaged during this entire conflict, only submarines were deployed for partrolling missions. With Sharif placing the onus of the Kargil attacks squarely on the army chief Pervez Musharraf, there was an atmosphere of uneasiness between the two. On October 12, 1999, General Musharraf staged a bloodless *coup d'état*, ousting Nawaz Sharif.

Benazir Bhutto, an opposition leader in the parliament and former prime minister, called the Kargil War "Pakistan's greatest blunder". Many ex-officials of the military and the Inter-Services Intelligence (Pakistan's principal intelligence agency) also believed that "Kargil was a waste of time" and "could not have resulted in any advantage" on the larger issue of Kashmir. A retired Pakistan Army's Lieutenant-General Ali Kuli Khan, lambasted the war as "a disaster bigger than the East Pakistan tragedy", adding that the plan was "flawed in terms of its conception, tactical planning and execution" that ended in "sacrificing so many soldiers." The Pakistani media criticized the whole plan and the eventual climbdown from the Kargil heights since there were no gains to show for the loss of lives and it only resulted in international condemnation.

Despite calls by many, no public commission of inquiry was set up in Pakistan to investigate the people responsible for initiating the conflict. The Pakistan Muslim League (PML(N)) published awhite paper in 2006, which stated that Nawaz Sharif constituted an inquiry committee that recommended a court martial for General Pervez Musharraf, but Musharraf "stole the report" after toppling the government, to save himself. The report also claims that India knew about the plan 11 months before its launch, enabling a complete victory for India on military, diplomatic and economic fronts. A statement in June, 2008 by a former X Corps commander and Director-General of Military Intelligence (M.I.) that time, Lieutenant-General (retired) Jamshed Gulzar Kianisaid that: "As Prime minister, Nawaz Sharif "was never briefed by the army" on the Kargil attack, reignited the demand for a probe of the episode by legal and political groups.

Though the Kargil conflict had brought the Kashmir dispute into international focus – which was one of the aims of Pakistan – it had done so in negative circumstances that eroded its credibility, since the infiltration came just after a peace process between the two countries was underway.

The sanctity of the LOC too received international recognition. President Clinton's move to ask Islamabad to withdraw hundreds of armed militants from Indian-administered Kashmir was viewed by many in Pakistan as indicative of a clear shift in US policy against Pakistan.

After the war, a few changes were made to the Pakistan armed forces. In recognition of the Northern Light Infantry's performance in the war – which even drew praise from a retired Indian Lt. General – the regiment was incorporated into the regular army.

The war showed that despite a tactically sound plan that had the element of surprise, little groundwork had been done to gauge the politico-diplomatic ramifications. And like previous unsuccessful infiltrations attempts, such as *Operation Gibraltar*, which sparked the 1965 war, there was little coordination or information sharing among the branches of the Pakistani Armed Forces.

One U.S. Intelligence study is reported to have stated that Kargil was yet another example of Pakistan's (lack of) grand strategy, repeating the follies of the previous wars. In 2013, General Musharraf's close collaborator and confidential subordinate Lieutenant-General (retired) Shahid Aziz revealed to Pakistan's news televisions and electronic media, that "[Kargil] adventure' was India's intelligence failure and Pakistan's miscalculated move, the Kargil operation was known only to General Parvez Musharraf and four of his close collaborators."

Casualties

Pakistan army losses have been difficult to determine. Pakistan confirmed that 453 soldiers were killed. The US Department of State had made an early, partial estimate of close to 700 fatalities. According to numbers stated by Nawaz Sharif there were over 4,000 fatalities. His PML (N) party in its "white paper" on the war mentioned that more than 3,000 Mujahideens, officers and soldiers were killed. Another major Pakistani political party, thePakistan Peoples Party, also says that "thousands" of soldiers and irregulars died. Indian estimates stand at 1,042 Pakistani soldiers killed. Musharraf, in his Hindi version of his memoirs, titled "Agnipath", differs from all the estimates stating that 357 troops were killed with a further 665 wounded. Apart from General Musharraf's figure on the number of Pakistanis wounded, the number of people injured in the Pakistan camp is not yet fully known although they are at least more than 400 according to Pakistan army's website. One Indian Pilot was officially captured during the fighting, while there were eight Pakistani soldiers who were captured during the fighting, and were repatriated on 13 August 1999;

India gave its official casualty figures as 527 dead and 1,363 wounded.

Kargil War in the Arts

The brief conflict provided considerable dramatic material for filmmakers and authors in India. Some documentaries which were shot on the subject were used by the ruling party coalition, led by Bharatiya Janata Party (BJP), in furthering its election campaign that immediately followed the war. The following is a list of the major films and dramas on the subject.

- "Lord John Marbury (The West Wing)" (1999), 11th episode of the first season depicts a fictionalized representation of the Kargil conflict.
- Pentagram's single, 'Price Of Bullets', released in 1999 dealt with the Kargil War.
- *LOC: Kargil* (2003), a Hindi movie which depicts many incidents from the war was one of the longest in Indian movie history, running for more than four hours.

- *Lakshya* (2004), another Hindi movie portraying a fictionalised account of the conflict. Movie critics have generally appreciated the realistic portrayal of characters. The film also received good reviews in Pakistan because it portrays both sides fairly.
- *Sainika* (2002), the Kannada film directed by Mahesh Sukhdhare depicted the life of a soldier with Kargil war as one of the events. Starring C.P.Yogishwar and Sakshi Shivanand.
- *Dhoop* (2003), Hindi film, directed by national award winner Ashwini Chaudhary, which depicted the life of Anuj Nayyar's parents after his death. Anuj Nayyar was a captain in the Indian army and was awarded Maha Vir Chakra posthumously. Om Puri plays the role of S.K. Nayyar, Anuj's father.
- *Mission Fateh – Real Stories of Kargil Heroes*, a TV series telecast on Sahara channel chronicling the Indian Army's missions.
- *Fifty Day War*–A theatrical production on the war, directed by Aamir Raza Husain, the title indicating the length of the Kargil conflict. This was claimed to be the biggest production of its kind in Asia, budget of Rs. 1.5 crore, involving real aircraft and explosions in an outdoor setting.
- *Kurukshetra* (2008) – A Malayalam film directed by a former Indian Army Major Ravi (Retd) based on his experience of Kargil War.
- *Laag* (2000)— A Pakistani film-drama based on the armed intrusions and struggle of Pakistan army soldiers in the conflict.

Many other movies like *Tango Charlie* drew heavily upon the Kargil episode, which still continues to be a plot for mainstream movies with a Malayalam movie *Keerthi Chakra*.

The impact of the war in the sporting arena was visible during the India-Pakistan clash in the 1999 Cricket World Cup, which coincided with the Kargil timeline. The game witnessed heightened passions and was one of the most viewed matches in the tournament.

CONSTRUCTIVISM AND CONFLICT: THE 'GOOD NORM' PROBLEM

Despite their richer ontology and more sophisticated analytical framework for studying the various facets of international relations, constructivists have nonetheless tended to disproportionately conduct research on the positive and progressive aspects of world politics—such as security cooperation and the role of global norms in stigmatising the use of nuclear weapons and aiding the demise of Apartheid—which has left conflict and war under-theorised.

Kowert and Legro first termed this the 'good norm problem,' and several constructivists have since emphasised the need to further explore the social construction of the 'nasty' aspects of world politics—such as violent nationalisms and war, and the conceptions of 'self' and 'other' (identity) which drive them—amidst the continuing constructivist bias and preference for 'nice' norms.

Indeed, this bias has been instrumental in providing realists such as Mearsheimer with the opportunity to (wrongly) dismiss constructivism as a theory of peace which is 'radically concerned with changing state behaviour' while being unable to account for power politics and war—the purported realm of realists. It might also be the case that such an impression has discouraged scholars and researchers of the India-Pakistan conflict from exploring constructivism as an alternative paradigm to rationalist theories.

However, as Wendt notes, Mearsheimer's critique is fundamentally flawed. Constructivism's focus on social construction is analytically neutral between conflict and cooperation. Moreover, Mearsheimer conflates description and explanation.

The former concerns the presence and extent of *realpolitik*-based practices in international relations. But even if power politics and war occur with regularity, this does not make realism true; the latter's theoretical value depends on its ability to *explain,* not merely describe or identify, *realpolitik*—in other words, on the strength of its materialist explanation of conflict and war, and whether constructivism's social explanation is superior. Realism, as Wendt and others correctly stress, 'does not have a monopoly on the ugly and brutal side of international life.' Thus, constructivists emphasise the ideational structures which lead states to define their identities and interests in conflictual terms. Nevertheless, the 'good norm problem' is certainly an issue. This paper will therefore aim to address the constructivist bias for 'nice' norms by exploring the centrality of intersubjective social structures in producing the India-Pakistan conflict—with a focus on the role of identity.

PRODUCING AN ANALYTIC FRAMEWORK FOR IDENTITY: BEYOND WENDT'S SYSTEMIC THEORY

Identities, writes Rogers Smith, 'are among the most normatively significant and behaviorally consequential aspects of politics,' and analyses that incorporate them present a powerful challenge to behaviouralist and rational-choice approaches. Constructivists have demonstrated, as discussed earlier, that Smith's observation extends to the realm of international relations. Accordingly, identity has been a central concept in constructivist arguments, particularly for Wendt and other influential 'middle-ground' constructivists. Indeed, the integrity of the former's theory hinges on the strength of his conceptualisation of identity. But Wendt's highly-influential conceptualisation suffers from important—even severe—flaws. Thus, this chapter will engage with and critique Wendt's 'middle-range' framework and attempt to formulate a more convincing conceptualisation of identity—as well as its relationship with conflict—based on the insights of alternative accounts. I will also aim to show that rationalist/ materialist explanations of identity formation and conflict are insufficient. Before proceeding, it is valuable first to elucidate what is meant by 'identity.' Identity essentially refers to our self-conception *in relation* to others.

Identities are not individualistic or personal, but are formed in a social context where individual and collective identities are co-constituted—leading us to identify with "our" social group—and 'defined [by our] interaction and relationship to others.' In the same way, national/state identities are also 'partly formed in relationship to other nations and states.' Accepting this, Wendt applies symbolic interactionist theory to the systems-level of inter-state relations and argues that states' social identities—and in turn their interests—are formed and sustained (or constituted) through *social interaction* with other states; an ongoing process which creates structures of shared knowledge (which are maintained by practices), leading to relatively stable identities as the social system into which states are embedded becomes a 'social fact.'

If social identities and structures of shared knowledge are competitive and zero-sum, conflict may ensue. However, while difficult to modify, identities 'are not carved in stone' and can change through 'social learning'; replacing, for example, Hobbesian cultures of anarchy and conflict with Kantian security communities. For Wendt, the 'daily life of international politics is an on-going process of states taking identities in relation to Others, casting them into corresponding counter-identities, and playing out the result.'

In contrast to Waltz's excessively materialistic 'proto-theory' of identity formation, Wendt endogenises states' social identities and regards them as socially constructed. Thus, 'anarchy is what states make of it.'Because he focuses on the level of the international system, Wendt also anthropomorphises states and distinguishes between their 'corporate' and 'social' identities—the latter referring to the sets of meanings about oneself a state derives from the social structures of international society through inter-state interaction, and the former denoting 'the intrinsic, self-organizing qualities that constitute actor individuality.' For states, this means domestic-level elements such as the constituent individuals, physical resources, and the shared beliefs and institutions which confer individuals with a collective function. Crucially, Wendt regards corporate identities as 'exogenously given' and 'ontologically prior to the state system'; in short, as 'fixed and pre-social entities'. Consequently, and because of his assumption of a unitary state, Wendt also brackets everything domestic.

Wendt's argument of social identities emerging through systemic interaction and his bracketing and exogenising of 'corporate' identities presents serious problems for his framework.

As Sujata Pasic argues, by attempting to avoid an 'oversocialized approach,' Wendt, in effect, strips identity of its social-cultural content. 'Social' identity formation in Wendt's constructivism is curiously missing a notion of society and is presented as 'simply a by-product of repeated state interactions.' Similar to realists/ rationalists, then, Wendt's conceptualisation of identity formation fails to engage 'the actual social levels of state sociality.'

Indeed, it is difficult to differentiate between identity and behaviour in Wendt's account; his framework demands us to deduce actors' self-conceptions/understandings merely from their behaviour. There is thus a compelling argument that Wendt's conceptualisation of identity does not entail 'identity' at all, but is simply an account of behaviour. The 'centrality of physical gestures' to Wendt's framework makes it 'impossible to analyse identity [formation and] transformation as a *discursive* process.' As does his treatment of 'corporate' identities. By bracketing the domestic, Wendt omits a considerable amount of the normative content that underlies identity formation and change.

Maja Zehfuss demonstrates this by showing how post-Cold War contestations over German identity were not limited to the level of inter-state relations, but were equally present in domestic discourse and exerted a deep influence on German identity construction. Moreover, by joining rationalists in regarding states and their corporate identities as 'exogenously given,' fixed and pre-social, Wendt obscures the complexity of identity formation/ change and the extent to which corporate identities are not 'bounded' categories or spatio-temprоally fixed, but are often contested and even unstable; with a profound effect not only on states' 'social' identities, but also in some cases—and this is extremely relevant to explanations of nationalist conflict—their very existence.

Cederman and Daase and Pasic thus correctly stress the need to move beyond 'static [and statist] conceptualisations of identity' and endogenise and problematise *corporate* identities; that is, actors' 'very existence and extension in space and time,' including their membership, boundaries, and domestic institutions. Runa Das argues this analytical approach is particularly important in the context of India-Pakistan relations. Contra Wendt, this requires an appreciation of state sociality beyond systemic interaction between fixed, unitary states. Importantly, this analytical shift can be achieved within a framework of constructivism without sliding into postmodern relativism.

In developing such a framework, I draw on sociology, social theory and social psychology by incorporating the insights of four main analytical perspectives—Abdelal et al.'s conceptualisation of collective identity; Cederman and Daase's application of Simmel's sociational theory; Peter Gries's adaptation of social identity theory, and the concept of 'ontological security.'

While some may criticise such analytical eclecticism, Katzenstein and Okawara offer a strong defense of this approach by arguing that it is intellectually more important to make sense of empirical anomalies than it is to privilege parsimony. I formulate the core assumptions of the model around Abdelal et al.'s framing of collective identity as 'a social category that varies along two dimensions—content and contestation.' The aim of the framework is to conceptualise the social construction of identities and its influence on actors, and to demonstrate the impact of *contestation* on the content of identities and on conflict in international relations.

Content

Content describes the *meaning* of a collective identity, and may entail four types; *constitutive norms,* which define the boundaries and formal and informal rules of group membership; *social purposes,* or the goals that a group attaches to its identity; *relational comparisons,* through which a group defines itself in reference to 'Others,' and *cognitive models,* which refers to the 'understandings of political and material conditions and interests' that are shaped by a group's identity. Three core assumptions can be inferred from this reading of the content of identities, which I place under two categories: *identity formation* and *influence over actors.*

Identity Formation. The first core assumption centres on the argument that identities are socially constructed, and emphasises the 'social origins of identity.' Collective identities are not primordial, essentialist or natural—as, for example, Huntington's 'clash of civilizations' paradigm or Posen's neo-realist reading of ethnic conflict would suggest—but are 'constructed and reconstructed through historical action.' Nationalism, for instance, is one key discursive process which constructs national identities around mythical, 'imagined communities.'

Arguments for unity and the boundaries of community (including nation-states') are also embedded into these mythical constructions through the use of language, socially meaningful cultural symbols and imagery or 'frames,' and narratives of national identity (storylines about a nation's origins and history).These might be employed strategically by purposeful agents ('political entrepreneurs'), but such action is not merely instrumental; it can be principled and takes place within a normative structure that enables or legitimises it. The endogenising of corporate identities central to Simmel's sociational theory—which privileges neither actor nor structure and emphasises the dynamic interaction of both—helps capture this and overcomes the structural-bias of constructivists like Wendt, who have been criticised for paying insufficient attention to human agents. Social psychology perspectives—notably social identity theory—also suggest that we might respond to the mythological social-cultural cues of collective identities and assimilate into groups because of the desire to gain—and maintain—collective self-esteem. The second core assumption, related to the content type *relational comparisons*, is that there is always an internal-external dynamic to identity formation. Collective identities do not simply emerge from internal group processes.

Rather, identities are incomplete without an 'understanding of oneself in relation to others.' Several scholars have shown, for example, that European identity construction has always needed—including contemporarily—a constituting 'Eastern' 'Other'. Similarly, central to social identity theory is the notion of the 'looking-glass self,' where groups gain knowledge about their own collective identities through comparisons with others, leading to identity formation through in-group/out-group differentiation. In the realm of international relations, Others are also vital to a state's identity. Carl Schmitt argues that a state's authority over its self-definition depends on framing Other(s) as 'public enemies.' But contra Wendt, states' 'social' identities are also partly the product of the domestic socio-cultural practices that constitute their national identities. Barnett captures the internal-external dynamics of identity formation succinctly with his definition of identity as 'a relational construct that emerges out of international and domestic discourse and interactions.'

Influence over actors. The third core assumption is that identities shape and influence actors' actions, interests and understandings of material and economic conditions. Here the content types *constitutive norms,social purposes*, and *cognitive models* are particularly relevant. With respect to the former, depending on the degree of internalisation of constitutive practices, norms may influence actors by biasing choice through a 'logic of appropriateness,' where behaviour that is inappropriate for an actor's identity is consciously dismissed. *Social purposes* highlights the *purposive* content of collective identities and emphasises the role of identity in leading actors to infuse their practices with group purposes and to interpret the world through frameworks partly defined by these purposes. An identity's purposive content—based on the notion that *who we are influences what we do*—thus assists in defining group interests, goals, and preferences, while also producing obligations for the group to pursue practices that increase the likelihood of achieving its set of goals. Purposive goals might range from specific territorial claims to an abstract moral purpose, which Reus-Smit argues deeply influences international state practices and institutions. Finally, the *cognitive content* of an identity entails a group's model of social reality, or its epistemology and ontology. This can be conceived of as a *worldview* which enables a group to 'make sense of social, political, and economic conditions.' Vitally, this cognitive perspective suggests that identities 'are not things in the world but ways of seeing the world,' which help us orient our actions and conceptualise ourselves (and Others), and our interests and predicaments or threats; as well as our 'subjective perception and understanding of [our] communal past' or history. Actors are not compelled into certain forms of behaviour by material forces or the objective instrumental logic of rational-choice. Rather, as Risse et al. argue, it is 'collective identities [that] define and shape how actors view their perceived instrumental and material interests and which preferences are regarded as legitimate and appropriate for enacting given identities.'

Contestation (and conflict)

Identities are not 'natural,' fixed or stable entities. As Yosef Lapid points out, taking constructivism seriously requires us to treat identities as socially constructed, rather than primordial; as optional, rather than deterministic; as fragmenting/diversifying, rather than integrating/homogenising; and as multidimensional and dynamic, rather than undimensional and static. In short, we must 'problematize [the] dominant ontology and epistemology of stability and continuity that [has] hitherto informed depictions of… collective identity.' Thus, the second key dimension of identity is *contestation*. Abdelal et al. challenge the reifying of collective identities and argue that the content of identities 'is the outcome of a process of social contestation within the group.' However, I diverge slightly from this perspective because of its one-dimensional focus on *internal*contestation, which obscures the importance of external challenges to the content of an identity from 'out-groups.' Instead, I frame contestation around Thomas Berger's argument that cultures and identities 'are not static entities hovering above society,' but are reproduced through often imperfect primary/secondary socialisation mechanisms, while being 'under constant pressure from *both* external developments and internal contradictions.' Crucially, utilising social identity theory and sociational theory, I centre the remaining core assumptions of the model on the argument that contestation dynamics are essential to understanding patterns of conflict in international relations, particularly 'enduring rivalries' such as India and Pakistan's.

Social Identity Theory (SIT). SIT emerged as a theoretical approach to intergroup relations in social psychology. Through robust experimental work using 'minimal-group' situations, SIT convincingly demonstrated that people seek a positive self-identity through identifying with a group, and favourably comparing this 'in-group' to 'out-groups.' These comparisons induce potential competition through in-group favouritism and out-group discrimination. Jonathan Mercer applied the insights of SIT to the level of the international system and argued that they provide theoretical and empirical support to neo-realist assumptions about state egoism, inter-state competition and conflict, self-help systems and the pursuit of relative gains—with the desire for a positive self-identity, rather than the anarchic international structure or material economic or security incentives, generating and driving inter-group and inter-state competition. Conflict, argues Mercer, is 'an inescapable feature of intergroup and interstate relations.' There are glaring errors in Mercer's application of SIT, however. Mercer conflates 'in-group love,' which SIT emphasises as emerging from in-group favouritism, and 'out-group hate/dislike,' which does not necessarily follow from favouritism towards in-groups. Inter-group competition, conflict, and aggression should thus be considered distinct from in-group bias. Many other applications of SIT to IR suffer from similar problems. Peter Gries challenges Mercer on the same grounds and offers a highly valuable framework for applying SIT to the identity-conflict debate in IR. Rather than viewing inter-state/inter-group competition or conflict as inevitable, Gries follows social psychologist Marilyn Brewer's argument that 'any relationship between ingroup identification and outgroup hostility is progressive and contingent rather than necessary and inevitable.'

Thus, Gries identifies conditions under which identification with nations may lead to international competition and conflict. To achieve this, he describes a four-stage process, with conflict as the final stage: (1) ingroup identification, (2) ingroup positivity, (3) intergroup competition, (4) intergroup conflict. According to SIT, once people identify with their 'ingroup,' they also attach positive attributes to it and favour it over outgroups. This creates a desire for *positive social identity*, and in order to obtain this and maintain ingroup positivity, groups engage in*intergroup social comparisons*, a process through which they seek external confirmation and recognition by outgroups of their social identity and the positive views they attach to it.

It is these *social comparisons processes* that lie at the heart of explaining when ingroup identification and ingroup positivity (stages one and two) may lead to intergroup competition and conflict (stages three and four). When ingroup positivity is not affirmed by significant Others, or when outgroups are perceived to impugn or *contest* the ingroup's identity, the latter's collective self-esteem is threatened, and anger and competition might follow. Here, argues Allen Whiting, nations may shift from espousing non-competitive 'affirmative nationalism' to competitive 'assertive nationalism,' and even 'aggressive nationalism':

> Affirmative nationalism centres exclusively on 'us' as a positive in-group referent with pride in attributes and achievements. Assertive nationalism adds 'them' as a negative out-group referent that challenges the in-group's interests and possibly its identity. Aggressive nationalism identifies a specific foreign enemy as serious threat that requires action to defend vital interests.

Contestation of one's identity from an 'outgroup' through social comparisons is thus a vital prerequisite to competition and conflict. However, Gries identifies three conditions which need to be satisfied for competition to ensue. First, the comparisons must be made with a *salient other*: an external group that is a relevant and 'desirable object of comparison.' With regards to Pakistan, for example, while India is a salient other, Ecuador is not. Second, the comparisons must entail something that is *consequential* to the groups' self-conceptions: something each group *cherishes as part of itself*. For Pakistan and India, this may be the ideological foundations of their national identities; for example Pakistan's 'Muslim' identity and India's 'secular' self-conception. Third, the comparisons must be framed in *zero-sum terms*. Here, the notion of 'status' is particularly important. Thus, under zero-sum comparisons, Pakistan's status as a 'Muslim' nation might require hurting India's status as a 'secular' or 'Hindu' nation, and vice versa. One group's 'gains' in this regard will be the other group's 'losses.' All three of these conditions need to be met; if comparisons are inconsequential or not framed in zero-sum terms with a salient other, competition will not ensue. Moreover, even if these conditions are met, competition can be inhibited through 'social mobility'—denoting 'exiting' from a threatened social identity—or 'social creativity,' which entails reframing threatening comparisons 'to allow for positive distinctiveness.' Therefore, contra

Mercer, competition is not an inevitable feature of ingroup favouritism.

Ontological Security and Sociational Theory. But how do we get from intergroup competition to intergroup conflict? Gries does not explore this in detail, but suggests the role of affect—particularly anger—might be crucial. Instead, I join Huysmans, Steele and Mitzen in emphasising the group/state's need for 'ontological security,' which is already implicit in the SIT framework. According to this perspective, states seek more than just the physical security that realists privilege. More importantly, they constantly require 'ontological security,' or security and stability in their self-understandings, which Anthony Giddens describes as essential to obtaining a sense of agency and self-identity.

States 'need to feel secure in who they are.' Deep uncertainty and anxiety—which in my model stems from threatening *contestations* (internal and external) to a group's identity—'renders the actor's identity insecure' (thus threatening collective self-esteem). To alleviate this ontological insecurity, states seek a stable cognitive environment. They thus pursue cognitive certainty by establishing *routinized relations* with significant others (such as those that threaten their ontological security), which in turn leads actors to 'get attached to these social relationships.'

Crucially, ontological security-seeking can conflict with physical security. If materially-harmful or 'self-defeating' conflicts can provide ontological security, states may become 'attached' to conflictual relationships because 'on-going, certain conflict' is preferable to deeply uncertain self-identities. This creates a sort of implicit 'dysfunctional [intergroup] collective identity' centred on physical insecurity and competition; a mutual, intersubjective social structure where each state nonetheless considers itself to be acting alone and contesting the 'Other.' In other words, a collective identity without a 'we' feeling. Here the traditional 'security dilemma' is turned on its head; the certainty conflict provides, rather than uncertainty, can cause and sustain conflict.

The need for ontological security offers a powerful structural explanation of 'intractable conflicts'/'enduring rivalries' (such as the India-Pakistan conflict) which seem pathological or irrational from a realist perspective—a perspective whose focus on 'material rationality' fails to explain the social construction of identities and the role identity plays in producing 'irrational' or 'self-defeating' conflicts. But the ontological security-conflict relationship also has a crucial *internal* component at the level of states' 'corporate' identities, which systemic theories omit by reifying nation-states. Threats to self-identity might emanate not only from external others, but also 'internal others'—a category Steele and Huysmans term *internal strangers*—who disturb the 'predictability and continuity' of a state's/nation's self-identity over time; thus endangering the 'realization of ontological security.' It is here that sociational theory is especially illuminating, for it also problematises 'corporate' identities—the boundaries of groups/ nations/states.

Rather than reifying the boundaries of nation-states, sociational theory regards spatial mappings as socially constructed. For Simmel, 'the boundary is not a spatial fact with social implications, but rather a sociological fact that forms spatially.' This highlights a crucial link between ontological (in)security and ontological *survival*, which Mitzen and others do not explore.

For as Pasic writes, 'states, even with stores of military might at their disposal, only survive if the historical arguments for unity within them continue to convince an audience.' Ontological survival in this context is especially pressing when the ingroup and outgroup hold incompatible spatial representations and the situation might involve potential boundary transformations—as is the case with 'irredentist' conflicts. Consequently, deep ontological uncertainty—stemming not only from external contestations but also 'internal strangers' who threaten 'national unity' and identity cohesion—may intensify levels of ingroup discrimination and bias as groups/ states urgently seek to establish firm and coherent boundaries.

This might be achieved through *internal violence*—which attempts to secure self-identities through efforts to homogenise populations and utilise violence as a 'vehicle for social integration' to 'defuse the danger that a "foreigner inside"' presents to the group's self-identity. More importantly, conflict with an outgroup might also be employed. Here, sociational theory highlights the importance of conflict—as an interaction process with an external Other—in creating the group consciousness necessary for secure identities. Applying the Framework: Identity and the Enduring India-Pakistan Conflict

In order to sufficiently analyse and contextualise the India-Pakistan rivalry, it is essential to firstly appreciate the nature of the conflict. As T.V. Paul et al. demonstrate, the relationship between the two states does not constitute an ordinary conflict, but an *enduring rivalry*, denoting 'a strategic competition between the same pair of states over an extended period of time.' While the majority of inter-state conflicts are concluded relatively quickly, a small percentage become *enduring*, 'locking' the competing states into a robust conflictual relationship.

These 'enduring' or 'intractable' conflicts are defined by an 'outstanding set of unresolved issues,' 'strategic interdependence,' 'psychological manifestations of enmity,' and 'repeated militarized conflict.' The aforementioned features evidently characterise the India-Pakistan relationship, which has experienced four wars (three of them over the disputed territory of Kashmir), continual crises and hostility, 'proxy wars', and has even been on the verge of nuclear conflict (in 1990 and 2001-2).

Interestingly, realist and rational-choice approaches have tremendous difficulty in explaining enduring rivalries. For realists, who place material*power* at the heart of explanations of conflict, enduring rivalries should only take place between states whose material capabilities are relatively similar (major powers, for example). In asymmetric conflicts—such as India and Pakistan's—where one state possesses a substantial power advantage (in our case India), enduring rivalries should not develop because of the stronger side's ability to militarily defeat and impose its will on the weaker state.

But contrary to realist assumptions, the asymmetric India-Pakistan conflict has endured for over sixty years, despite Pakistan's repeated failures to militarily defeat or challenge India. Such conflicts appear similarly enigmatic to rational-choice theorists, with some even suggesting that repeated military conflicts are not 'enduring rivalries' with strong historical interconnections, but 'random events' occurring by chance. However, not only has this argument been challenged empirically, but it also seems 'ludicrous' to suggest that India and Pakistan's various conflicts have taken place 'randomly,' with no interconnections. Some realists/ rationalists accept the substantive presence of these seemingly 'irrational' conflicts, but tend to implicitly regard them as aberrations or deviations from the 'rational' systems-level realist logic, and explain them with reference to 'second-image' causes such as bureaucratic self-interest.

However, this chapter will move beyond realism's materialism and methodological individualism and seek to analyse the enduring India-Pakistan rivalry utilising the identity framework developed—exploring the social construction of both states' identities and the influence of these intersubjective social structures on their interests, preferences, and understandings of the material world, and, vitally, on their conflictual relationship.

It will be concluded that the India-Pakistan relationship constitutes a 'dysfunctional [intergroup] collective identity,' characterised by deep ontological uncertainty—stemming from both 'domestic' and 'systemic' turbulence in the form of *threatening contestations to each state's 'social' but also 'corporate' identities*—and an on-going, zero-sum social comparisons process, with conflict providing an avenue for the realisation of ontological security and the maintenance of collective (in-group) self-esteem. To strengthen my argument and test its plausibility, alternative explanations of the conflict will then be critically analysed, before concluding the paper by situating its contribution within the wider debate on the India-Pakistan conflict and suggesting that constructivism offers researchers the opportunity to introduce IR theory as a serious tool in the study of the conflict without being constrained by excessively materialistic or parsimonious, systemic—and wholly inadequate—theories such as neo-realism.

Indian and Pakistani Identity Formation

In analysing the role of identity in India-Pakistan relations, it is crucial to recognise the socially constructed, as opposed to primordial or instrumental, quality of identity formation. Many adopt a primordialist interpretation and attribute the enduring rivalry to the irreconcilable worldviews of, and entrenched hostilities between, monolithic 'Muslim' Pakistan and 'Hindu' India—essentially explaining the conflict as an offshoot of Hindu-Muslim communalism. While superficially appealing, this argument fails to account for the centuries of relative coexistence and inter-social, cultural and religious connections and exchanges between generally pluralistic Hindu and Muslim communities prior to the twentieth century.

More fundamentally, it ignores the *socially constructed,* rather than natural, quality of both states' national and state identities; something this section aims to address, beginning with India. Much of 'modern' India's self-conception was originally formulated around Indian nationalist discourse and spearheaded by the highly-dominant Congress party before and following independence.

In particular, Jawaharlal Nehru was pivotal in helping to articulate the central features of Indian identity—not in a liberal-individualist sense, but as a purposeful agent embedded in a social structure consisting of the intersubjective ideas of the wider Indian nationalist movement. The first core element of India's self-conception was *Sarva Dharma Samabhava* (secularism), which was key in distinguishing India from the 'communal' and 'reactionary' Pakistani 'other,' highlighting the in-group/out-group differentiation element of identity formation. Indeed, Nehru himself defined India's self-image as 'a secular nation' by differentiating it with ' two-nation theory which Pakistan is sponsoring.'

The 'exceptionalism' of Indian democracy in South Asia as well India's espousal of non-alignment and its claim to moral leadership in the developing world were the other core 'differentiating markers' from the Pakistani 'other' in India's self-image. In addition, India was deemed a *modern* 'major power'; a successor to the British with a powerful regional and global mission that reflected its 'national greatness.' Narratives and frames were utilised to reify this self-conception; history was interpreted anew and multiculturalism presented as a natural feature of Indian civilisation, while 'pacific' ancient cultural and social traditions coupled with stories exalting the glories of India's past civilisations helped legitimise its 'benign' global role in the international system. Moreover, 'India' was transformed from a vast land of disparate provinces and princely states—described as a 'porridge of irregular and improbable jigsaw puzzle shapes' —into an 'imagined community' whose territorial borders were naturalised and embedded into the national consciousness through 'the popular sacralisation of territory,' embodied in the metaphor of *Bharat Mata*('Mother India').

While India's self-image has been based on secularism, Pakistan's identity was constructed on the mythical narrative of the 'two-nation' theory, popularly articulated by the Muslim League, which posited that the Muslims and Hindus of India represented two monolithic, incompatible civilisations who were based, as Jinnah declared, 'on conflicting ideas and conceptions.' Crucially, Pakistan's national (and state) identity as the homeland of India's Muslims and its self-image as an advanced, *modern* Islamic state was (and continues to be) constructed against the perceived threat of Hindu (the 'other') domination and majoritarianism. Thus, the notion of *parity* between 'Muslim' Pakistan and 'Hindu' India has been central to Pakistan's self-conception. As former Prime Minister Zulifkar Bhutto wrote:

One of the dominant urges for Pakistan has been to dispel the notion of seniority or superiority of Hindu India over Muslim India by creating a Muslim State equal and sovereign to the other State.

Moreover, being different from the Indian 'other' has been essential in providing 'a rationale for the two-nation theory and for Pakistan's battle for a separate identity.' Narratives have thus emphasised Pakistan's Islamic-Arabic roots and '[rejected] everything that was Indian' about Pakistan. Some have suggested the narratives and cultural symbols associated with the 'two-nation' theory were merely instruments in the power struggle between elites (and thus without normative content). However, while the 'two-nation' theory was certainly employed strategically by political entrepreneurs, such activity took place within a normative structure influenced by a mass, broad-based movement, and arose from a genuine fear of 'Hindu domination,' as elements of the Congress-led 'nationalist-secular' movement increasingly incorporated 'Hindu' symbols and policies. Similarly to India, Pakistan was socially constructed as an 'imagined community,' based on the narrative of the two-nation theory. This was achieved not merely through territorial state/nation-building, but more importantly through 'representational practices,' that 'in various ways attempted to inscribe something called India [and Pakistan] with a content, history, meaning, and trajectory.'

The identities of the two states, however, have not been stable and unchanging. Beginning in the 1980s, India's secularism began to decline and its conception of 'self' and 'other' was increasingly informed by the discourse of Hindu nationalism framed by the *Hindutva* movement, which attacked the 'pseudo-secularism' of the Congress for purportedly empowering religious minorities, particularly Muslims (the 'other'), at the expense of Hindus, and sought to 're-imagine' India as a virile and masculine Hindu *rashtra* (state). Narratives were employed to reconstruct Hindus as a homogenous in-group, with India's identity being re-articulated on the principle of *akhand bharat*, or 'one nation, one people, and one culture.' Critically, Hindu nationalism was invigorated by the 'Muslim question' and Pakistan; the Hindu *rashtra* was constructed in contradistinction to the Muslim and Pakistani 'other.'

Hindutva was further empowered by the formation of BJP governments, notably in 1998. Nevertheless, Hindu nationalist parties were compelled to moderate their agendas to remain in power because of the constraining effects of India's liberal-democratic structures. Thus, rather than forging a Hindu *rashtra*, India's self-conception has been defined by the tensions, compromises and even convergences between secular and Hindu nationalist narratives.

Pakistan also underwent 're-imagining' in the 1980s, as processes of *Islamisation*, particularly under Zia-ul Haq, sought to redefine Pakistan's identity on the basis of orthodox Islam. *Madrassas* and *Jihad* symbolised the new discourse, and fresh narratives about the nation's birth were employed to reconstruct Jinnah and the anti-colonial freedom struggle as Islamists that aimed to establish an Islamic state. Moreover, protecting Pakistan's Islamic identity and defending its 'ideological frontiers' became crucial for achieving national unity and stability in Pakistan's self-conception. As Zia-ul Haq declared, the 'preservation of [Pakistan's ideology] and the Islamic character of the country ... as important as the security of the country's geographical boundaries.' Islamisation has also been considered vital to the core aim of distinguishing Pakistan from the Indian 'other,' which is reflected in the fear that 'if Pakistan does not become and remain aggressively Islamic, it will become India again.'

Role of identity in shaping actors and foreign policies

The conceptions of identity discussed above have played a pivotal role in shaping both states' actions and understandings of their material and instrumental geopolitical and strategic interests—or their *social purposes*and *cognitive models*—as well as their foreign policies. As Gupta argues, 'cultural and ideological factors [have been] enmeshed with strategic calculations' of both states, which is reflected in their respective*strategic cultures,* which Ken Booth defines as perceptual frameworks entailing the 'traditions, values, attitudes [and] patterns of behaviour' of nations—or in Alistair Johnston's words their 'integrated set of symbols' —that shape states' security discourses and interactions (which are not merely determined by the 'rational' pursuit of instrumental interests). Within this context, one of the 'key elements of Pakistan's strategic culture,' notes Peter Lavoy, has been opposition to Indian hegemony.

This is characterised by what many describe as Pakistan's primary foreign policy goal; to achieve *parity*—politically, diplomatically and even militarily—with India, and to eventually balkanise 'akhand bharat' (united India) in order to make it more manageable and less threatening. This *purposive goal* is not merely a prudent geopolitical strategy arising from threats to state survival by a hegemonic neighbour in an anarchic world, but has been intimately shaped by Pakistan's long-standing self-conception as a strong 'Muslim' state that is equal to 'Hindu' India and must challenge 'Hindu' majoritarianism and domination. For its part, India's own security and strategic discourses have centred on—

even 'obsessed' over—the Pakistani 'other.' While realist analysts have derided the 'irrationality' of this preoccupation with a far smaller power, the strategy has been motivated by India's self-image as a secular nation that needs to challenge and demonstrate the artificiality of Pakistan's two-nation theory. The disputed territory of Kashmir attests to the centrality of identity to both states' geostrategic understandings, for the meaning and significance attached to it has been defined by their respective self-conceptions rather than narrow material incentives. For Pakistan, Kashmir is crucial to its 'Muslim' (and pan-Islamic) identity and the two-nation theory, while for India, as former Prime Minister Vajpayee commented in 2002, 'Kashmir is not a piece of land; it is a test case of secularism.' Identity has also played a fundamental role in the most significant security issue—the nuclearisation of the subcontinent. As Das and others have demonstrated, India and Pakistan's nuclear trajectories have been—to a considerable degree—shaped by their self-images. Thus, by pursuing a nuclear capability, India sought to act out its identity as a *modern* post-colonial state (and indeed a major power) established on the *modernist*principles of secularism, democracy, and scientific and technological progress. Similarly, Pakistan's nuclear programme sought to confirm its 'scientific and technological greatness' and self-image as 'the most advanced Muslim country,' while also being 'a symbol of defiance' to the Indian 'other,' and furthering its goal of *parity* with 'Hindu' India. Indeed, Pakistan originally contextualised its nuclear policy around its 'Islamic' identity, with Bhutto coining the term 'the Islamic bomb' and reasoning that:

> The Christian, Jewish, and Hindu civilizations have [a full nuclear capability]... Only the Islamic civilization was without it ... but this was about to change.

The 1998 nuclear tests further demonstrated how conceptions of 'self' and 'other' have shaped both states' security discourses. For India, the tests reflected the increasing salience of *Hindutva* as a source of Indian identity, as the Hindu-Right BJP government overturned India's longstanding policy of nuclear ambiguity to showcase the nation's 'nuclear teeth,' dubbing the tests 'Operation Shakti' as Hindu nationalist discourse situated it in the context of 'the cult of manliness and virility' that defined the Hindu *rashtra*—in contradistinction to the Muslim and Pakistan 'other.' Realist analysts explained the tests as instances of instrumental power politics vis-a-vis Pakistan, and especially China, but this fails to appreciate that the tests were actually strategically counter-productive and *not* constructed against 'the China threat.' Rather, the tests most importantly represented what Talbot terms the 'Hindutva bomb'—aimed primarily at the Pakistani/Muslim 'other.' Pakistan's subsequent 'tit-for-tat' explosions were also framed within the context of its Islamic identity as an advanced Muslim state reacting to the domineering threat of the Hindu 'other.' Thus, the tests were constructed as the 'Islamic bomb' responding to the 'Hindu bomb,' which also reflected the increasing importance of an orthodox Islamic identity to Pakistan's strategic culture and its foreign policy and security discourses. In India, *Hindutva* was further energised by the post-September 11th security context, as the 'cult of manliness and virility' informed India's new, more aggressive, policy of 'coercive diplomacy' vis-a-vis Pakistan. The Pakistani/Muslim 'other' was now constructed as a despotic *Jihadi* state and 'the epicentre of world terrorism'; as well as a threat to Indian civilisation.

As the preceding discussion has shown, India and Pakistan's identities have shaped their respective understandings of the material world, informed their interests and influenced their foreign policy and security discourses.

TALKS AND OTHER CONFIDENCE BUILDING MEASURES

After the 1971 war, Pakistan and India made slow progress towards the normalisation of relations. In July 1972, Indian Prime Minister Indira Gandhi and Pakistani PresidentZulfikar Ali Bhutto met in the Indian hill station of Simla. They signed the Simla Agreement, by which India would return all Pakistani personnel (over 90,000) and captured territory in the west, and the two countries would "settle their differences by peaceful means through bilateral negotiations." Diplomatic and trade relations were also re-established in 1976.

In 1997, high-level Indo-Pakistan talks resumed after a three-year pause. The Prime Ministers of Pakistan and India met twice and the foreign secretaries conducted three rounds of talks. In June 1997, the foreign secretaries identified eight "outstanding issues" around which continuing talks would be focused. The dispute over the status of Kashmir, (referred by India as Jammu and Kashmir), an issue since Independence, remains the major stumbling block in their dialogue. India maintains that the entire former princely state is an integral part of the Indian union, while Pakistan insists that UN resolutions calling for self-determination of the people of the state/province must be taken into account. It however refuses to abide by the previous part of the resolution, which calls for it to vacate all territories occupied.

In September 1997, the talks broke down over the structure of how to deal with the issues of Kashmir, and peace and security. Pakistan advocated that the issues be treated by separate working groups. India responded that the two issues be taken up along with six others on a simultaneous basis.

Attempts to restart dialogue between the two nations were given a major boost by the February 1999 meeting of both Prime Ministers in Lahore and their signing of three agreements.

A subsequent military coup in Pakistan that overturned the democratically elected Nawaz Sharif government in October of the same year also proved a setback to relations.

In 2001, a summit was called in Agra; Pakistani President Pervez Musharraf turned up to meet Indian Prime Minister Atal Behari Vajpayee. The talks fell through.

On 20 June 2004, with a new government in place in India, both countries agreed to extend a nuclear testing ban and to set up a hotline between their foreign secretaries aimed at preventing misunderstandings that might lead to a nuclear war.

Baglihar Dam issue was a new issue raised by Pakistan in 2005. After Dr. Manmohan Singh become prime minister of India in May 2004, the Punjab provincial Government declared it would develop Gah, his place of birth, as a model village in his honour and name a school after him. There is also a village in India named

Pakistan, despite occasional pressure over the years to change its name the villagers have resisted. Violent activities in the region declined in 2004. There are two main reasons for this: warming of relations between New Delhi and Islamabad which consequently lead to a ceasefire between the two countries in 2003 and the fencing of the LOC being carried out by the Indian Army. Moreover, coming under intense international pressure, Islamabad was compelled to take actions against the militants' training camps on its territory. In 2004, the two countries also agreed upon decreasing the number of troops present in the region.

Under pressure, Kashmiri militant organisations made an offer for talks and negotiations with New Delhi, which India welcomed.

India's Border Security Force blamed the Pakistani military for providing cover-fire for the terrorists whenever they infiltrated into Indian territory from Pakistan. Pakistan in turn has also blamed India for providing support to terrorist organisations operating in Pakistan such as the BLA.

In 2005, Pakistan's information minister, Sheikh Rashid, was alleged to have run a terrorist training camp in 1990 in N.W. Frontier, Pakistan. The Pakistani government dismissed the charges against its minister as an attempt to hamper the ongoing peace process between the two neighbours.

Both India and Pakistan have launched several mutual confidence-building measures (CBMs) to ease tensions between the two. These include more high-level talks, easing visarestrictions, and restarting of cricket matches between the two. The new bus service between Srinagar and Muzaffarabad has also helped bring the two sides closer. Pakistan and India have also decided to co-operate on economic fronts.

Some improvements in the relations are seen with the re-opening of a series of transportation networks near the India–Pakistan border, with the most important being bus routes and railway lines.

A major clash between Indian security forces and militants occurred when a group of insurgents tried to infiltrate into Kashmir from Pakistan in July 2005. The same month also saw a Kashmiri militant attack on Ayodhya and Srinagar. However, these developments had little impact on the peace process. An Indian man held in Pakistani prisons since 1975 as an accused spy walked across the border to freedom 3 March 2008, an unconditional release that Pakistan said was done to improve relations between the two countries.

In 2006, a "Friends Without Borders" scheme began with the help of two British tourists. The idea was that Indian and Pakistani children would make pen pals and write friendly letters to each other. The idea was so successful in both countries that the organisation found it "impossible to keep up". The World's Largest Love Letter was recently sent from India to Pakistan.

In December 2010, several Pakistani newspapers published stories about India's leadership and relationship with militants in Pakistan that the papers claimed were found in theUnited States diplomatic cables leak. A British newspaper, *The Guardian,* which had the Wikileaks cables in its possession reviewed the cables and concluded that the Pakistani claims were "not accurate" and that "WikiLeaks [was] being exploited for propaganda purposes."

On 10 February 2011, India agreed to resume talks with Pakistan which were suspended after 26/11 Mumbai Attacks. India had put on hold all the diplomatic relations saying it will only continue if Pakistan will act against the accused of Mumbai attacks.

On 13 April 2012 following a thaw in relations whereby India gained MFN status in the country, India announced the removal of restrictions on FDI investment from Pakistan to India.

The Foreign Minister of Pakistan on 11 July 2012, stated in Pnom Penh that her country is willing to resolve some of the disputes like, Sir Creek and Siachan on the basis of agreements reached in past. On 7 September 2012, Indian External Affairs Minister would pay 3-day visit to Pakistan to review the progress of bilateral dialogue with his Pakistani counterpart.

RESPONSE TO NATURAL CALAMITIES

2001 Gujarat Earthquake in India

Pakistani President Pervez Mushrraf sent a plane load of relief supplies to India from Islamabad to Ahmedabad. That carried 200 tents and more than 2,000 blankets. Furthermore the President called Indian PM to express his 'sympathy' over the loss from the earthquake.

2005 Earthquake in Pakistan

India offered generous aid to Pakistan in response to the 2005 Kashmir earthquake on 8 October. Indian and Pakistani High Commissioners consulted with one another regarding cooperation in relief work. India sent 25 tonnes of relief material to Pakistan including food, blankets and medicine. Large Indian companies such as Infosys have offered aid up to $226,000. On 12 October, an Ilyushin-76 cargo plane ferried across seven truckloads (about 82 tons) of army medicines, 15,000 blankets and 50 tents and returned to New Delhi. A senior airforce official also stated that they had been asked by the Indian government to be ready to fly out another similar consignment. On 14 October, India dispatched the second consignment of relief material to Pakistan, by train through the Wagah Border.

The consignment included 5,000 blankets, 370 tents, 5 tons of plastic sheets and 12 tons of medicine.

A third consignment of medicine and relief material was also sent shortly afterwards by train. India also pledged $25 million as aid to Pakistan. India opened the first of three points at Chakan Da Bagh, in Poonch, on the Line of Control (LoC) between India and Pakistan for the 2005 Kashmir earthquake relief work. (Rediff) Such generous gestures signalled a new era of confidence, friendliness and cooperation between both India and Pakistan.

Fugitives

India has accused some of the most wanted Indian fugitives, such as Dawood Ibrahim, of having a presence in Pakistan. On 11 May 2011, India released a list of 50 "Most Wanted Fugitives" hiding in Pakistan. This was to tactically pressure Pakistan after the killing of Osama bin Laden in his compound in Abbottabad.

After two errors in the list received publicity, the Central Bureau of Investigation removed it from their website pending a review. After this incident the Pakistani interior ministry rejected the list of 50 Most Wanted men forwarded by India to Islamabad, saying it should first probe if those named in the list were even living in the country.

SOCIAL RELATIONS

Cultural links

India and Pakistan, to some degree have similar cultures, cuisines and languages which underpin the historical ties between the two. Pakistani singers, musicians, comedians and entertainers have enjoyed widespread popularity in India, with many achieving overnight fame in the Indian film industry Bollywood. Likewise, Indian music and film are very popular in Pakistan. Being located in the northernmost region of the South Asia, Pakistan's culture is somewhat similar to that of North India.

The Punjab region was split into Punjab, Pakistan and Punjab, India following the independence and partition of the two countries in 1947. The Punjabi people are today the largest ethnic group in Pakistan and also an important ethnic group of northern India.

The founder of Sikhism was born in the modern-day Pakistani Punjab province, in the city ofNankana Sahib. Each year, millions of Indian Sikh pilgrims cross over to visit holy Sikh sites in Nankana Sahib. The Sindhi people are the native ethnic group of the Pakistani province of Sindh. Many Hindu Sindhis migrated to India in 1947, making the country home to a sizable Sindhi community. In addition, the millions of Muslims who migrated from India to the newly created Pakistan during independence came to be known as the Muhajir people; they are settled predominantly in Karachi and still maintain family links in India.

Relations between Pakistan and India have also resumed through platforms such as media and communications. Aman ki Asha is a joint venture and campaign between *The Times of India* and the *Jang Group* calling for mutual peace and development of diplomatic and cultural relations.

Geographic links

The Indo-Pakistani border is the official international boundary that demarcates the Indian states of Punjab, Rajasthan andGujarat from the Pakistani provinces of Punjab and Sindh. The Wagah border is the only road crossing between India and Pakistan and lies on the famous Grand Trunk Road, connecting Lahore, Pakistan with Amritsar, India. Each evening, theWagah border ceremony takes place at the Wagah border in which the flags are lowered and guards on both sides make a pompous military display and exchange handshakes.

Linguistic ties

Hindustani is the linga franca of North India and Pakistan, as well as the national language of both countries, under the nameHindi and Urdu, respectively. Standard Urdu is mutually intelligible with Standard Hindi.

Both languages share the same Indic base and are all but indistinguishable in phonology and grammar.

Most linguists consider them to be two standardised forms of a same language; when speaking colloquially, a speaker of Urdu has no trouble understanding a speaker of Hindi, and vice-versa.

Apart from Hindustani, India and Pakistan also share a distribution of the Punjabi language (written in the Gurmukhi script in Indian Punjab, and the Shahmukhi script in Pakistani Punjab), Kashmiri language and Sindhi language.

Matrimonial ties

Some Indian and Pakistani people marry across the border, particularly with present generation of relatives who had migrated from India at the time of partition.

In April 2010 a high profile Pakistani cricketer, Shoaib Malik married the Indian tennis star Sania Mirza. The wedding received much media attention and was said to transfix both India and Pakistan.

Sporting ties

Cricket and hockey matches between the two (as well as other sports to a lesser degree such as those of the SAARC games) have often been political in nature.

During theSoviet invasion of Afghanistan General Zia-ul Haq traveled to India for a bout of "cricket diplomacy" to keep India from supporting the Soviets by opening another front. Pervez Musharaff also tried to do the same more than a decade later but to no avail.

In tennis, Rohan Bopanna of India and Aisam-ul-Haq Qureshi of Pakistan have formed a successful duo and have been dubbed as the "Indo-Pak Express."

Diasporic relations

The large size of the Indian diaspora and Pakistani diaspora in many different countries throughout the world has created strong diasporic relations. British Indians and British Pakistanis, the largest and second-largest ethnic minorities living in the United Kingdom respectively, are said to have friendly relations with one another. It is quite common for a "Little India" and a "Little Pakistan" to co-exist in South Asian ethnic enclaves in overseas countries. There are various cities such as Birmingham, Blackburn and Manchesterwhere British Indians and British Pakistanis live alongside each other in peace and harmony. Both Indians and Pakistanis living in the UK fit under the category of British Asian. The UK is also home to the Pakistan & India friendship forum. In the United States, Indians and Pakistanis are classified under the South Asian American category and share many cultural traits. The British MEP Saj Karim is of Pakistani origin. He is a member of the European Parliament Friends of India Group, Karim was also responsible for opening up Europe to free trade with India. He narrowly escaped the Mumbai attacks at Hotel Taj in November 2008. Despite the atrocity, Mr Karim does not wish the remaining killerAjmal Kasab to be sentenced to death. He said: "I believe he had a fair and transparent trial and I support the guilty verdict. But I am not a supporter of capital punishment. I believe he should be given a life sentence, but that life should mean life."

ECONOMIC RELATIONS

Trade links

Trade across direct routes has been curtailed formally, so the bulk of India-Pakistan trade is routed through Dubai.

Re-evaluation

The insurgents who initially started their movement as a pro-Kashmiri independence movement, have gone through a lot of change in their ideology. Most of the insurgents portray their struggle as a religious one.

Indian analysts allege that by supporting these insurgents, Pakistan is trying to wage a proxy war against India while Pakistan claims that it regards most of these insurgentgroups as "freedom fighters" rather than terrorists

Internationally known to be the most deadly theatre of conflict, nearly 10 million people, including Muslims, Hindus, and Buddhists, have been fighting a daily battle for survival. The *cross-border firing* between India and Pakistan, and the terrorist attacks combined have taken its toll on the Kashmiris, who have suffered poor living standards and an erosion of human rights.

6

Kashmir Dispute and Security Council Mediation

ROOTS OF CONFLICT IN DECOLONIZATION

The roots of the conflict over Kashmir lie in the demise of the British Empire in South Asia. During colonial rule, the Kashmir region was the princely state of Jammu and Kashmir, an amalgam of five different areas with a Muslim-majority population ruled by a Hindu maharajah. As one of the 584 princely states within the "paramountcy" of the British Empire, Kashmir's legal status was that of a closely held protectorate whose status was tantamount to that of a direct colony but that was not technically part of British India.

In 1947, when the British government transferred power and partitioned its former colonies in British India into the new states of India and Pakistan, the British government determined that the legal status held by Kashmir and the other princely states would lapse. In place of this legal status, the princely states, which were scattered throughout various pockets of South Asia, were given a choice to accede to either India or Pakistan. According to the Indian Independence Act and the British Viceroy's strong wishes, independence from either India or Pakistan was strongly discouraged. Although the princely states' choices produced heated controversy among India, Pakistan, and the people of each region, each princely state was incorporated into either India or Pakistan within two months of the official British departure and transfer of power in August 1947, except for Kashmir. The ruler of Kashmir, Maharajah Hari Singh, stalled in making a decision about accession in the hopes of negotiating to become an independent state, which placed the region in a legal no-man's-land. All such negotiations, however, came to a halt in early October 1947 when Pakistani "tribesmen" crossed the northern border of Kashmir with cooperation from pro-Pakistani Muslims in the northern part of Kashmir and occupied one-third of the region. In response to what he saw as an invasion of his state, Hari Singh appealed to neighboring India for military assistance.

India would not cross the border into Kashmir, however, unless Hari Singh signed the Instrument of Accession, through which Kashmir would legally accede to India and come under its sovereign control. In addition, although not stated explicitly in the Instrument of Accession, the Indian leadership had made broad but vague political statements suggesting that the accession would be provisional and that the people of Kashmir would have to ratify accession.

Once Hari Singh signed the instrument, thus changing Kashmir's legal status, Indian troops entered the territory and stopped the tribal advance toward the capital city of Srinagar. In the process, Indian troops took control of the southern two-thirds of Kashmir. The Pakistani military entered the region in November 1947 to support the invading tribal parties, bringing about the first full-scale Indo-Pakistani war over Kashmir.

THE SECURITY COUNCIL'S INITIAL MEDIATION ATTEMPTS

With no obvious end in sight to the fighting, India approached the U.N. Security Council to lodge a complaint, pursuant to Article 35 under the U.N. Charter, invoking the Security Council's dispute resolution capacity.

For India, the issue before the Security Council was the relatively simple one of Pakistani-supported aggression in the face of Indian sovereignty in Kashmir. India contended that Kashmir's accession was legally binding, bringing the entire region under

Indian sovereignty and making any Pakistani or Pakistani-supported fighters "invaders."

Within two weeks, Pakistan filed a response and counterclaim, pursuant to Article 35 of the U.N. Charter, and framed the situation in a fundamentally different way. First, Pakistan denied the charge of directly giving aid and assistance to the tribesmen, claiming that they were actors independent from the Pakistani government. Second, Pakistan broadened the focus of the dispute by raising a litany of objections. One of these objections was to the validity of Kashmir's accession to India. Pakistan claimed that the accession had occurred by "fraud and violence" and alleged conspiracy between India and Hari Singh. Pakistan argued that any arrangement between India and Hari Singh was illegitimate. Any decision about Kashmir's legal status should thus be made in reference to the Kashmiri people's will through a plebiscite.

Upon receiving these letters from India and Pakistan, the Security Council assumed jurisdiction to examine the conflict, pursuant to Article 34 of the U.N. Charter, and passed Resolutions 38 and 39, its first statements on the dispute. Resolution 39 established the United Nations Commission for India and Pakistan (UNCIP) on January 20, 1948. The UNCIP's established function was (1) to investigate the facts that gave rise to the Kashmir dispute, and (2) to exercise any mediatory influence likely to smooth away difficulties, to carry out directions given by the Security Council, and to report on the progress of executing the advice and directions of the Security Council.

Before the UNCIP reached the region to follow through on its mandate, the Security Council passed Resolution 47 in April 1948, which was and still remains the Security Council's outlined structurea recommended permanent solution. Resolution 47 set forth a two-part recommendation consisting of demilitarization and plebiscite. The resolution called for Pakistan to secure the withdrawal of the tribesmen and Pakistani nationals from the region, after which India would have to withdraw to a military level minimally necessary to maintain law and order. Once the region had been demilitarized, a U.N.-appointed Plebiscite

Administrator would supervise a free and impartial plebiscite, through which the Kashmiri people would determine to which state they would accede. The Security Council, however, avoided mention of the Instrument of Accession, whose validity India asserted and Pakistan explicitly challenged.

Neither India nor Pakistan was fully satisfied with Resolution 47. Despite their disapproval, India and Pakistan both agreed to accept the good offices of the UNCIP to their states pursuant to Resolution 47. However, in May 1948, before the UNCIP reached South Asia to conduct investigations, regular Pakistani troops entered the northern part of Kashmir to support the tribesmen and Pakistani nationals, who were occupying the area, against the Indian military. When the UNCIP arrived in July, the presence of Pakistani regular military caught the UNCIP by surprise and made it concentrate on the first and primary challenge of demilitarization.

The first UNCIP Resolution passed on August 13th of the same year reflected this development. In addition to calling for a ceasefire, the UNCIP resolution reiterated the recommendations in Resolution 47 and emphasized the importance of the withdrawal of the Pakistani military, whose presence constituted a "material change" from the situation originally presented to the Security Council. Again, however, aside from noting a "material change," there was little mention of the Instrument of Accession, which, if valid, made any Pakistani military presence in the region an act of aggression.

India accepted the UNCIP Resolution, even though the UNCIP did not condemn the presence of the Pakistani military. Pakistan also accepted the Resolution, but with so many qualifications that the UNCIP deemed the answer as "tantamount to rejection." First, Pakistan objected to the absence of definite details for a free plebiscite. Second, Pakistan wanted its military withdrawal to be synchronized, both in timing and number, with the withdrawal of the Indian military.

After much deliberation, India and Pakistan eventually agreed to a ceasefire, which went into effect on January 1, 1949, exactly one year after India's complaint to the Security Council. The ceasefire created a border that gave India two-thirds control of the region and Pakistan one-third control. However, the two states were not able to come to an agreement on the demilitarization of Kashmir. To India, this disagreement precluded further talks about a plebiscite; to Pakistan, this situation demonstrated India's lack of commitment to a plebiscite, which Pakistan saw as the ultimate goal.

After further attempts at mediation, the UNCIP was terminated in favour of a single person vested as a U.N. Representative to conduct negotiations. Until 1958, various U.N. Representatives attempted to negotiate ways to achieve demilitarization and to conduct a plebiscite, but none came to a permanent resolution.

After this time, the Security Council seemed to abandon its mediatory role. The evidence of this shift away from its mediatory role can be seen in 1965, during the Second War in Kashmir. The Security Council passed Resolutions 210 and 211, its last statements on the Kashmir conflict. Both resolutions omitted reference to earlier Security Council or UNCIP recommendations to a permanent resolution and implicitly pushed India and Pakistan toward using mediators outside of the U.N.

POST-1965 NEGOTIATIONS AND TENSIONS

After 1965, India and Pakistan have almost exclusively dealt with the conflict bilaterally. The ceasefire line has become a de facto legal border called the "Line of Control" through an arrangement created by the Simla Agreement in 1972. Pakistan has repeatedly tried to raise the conflict in an international forum. However, India insists on dealing with Kashmir's legal status bilaterally and has resisted attempts at international mediation for the last thirty years.

Since the rise of the separatist movement in the late 1980s, the stakes in Kashmir have altered and intensified. India has accused Pakistan of conducting a "proxy war" and "sponsoring terrorism" in the region by providing military support and training to the militants and by allowing infiltration across the Line of Control into Indian-controlled Kashmir, in violation of the existing bilateral treaty regime. Pakistan has denied all claims of direct military and other material support and, in turn, alleges that India has not abided by its obligations according to the Security Council resolutions. Tensions seesaw between a precarious stalemate and the brink of war, with the threat to peace ever present.

SECURITY COUNCIL'S VIEW OF THE KASHMIR DISPUTE WEAKENED ITS ABILITY TO BRING PERMANENT RESOLUTION

One reason for the Security Council's failure in bringing a permanent resolution to the Kashmir conflict is the Council's view of the conflict as political rather than legal. From the beginning, the Security Council framed the problem as primarily a political dispute rather than looking to a major legal underpinning of the dispute: the Instrument of Accession's validity or lack thereof.

The Security Council, unlike the International Court of Justice (ICJ), often deals with dispute resolution in a political mode and does not have the capacity to adjudicate on purely legal terms. Nevertheless, the Kashmir dispute represents a situation where the Security Council could have given a stronger voice and stiffer backbone to its binding recommendations by taking a "quasi-judicial" stance and referring to the legal basis of the conflict. But, by side-stepping overt references to the Instrument of Accession, which lies at the centre of the legal dispute over Kashmir, the Security Council could not give a forceful rationale for its two-pronged recommendations, which ultimately weakened its recommendations for permanent solution.

Instead, the Security Council took a merely implicit stance that the Instrument of Accession was valid yet incomplete. The two- pronged plan, demilitarization and plebiscite, was one clear demonstration of this implicit stance that the Security Council articulated in Resolution 47. For instance, by asking Pakistan to secure the withdrawal of "tribesmen and Pakistani nationals not normally resident therein" before any withdrawal of Indian troops, the Security Council made a tacit statement accepting the textual validity of the Instrument of Accession and India's claim to sovereignty in Kashmir, even if provisional. However, by outlining the details of a plebiscite, the Security Council implicitly found that the plain language of the Instrument, which did not state that

Kashmir's accession was provisional or that a plebiscite was necessary, was incomplete. Recommending a plebiscite was a way of holding India to its political commitment, even though it had made no legal obligation as such.

The Security Council chose not to explicitly mention the Instrument of Accession in the language of Resolution 47. The Security Council simply called for Pakistan to "secure the withdrawal" of the tribesmen and Pakistani nationals from Kashmir, but stopped short of labelling their presence as an act of aggression. Similarly, the Council called for a plebiscite without saying that the plain language of the Instrument was incomplete in reflecting India's obligations in the region. Dealing with the situation as a political dispute requiring quid pro quo concessions, rather than legal obligations, was a more conciliatory choice that proved to be too weak to compel India and Pakistan to take steps toward a final resolution.

This lack of force behind Resolution 47 was part of the reason India and Pakistan disapproved of the resolution. India believed that the Security Council did not take into account or give credence to the legality of Kashmir's accession to India, even if accession were only a provisional arrangement until normalcy in the region was achieved. On the other hand, Pakistan wanted to emphasize the second element of the recommendation—the plebiscite—and deemphasize demilitarization.

The purely political characterization of the conflict continued into the August 13th UNCIP Resolution of 1948. For instance, the UNCIP dealt with the entrance of the regular Pakistani military in May 1948, an overt act of aggression in India's view, by simply calling it a "material change" in circumstances in violation of Security Council Resolution 38. The UNCIP Resolution reprimanded Pakistan but did not declare the entrance of Pakistani troops a violation of Indian sovereignty, regardless of whether that sovereignty was provisional or permanent. Although India accepted the UNCIP Resolution, it was disappointed that the UNCIP or Security Council did not condemn Pakistan for violating Resolution 38, which would have helped bolster recognition of the legality of Kashmir's accession to India.

The entanglement of demilitarization and plebiscite thus remained unresolved. Since no return to normalcy had occurred by 1951, India constitutionally integrated into the Indian Union the portion of Kashmir that it occupied, relying on the idea that it had the legality of the Instrument of Accession's text on its side, despite Pakistan's strenuous protests. By 1965, largely because of the political realities of the Cold War and likely because of the repeated failure to demilitarize Kashmir, the Security Council disengaged from its mediatory efforts by conspicuously not assuming its previous mediatory role.

ACTIONS THE SECURITY COUNCIL COULD TAKE TO REINSERT

Itself as a Mediator

Considering the dangers to the region, renewed efforts toward mediation appear to be an option that could save India, Pakistan, South Asia, and the international order from further uncertainty. According to Jacob Bercovitch, two of the conditions under which mediation is likely to be used are (1) when "both parties' own conflict management efforts have reached an impasse," and (2) when "both parties are prepared to cooperate to break their stalemate." However, at this point, such mediation is only possible if the Security Council reengages India, whose various governments have become resistant to Security Council mediation.

The problem remains that, even if India admits that it has reached an impasse over the Kashmir conflict under current bilateral negotiation attempts, India will likely continue to resist cooperating with Pakistan in seeking outside mediation. One of several reasons is that India's initial attempt to use the Security Council to resolve the dispute failed to bring peace. However, Pakistan seems amenable to international mediation. Should the Security Council act as that mediator, it should attempt to reengage India in the mediatory process, which entails considering why its efforts failed initially, and what India would require for its faith to be restored in the powers of the Security Council.

To reengage India, the Security Council should consider refocusing the legal framework of the conflict, rather than treating the dispute in political terms as it had in earlier mediatory attempts, especially if the Security Council continues to deal with the Kashmir dispute under Article 34. Considering the changes of the last thirty years, referring to the Instrument of Accession's validity, while a useful starting point, does not seem to be the most realistic way to approach the conflict. Instead, the proper legal starting point to reengage India at this juncture should be the policing of the Line of Control, which has ripened into the de facto border in the last three decades since the Simla Agreement, the current Indo-Pakistani treaty that controls the two countries' actions in Kashmir.

Since the rise of the separatist movement in Kashmir, India's major and consistent complaint against Pakistan has been its support of infiltration across the Line of Control in violation of the Simla Agreement, its current bilateral treaty arrangement. Interestingly, India's current accusations are analogous to those that it lodged against Pakistan's alleged support of the tribesmen and other "invaders" at the beginning of the Kashmir conflict. Pakistan's denial of support, claiming that the infiltrators are independent actors whose movements Pakistan is not able to control officially, sounds similar as well. In bilateral negotiations, India has claimed that it will not make meaningful concessions to Pakistan until sponsorship, direct or indirect, of cross-border infiltration ceases. If the Line of Control becomes the new focus, then the Security Council could avoid its earlier mistake: first, by making a good faith effort to investigate, and then, if necessary, by denouncing cross-border infiltration across the Line of Control.

Taking a strong stance against cross-border infiltration does not mean that the Security Council has to grant an absolute moral superiority to the Indian case by treating Pakistan as the naked aggressor. Since January 2002, even Pakistan has attempted to address the supposedly unauthorized crossing over into Indian-controlled Kashmir by its nationals, particularly as to members of Islamic fundamentalist groups that incite and respond with violence in the region. However, to have the Security Council or a Security Council-mandated committee such as the UNCIP to investigate these discreet issues—the alleged crossing of the Line of Control and violation of the Simla Agreement—might give India the incentive to reengage in mediation. India has an interest in taking help from the Security Council in this respect because India's major challenge in the region has been controlling illegal movement across the Line of Control. This investigation of, and stance against, cross-border infiltration could be a starting point for reengaging India.

RESOLVING THE CONFLICT DISPUTED AREA OF JAMMU AND KASHMIR

We will present various solutions that we have considered that could bring peace to the disputed area of Jammu and Kashmir. The precise contours of solutions to the conflict in Kashmir are, of course, uncertain. There are many proposed resolutions from which to choose; new ones could still be devised, but it is important to consider the present status of the Line of Control while devising a plan for the future. All the feasible options can only be long lasting if the actions are undertaken while keeping the aspirations of Kashmiris living on both sides of the LOC in mind. While resolving the problems in Kashmir is an integral aspect of the peace process, it is equally important to remember to keep the wishes of Kashmiri people in mind. A solution without the participation, wishes and aspirations of Kashmir people would not last.

Past solutions that have been suggested include recognition of the Line of control as it is. Currently a boundary - the Line of Actual Control - divides the region in two, with one part administered by India and one by Pakistan. India would like to formalize this status quo and make it the accepted international boundary. But Pakistan and Kashmiri activists reject this plan because they both want greater control over the region. Pakistan has consistently favored the idea that Kashmir should join Pakistan. In view of the state's majority Muslim population, it believes that it would vote to become part of Pakistan. However a simple majority (plebiscite) held in a region which comprises peoples that are culturally, religiously and ethnically diverse, would create large, disaffected minorities. The Hindus and Sikhs of the Kashmir Valley, the Hindu majority of Jammu, and the Buddhist majority of Ladakh have never shown any desire to join Pakistan and would protest such an outcome.

In the same spirit of the argument, India, of course, believes that the entire state of Kashmir should be a part of India. Such a solution would be unlikely to bring stability to the region, as the Muslim inhabitants of Pakistani-administered Jammu and Kashmir, including the Northern Areas, have never shown any desire to become part of India.

In addition to making decisions about the whole region, there have also been proposal of a smaller independent Kashmir. An independent Kashmir could be created from the Kashmir Valley - currently under Indian administration - and the narrow strip of land that Pakistan calls Azad Jammu and Kashmir. This would leave the strategically important regions of the Northern Areas and Ladakh, bordering China, under the control of Pakistan and India respectively. However both India and Pakistan would be unlikely to enter into discussions that would have this scenario as a possible outcome.

Some have considered the possibility of having an independent Kashmir Valley as an option. This possibility is supposed to address the grievances of those who have been fighting against the Indian Government since the insurgency began in 1989. But critics say that, without external assistance, the region would not be economically viable. The rest of the paper considers the possibility of an Independent Economic Zone of Kashmir and some of the policies that need to be implemented for this option to be a viable one. We argue that Kashmir can become an independent entity that is economically sustainable if proper resources and policies are filtered into the region by the State as well as the Central Government.

Independent Economic Zone

One creative proposal is to turn the entire area into an Independent Economic Zone where both India and Pakistan can engage in free Trade. This would require both armies to withdraw under conditions of honour and dignity; it would not prejudice their positions on Kashmir as a whole; it would stop further degradation of a magnificent mountain area; it would save thousands of lives and billions of rupees that are spent on special military forces by the government; and more importantly, try to heal a running sore among Kashmiri hearts. Any agreement to withdraw forces would, of course, have to be backed by assurances. An independent entity such as the United Nations can be involved as an "enforcer" in such scenarios. There have been examples in the past where such actions have been undertaken. Ground-based and air surveillance, such as is used along the Mexico–US border, or was used in 1973 to monitor the Sinai Desert Cease Fire, could ensure this. The mountain terrain would present special difficulties, but from reports of recent discussions, it may be assumed that these can be overcome.

This scenarios requires detailed knowledge of the situation on the ground with a deep understanding of political considerations. Both sides need to recognize each other's claims, agree not to change the status quo by force, and agree not to introduce irregulars. This would be followed by 3 steps:

1 End the fighting without disengaging or redeployment.
2 Introduce technical means of monitoring and surveillance, permitting meaningful reductions of forces to be negotiated.
3 Work out a complete demilitarization.

At present, with possibly up to a million armed men facing each other across the Kashmir border, talk of ending the fighting and of bringing peace to the region seems remote. But the dawn always comes after the darkest period: perhaps there will also be a dawn for the state of Jammu and Kashmir.

It is also crucial to look at the feasibility of the option. Kashmir has a sizable population and enough land and infrastructure to support itself. However, it requires a lot more resources to continue building the necessary framework to be a successful entity, in the purely economic as well as social sense. Both the Government of India and Pakistan needs to be actively involved in the development process of the region to build the necessary infrastructure of the well beings of its residents as well as foster good educational institutions and aid the tourism industry for long term growth.

In retrospect, India and Pakistan have spent a lot of resources, both in terms of monetary contribution as well as human capital, in trying to resolve or perpetuate the problem. Thus, the proposed solution is much cheaper in comparison to the past willingness to pay in both countries. The costs of the Kashmir conflict are said to be increasingly unbearable for all involved. Over 40,000 lives have been lost since the insurgency began in 1989. The governments have spent tens of billions of rupees on feeding and fighting the conflict rather than on alleviating poverty and improving literacy and health programs for the staggering number of poor in all of India and Pakistan.

VIABILITY OF KASHMIR AS AN INDEPENDENT ECONOMIC REGION

In terms of considering the viability of Kashmir as an independent Economic region, it is important to look at its available resources as well as its past history. Kashmir is a unique region since it is land-scarce and yet labor-abundant state, with less than 30% of its total area suitable for cultivation. The majority of the land comprises mountains and hillsides. The Government of India attempted to overcome these handicaps by heavily subsidizing the state with grants in the early years. Between 1950 and 1970 nearly the Central funded 90% of the state's Five Year Plans, whilst other backward states such as Bihar only received 70% aid. One major side effect of this policy was that it failed to give the state an impetus to mobilize its own resources for economic growth. As a result, Kashmir has not tapped its potential tax revenue and developed into the lowest taxed state in India because of the lack of incentives provided by the Central Government's aid.

In the 1970s, the central Government reversed its aid policy to 30% grants and 70% loans. As a result, more than 50% of the state's expenditure began to comprise of debt and interest repayments. This debt servicing liability on one rupee loaned by the center to J&K today is a staggering amount (5.35 rupees for every rupee borrowed by the State Government). The situation is similar to the debt crisis facing Africa, whereby resources required for productive investments are being diverted to debt repayments.

Kashmiri militants who were fighting for independence have cited such evidence to justify their claims that 'India is guilty of treating Kashmir as a colony.' In hindsight, while certain decision taken by the government of India were misguided, the economic policies implemented by various state governments in Kashmir played a much greater role in explaining the problems confronting the state today. State interventions in agriculture and industry were constantly subjected to the pressures and pulls of various interest groups. As a result, policies that were conceived to benefit to society at large were often implemented by a small group of the population to beneficial to themselves. It would be crucial for the Central Government to forgo the future debt payments and allow the state to spend the financial capital on building the infrastructure and providing the right resources and opportunities to its population.

Rural Areas of Kashmir

The rural areas of Kashmir need an active involvement by the State Government to make agriculture an active and vibrant part of the economy. Agriculture contributes over 40% of the state domestic product and employs two thirds of the total working population of the state. Official government publications suggest that 'agricultural activities have remained uninterrupted during all these years of turmoil' and the figures show impressive increases in productivity. The farmers in the region have underutilized the technology despite the staggering gains by other states such as Punjab, who have benefited tremendously from the Green Revolution. In the past, state intervention has not always resulted in optimal outcomes. The major thrust of policies aimed at raising agricultural production has been concentrated on cereal production, although non-cereal production activities also have recorded gains. As a result of state expenditure, cereal production has increased, but the state's food grain requirements have exceeded local production levels. Over the years, the state's dependence on outside markets for milk, mutton, cereals, vegetables and wool has consistently risen.

The growth in the demand for food and cereals has not been able to keep up with the increase in the population. Lack of proper incentives and resources for the farmers have resulted in such outcomes. In order to encourage small farmers to adopt Green Revolution technology, the government has to offer high prices for their crops, as had occurred in the rest of India. The 1975 Development Review Committee's Report suggests that the state government was pursuing a mistaken price policy with regard to food grains. The Report concludes that, 'food farmers are left with the depressed price offer and the law of supply clearly says that the lower the price the lower will be the production '. As a result of low profitability, small farmers in Kashmir have often lacked the capital to invest in costly technological changes, unlike other parts of India. Moreover, by creating small farms below the optimal size, the land reforms were not the best base for the Green Revolution to flourish. The poverty in the rural areas perpetuates the conflict, forcing the farmers to look for extra income elsewhere. For example, in some regions, farmers will often house the militants to earn the extra cash. Thus, it is crucial that the Government takes action to provide proper opportunities to the farmers.

In addition to the rural areas, there is also a need to understand why there is dissatisfaction in the urban community, which has become the center of militancy. Since 1989, the majority of terrorist activity reported to date has tended to be concentrated in the summer capital Srinagar.

The 1975 Development Review Committee's Report on industrial development stated that, "with a rapidly increasing population, expanding and easily accessible education and the growing pressure on land, the creation of new and productive avenues of non-agricultural employment has become a pressing need."

The development of modern industry would be one such avenue to provide opportunities for absorbing technically qualified people. It is argued that the urban bias discussed earlier did not provide sufficient benefits to the urban population. Self-seeking bureaucrats and private individuals manipulated government subsidies. This accounts for the state's poor industrial performance over a period of 40 years as a result of which underemployment and unemployment have grown into severe problems that may have fuelled the disagreements. Therefore, if Kashmir has to become an Independent Economic entity, it is important to take steps that welcome the maximum possible investment of private capital and entrepreneurship in the state. Unfortunately the incentives available to private investors have not been as attractive in other states, which meant that Kashmir failed to generate sufficient capital from the private sector. Unlike rapid movement towards Privatization in other parts of the country, most of the existing large and medium scale industries are state owned. There are several factors responsible for such poor outcomes. Kashmir is a land locked region and it was given a special status granted to the state by the central Government under Article 370 which bars non-Kashmiris from owning property within the State.

Since most of the State owned enterprises are highly inefficient, the contribution of the industrial sector to the state's economy over the past four decades has been minimal. This is because most of the industrial units run by the state have consistently suffered huge losses, developing into a permanent drain on the state exchequer. All the revenue from sales of these units is being absorbed by costs. Since none of the revenue is generating profits or being used to create efficiency in production, the enterprises fail to be efficient or even profitable for that matter.

Such economic problems have perpetuated the problems in Kashmir. It is clear that the alienation of the Kashmiri people has been driven disillusionment in the state's economic policies. Their ideals and aspirations have been thwarted by a series of the corrupt government officials, as well as the misguided policies of the central government. Therefore, a genuine solution to the conflict depends on restoring Kashmir's confidence in a democratic and secular India with the creation of new job opportunities (within the state and in other parts of the country), a clean administration and political freedom.

PAKISTAN'S RELATION WITH MILITANTS

According to Indian Prime-minister Manmohan Singh, one of the main reasons behind the conflict is Pakistan's "terror-induced coercion". Indian Prime-minister Manmohan Singh stated in a

Joint Press Conference with United States President Barack Obama in New Delhi that India is not afraid of resolving all the issues with Pakistan including the kashmir *"but it is our request that you cannot simultaneously be talking and at the same time the terror machine is as active as ever before. Once Pakistan moves away from this terror-induced coercion, we will be very happy to engage productively with Pakistan to resolve all outstanding issues."*

In 2009, the President of Pakistan Asif Zardari asserted at a conference in Islamabad that Pakistan had indeed created Islamic militant groups as a strategic tool for use in its geostrategic agenda and "to attack Indian forces in Jammu and Kashmir". Former President of Pakistan and the ex-chief of Pakistan military Pervez Musharraf also stated in an interview that Pakistani government helped to form underground militant groups to fight against Indian troops in Jammu and Kashmir and "turned a blind eye" towards their existence because it wanted to force India to enter negotiations. The British Government have formally accepted that there is a clear connection between Pakistan's Inter-Services Intelligence and three major militant outfits operating in Jammu and Kashmir, Lashkar-e-Tayiba, Jaish-e-Mohammed and Harkat-ul-Mujahideen. The militants are provided with "weapons, training, advice and planning assistance" in Punjab and Kashmir by the ISI which is *"coordinating the shipment of arms from the Pakistani side of Kashmir to the Indian side, where Muslim insurgents are waging a protracted war"*.

Throughout the 1990s, the ISI maintained its relationship with extremist networks and militants that it had established during the Afghan war to utilize in its campaign against Indian forces in Kashmir. Joint Intelligence/North (JIN) has been accused of conducting operations in Jammu and Kashmir and also Afghanistan. The Joint Signal Intelligence Bureau (JSIB) provide support with communications to groups in Kashmir. According to Daniel Benjamin and Steven Simon both former members of the National Security Council the ISI acted as a "kind of terrorist conveyor belt" radicalizing young men in the Madrassas in Pakistan and delivering them to training camps affiliated with or run by Al-Qaeda and from there moving them into Jammu and Kashmirto launch attacks. Reportedly, about Rs. 2.4 crore are paid out per month by the Inter-Services Intelligence, in order to fund its activities in Jammu and Kashmir. Pro-Pakistani groups were reportedly favored over other militant groups. Creation of six militant groups in Kashmir, which included Lashkar-e-Taiba (LeT), was aided by the ISI. According to American Intelligence officials, ISI is still providing protection and help to LeT. The Pakistan Army and ISI also LeT volunteers to surreptitiously penetrate from Pakistan Administrated Kashmir to Jammu and Kashmir.

Indian authorities in past has alleged several times that Pakistan was involved in training and arming underground militant groups to fight Indian forces in Kashmir.

Human Rights Abuse

Claims of human rights abuses have been made against the Indian Armed Forces and the armed insurgents operating in Jammu and Kashmir. Since 1989, over 50,000 and by some reports nearly 100,000 Kashmiris are claimed to have died during the conflict. Some human rights organizations have alleged that Indian Security forces have killed hundreds of Kashmiris by indiscriminate use of force and torture, firing on demonstrations, custodial killings, encounters and detensions.

The government of India denied that torture was widespread. It stated that some custodial crimes may have taken place but stated "these are few and far between". According to one human rights report in Kashmir there were more than three hundred cases of "disappearances" since 1990. State Human Rights Commission (SHRC) has found 2,730 bodies buried into unmarked graves scattered all over Kashmir believed to contain the remains of victims of unlawful killings and enforced disappearances by Indian security forces.

SHRC stated that about 574 of these bodies have already been identified as those of disappeared locals. SHRC also accused Indian army of forced labour. According to the cables leaked by website WikiLeaks, US diplomats in 2005 were informed by the International Committee of the Red Cross (ICRC) about the use of torture and sexual humiliation against hundreds of Kashmiri detainees by the security forces. The cable said Indian security forces relied on torture for confessions and the human right abuses are believed to be condoned by the Indian government. In 2012, the Jammu and Kashmir State government stripped its State Information Commission (SIC) department of most powers after the commission asked the government to disclose the information about the unmarked graves. This action of the state was reportedly denounced by the former National Chief Information Commissioner. A state government inquiry into the Oct 22, 1993 Bijbehara killings, in which the Indian military fired on a procession and killed 40 people and injured 150, found out that the firing by the forces was 'unprovoked' and the claim of the military that it was in retaliation was 'concocted and baseless'. However, the accused are still to be punished.

According to a report of Human rights watch, "Indian security forces have assaulted civilians during search operations, tortured and summarily executed detainees in custody and murdered civilians in reprisal attacks. Rape most often occurs during crackdowns, cordon-and-search operations during which men are held for identification in parks or schoolyards while security forces search their homes. In these situations, the security forces frequently engage in collective punishment against the civilian population, most frequently by beating or otherwise assaulting residents, and burning their homes. Rape is used as a means of targetting women whom the security forces accuse of being militant sympathizers; in raping them, the security forces are attempting to punish and humiliate the entire community."

The allegation of mass rape incidents as well as forced disappearances are reflected in a Kashmiri short documentary film by an Independent Kashmiri film-maker, the *Ocean of Tears* produced by a non-governmental non-profit organization called *the Public Service Broadcasting Trust of India* and approved by the Ministry of Information and Broadcasting (India). The film also depicts mass rape incidents of Kunan Poshpora and Shopian as facts alleging that state forces are responsible despite the fact that the Central Bureau of Investigation itself has described both the incidents as "propaganda". A report from the Indian Central Bureau of Investigation (CBI) claimed that the seven people who were killed in 2000 by the Indian military, were innocent civilians. The Indian Army has decided to try the accused in the General Court Martial. It was also reported that the killings that were allegedly committed in "cold-blood" by the Army, were actually in retaliation to the murder of 36 civilians [Sikhs] by militants at Chattisingpora in 2000. The official stance of the Indian Army was that, according to its own investigation, 97% of the reports about the human rights abuse have been found to be "fake or motivated". However, there have been at least one case where civilians were killed in 'fake encounters' by Indian army personnel for cash rewards.

The violence was condemned and labeled as ethnic cleansing in a 2006 resolution passed by the United States Congress. It stated that the Islamic terrorists infiltrated the region in 1989 and began an ethnic cleansing campaign to convert Kashmir to a Muslim state. According to the same, since then nearly 400,000 Pandits were either murdered or forced to leave their ancestral homes.

According to Hindu American Foundation report, the rights and religious freedom of Kashmiri Hindus have been severely curtailed since 1989, when there was an organized and systematic campaign by Islamist militants to cleanse Hindus from Kashmir. Less than 4,000 Kashmiri Hindus remain in the valley, reportedly living with daily threats of violence and terrorism.

According to an op-ed published in BBC journal, the emphasis of the movement after 1989, 3 soon shifted from nationalism to Islam. It also claimed that the minority community of Kashmiri Pandits, who had lived in Kashmir for centuries, were forced to leave their homeland. The displaced Pandits, many of whom continue to live in temporary refugee camps in Jammu and Delhi, are still unable to safely return to their homeland. The lead in this act of ethnic cleansing was initially taken by the Jammu & Kashmir Liberation Front and the Hizbul Mujahideen. And all this, according to Indian Media at least, happened at the instigation of Pakistan's Inter-Services Intelligence (ISI) by a group of Kashmiri terrorist element who were trained, armed and motivated by the ISI. Reportedly these type of organizations which subsequently came into existence after having been trained and armed by the ISI, kept the ethnic cleansing going till practically all the Kashmiri Pandits were driven out after having been subjected to numerous indignities and brutalities such as rape of women, torture, forcible seizure of property etc. The separatists in Kashmir deny these allegations. The Indian government is also trying to reinstate the displaced Pandits in Kashmir. Tahir, the district commander of a separatist Islamic group in Kashmir, stated: "We want the Kashmiri Pandits to come back. They are our brothers. We will try to protect them." But the majority of the Pandits, who have been living in pitiable conditions in Jammu, believe that, until insurgency ceases to exist, return is not possible.

Mustafa Kamal, brother of Union Minister Farooq Abdullah, blamed security forces, former Jammu and Kashmir governor Jagmohan and PDP leader Mufti Sayeed for forcing the migration of Kashmiri Pandits from the Valley. Jagmohan denies these allegations.

Reports by Indian government state 219 Kashmiri pandits were killed and around 1,40,000 migrated due to millitancy while over 3000 stayed in the valley The local organisation of pandits in Kashmir, Kashmir Pandit Sangharsh Samiti claimed that 399 Kashmiri Pandit were killed by insurgents.

The CIA has reported that at least 506,000 people from Indian Administered Kashmir are internally displaced, about half of which are Hindu Pandits. The United Nations Commission on Human Rights reports that there are roughly 1.5 million refugees from Indian-administered Kashmir, bulk of whom arrived in Pakistan-administered Kashmir and in Pakistan after the situation on the Indian side worsened in 1989 insurgency.

Médecins Sans Frontières conducted a research survey in 2005. The survey states that 11.6% of the interviewees who took part in the study responded that they had been victims of sexual abuse since 1989. Some surveys have found that in the Kashmir region itself (where the bulk of separatist and Indian military activity is concentrated), popular perception holds that the Indian Armed Forces are more to blame for human rights violations than the separatist groups. Amnesty International has called on India to "unequivocally condemn enforced disappearances" and to ensure that impartial investigation is conducted on mass graves in its Kashmir region.

The Indian state police confirms as many as 331 deaths while in custody and 111 enforced disappearances since 1989. Amnesty International criticised the Indian Military regarding an incident on 22 April 1996, when several armed forces personnel forcibly entered the house of a 32-year-old woman in the village of Wawoosa in the Rangreth district of Jammu and Kashmir. They reportedly molested her 12-year-old daughter and raped her other three daughters, aged 14, 16, and 18. When another woman attempted to prevent the soldiers from attacking her two daughters, she was beaten. Soldiers reportedly told her 17-year-old daughter to remove her clothes so that they could check whether she was hiding a gun. They molested her before leaving the house.

Several international agencies and the UN have reported human rights violations in Indian-administered Kashmir. In a recent press release the OHCHR spokesmen stated "The Office of the High Commissioner for Human Rights is concerned about the recent violent protests in Indian-administered Kashmir that have reportedly led to civilian casualties as well as restrictions to the right to freedom of assembly and expression." A 1996 Human Rights Watch report accuses the Indian military and Indian-government backed paramilitaries of "committ serious and widespread human rights violations in Kashmir." One such alleged massacre occurred on 6 January 1993 in the town of Sopore.

TIME Magazine described the incident as such: "In retaliation for the killing of one soldier, paramilitary forces rampaged through Sopore's market, setting buildings ablaze and shooting bystanders. The Indian government pronounced the event 'unfortunate' and claimed that an ammunition dump had been hit by gunfire, setting off fires that killed most of the victims." There have been claims of disappearances by the police or the army in Kashmir by several human rights organizations. Jammu and Kashmir Public Safety Act, 1978: Human rights organizations have asked Indian government to repeal the Public Safety Act, since "a detainee may be held in administrative detention for a maximum of two years without a court order."

Many human rights organizations such as Amnesty International and the Human Rights Watch (HRW) have condemned human rights abuses in Kashmir by Indians such as "extra-judicial executions", "disappearances", and torture.

The "Armed Forces Special Powers Act" grants the military, wide powers of arrest, the right to shoot to kill, and to occupy or destroy property in counterinsurgency operations. Indian officials claim that troops need such powers because the army is only deployed when national security is at serious risk from armed combatants.

Such circumstances, they say, call for extraordinary measures. Human rights organizations have also asked Indian government to repeal the Public Safety Act, since "a detainee may be held in administrative detention for a maximum of two years without a court order."

A 2008 report by the United Nations High Commissioner for Refugees determined that Indian Administered Kashmir was only 'partly free'. A recent report by Amnesty International stated that up to 20,000 people have been detained under a law called AFSPA in Indian-administered Kashmir.

TERRORISM RESPONSIBLE FOR THE CURRENT SITUATION IN KASHMIR

A look at the situation in Kashmir gives a firm negative answer. It is, of course, true that the people and government of Pakistan have extended a degree of support, some material, most of it moral, to the struggle in Kashmir. But there is no question that the Resistance is essentially indigenous. Were Pakistan, for instance, to get completely out of the picture, the movement would still continue, however, bereft and straitened. Actually, it is grossly unfair and unrealistic to expect Pakistan to stand aside when the people of Kashmir are engaged in a struggle for which Pakistan and its people have made enormous sacrifices since 1947, and with which they have heartfelt sympathy. Kashmir and Pakistan are intertwined in such a variety of ways that it is not possible for events in the one not to have strong repercussions in the other.

Rendering aid to Kashmiris for their freedom from despotic rule has been a recurrent phenomenon in the areas, which now constitute Pakistan. It began as far back as 1835, more than a hundred years before the birth of Pakistan. In 1933-34, as many as 20,000 people from the Sialkot-Lahore area were jailed by the British Indian government to prevent them from marching into Kashmir to agitate against the ruling Hindu prince's repression. In 1947, when there were scattered and large-scale uprisings against the despot in many parts of the State, people from Pakistan felt compelled by what they considered their moral and political duty join ranks with the freedom fighters in Kashmir. It happened again in 1965. It is understandable and consistent with history if it happened (though to a much reduced extent) following the brutal and continuing Indian onslaught against the resurgent movement in Kashmir that we now date from 1989.

Pakistan is an irremovable factor in the Kashmir equation. It has fought two wars to secure the right of self-determination for Kashmiris. The first war in 1947-48 led to the resolutions of the United Nations Commission for India and Pakistan (UNCIP), which called for a plebiscite in the State to ascertain the people's wishes. The second in 1965 was brought to an end with the resolution of the UN Security Council stating the "decision" of the Council to consider after the end of hostilities "what steps should be taken to assist towards a settlement of the political problem underlying the conflict", namely Kashmir. Even the Simla Agreement in 1971 called for a "final settlement of Jammu and Kashmir", though the meeting between the President of Pakistan and the Prime Minister of India which produced the accord, was not convened to deal with Kashmir but with the aftermath of the dismemberment of Pakistan through Indian military intervention in East Pakistan. None of these undertakings has been fulfilled. Pakistan cannot be expected to force amnesia on itself and consign all this to oblivion.

After the Soviet invasion of Afghanistan, the Afghan resistance sought help from volunteers in many Muslim countries. A number of Kashmiri young men also joined the combat, which they viewed as a just and even holy war against an invader. When the Soviet Union decided to pull out of Afghanistan, having failed to overcome the popular armed struggle against the communist-backed regime in Kabul, the Kashmiri youth, like their other foreign comrades, had to leave Afghanistan and return home. By then they were battle-hardened and imbued with the zeal to carry on a similar fight against Indian occupation. They were also confident that if a superpower like the Soviet Union could be humbled by disorganized but dedicated Afghan fighters, surely they could also combat the occupation of their land by the India Union.

The fall of communism is a watershed in history and its impact on developing countries has been especially powerful. The message that went forth to societies as diverse as those of Africa and Eastern Europe was that any system that owed its hold solely to military power and its authority to force and coercion could not endure. The Kashmiris, it must be repeated, never asked for the annexation of their land by India. So the great wind of freedom blowing across the world also swept Kashmir and its youth, leading eventually to the heroic upsurge witnessed in 1989.

THE ACCESSION OF KASHMIR TO INDIA LEGAL

The ostensible accession of Kashmir to India is a fiction entrenched in the Indian position. The fact that the act was performed by a feudal ruler who had fled his capital in the face of popular revolt is well established in the official record of the dispute. But the facts of the elaborate conspiracy are no so well known but they are being exposed by the painstaking historical research conducted by such unimpeachable authorities as the Oxford historian, Alistair Lamb. The details would need a lengthy narration. Let the following facts, all beyond contradiction, therefore suffice:

1. For months prior to the so-called accession, the Maharaja (the feudal despot) was in contact not only with the Indian leaders but also with other Maharajas who had brought about the mass killings and exodus of their Muslim subjects and acceded to India. Ten weeks earlier, he had dismissed his Kashmiri Pandit Prime Minister who had counseled against a move hostile to Pakistan. The Maharaja had brought in troops and murderous gangs from outside to

overawe his Muslim subjects (the majority of the people) and crush any movement for accession to Pakistan.

2. At the moment that he offered to accede to India, his authority over the bulk of the State had crumbled.
3. India flew in its troops to restore his authority even before he had signed and delivered the instrument of accession. His accompanying letter was composed in Delhi.
4. An erstwhile Kashmiri popular leader, Sheikh Muhammad Abdullah, who had become a cohort of Indian leaders, was installed in office for his support of the Maharaja's accession. But this same person, when he insisted that the accession was provisional and depended on a plebiscite, was dismissed and put in jail in 1953. He languished in prison for about thirteen years. It was his followers who mainly formed what was called the Plebiscite Front. (He was reinstated when he was a tired, old man and had given up the fight.)
5. The Constituent Assembly was convened without a poll in Kashmir itself. Seventy-three out of 75 candidates were declared to have been elected unopposed.
6. Before this Assembly was convened, India assured the Security Council that the Assembly would not "come in the way" of the holding of a plebiscite under the auspices of the United Nations. One representative of India (an eminent jurist. Benegal Rao, later a judge of the International Court of Justice at the Hague) in his formal statement before the Council termed the State's accession to India as "tentative", pending a plebiscite.
7. The Security Council adopted the resolution of 30 March 1951 that any action of the so-called Constituent Assembly "would not constitute a disposition of the State" in accordance with the principles enunciated in the Council's earlier resolutions and accepted by both India and Pakistan - namely the synchronized withdrawal of the forces of both sides preparatory to the plebiscite and the holding of the plebiscite under the control and supervision of the United Nations.

8. When in defiance of the Security Council and in violation of the international argument embodied in the resolutions of the United Nations Commission for India and Pakistan (UNCIP), India in November 1956 nevertheless got the Assembly to declare Kashmir as a part of India, the Security Council adopted the resolution of 24 March 1957, again reminding the parties that "the final disposition of the state of Jammu and Kashmir will be made in accordance with the will of the people expressed through the democratic method of a free and impartial plebiscite conducted under the auspices of the United Nations". It also reiterated its earlier declaration that, "any action that the Assembly may have taken or might attempt to take to determine the future shape and affiliation of the entire State or any part thereof, or action by the parties concerned in support of any such action by the Assembly, would not constitute a disposition of the State in accordance with the above principle."

If India were as certain of the legal strength of its claim as it professes to be, would it not agree to the whole question being examined by the World Court? A process lasting a few months would vindicate its position and bring it resounding victory. But India knows that an impartial investigation would be fatal to its claim. Hence the loud, indignant insistence on "sovereignty". Said an experienced lawyer to his young apprentice: "If you are weak in law, stress the facts; if you are weak in facts, stress the law; but if you are weak in both facts and law, give them hell!" The way India has been giving hell to all its critics would please that lawyer.

To recapitulate, the question needs to be faced: at what point of time and by what justifiable means did Kashmir become a part of India? By the Maharaja's accession? But India itself acknowledges that the accession was subject to plebiscite under international auspices. By the decision of the Constituent Assembly? But India assured the Security Council that the decision would not prejudge the plebiscite and come in its way. By the sheer passage of time? But, despite the lapse of decades, Kashmiris have shown themselves that they have not reconciled to Indian occupation and rule. By the elections held periodically in the Indian-occupied area? But these elections are known to have been rigged and their outcome is totally disowned by the people of Kashmir, as the mass uprising amply bears out.

Resolutions of the United Nations Obsolete

Even if those resolutions had never been adopted, the principle which the articulate - the consent of the people - would have to be summoned to provide the basis, the rationale, the framework of a negotiated settlement. There is no alternative to popular will except force and fraud.

The right of self-determination does not lapse, nor the passage of time invalidate agreements, much less release a state from the international obligations it has solemnly accepted. The Indian argument to the contrary subverts the foundations of a viable order of international relations.

Without sanctity of agreements and treaties, order would be turned into anarchy. India's own founding father Jawaharlal Nehru stated in 1952. "Kashmir is not the property of India or Pakistan. It belongs to the Kashmiri people.

When Kashmir acceded to India, we made it clear to Kashmiri people that we would abide by the verdict of their plebiscite, and if they tell us to walk out, I would have no hesitation in quitting Kashmir. We have taken the issue to the United Nations and given our word of honour for a peaceful solution. As a great nation, we cannot go back on it."

As Zulfikar Ali Bhutto said at the United Nations, "Forcible annexation of Jammu and Kashmir by India is not a guarantee of Indian secularism, democracy or territorial integrity." Communal peace is not a new concern in India.

Did it not exist when India committed itself to the holding of a plebiscite in Kashmir? How can the security of India Muslims be made dependent on the occupation of Kashmir by force, if blackmail is not be countenanced? Secularism should be a function of India's own history, the composition of its population, its diversified cultural heritage, as well as its international contacts. If India's Mughal heritage and its living reminders such as the Red

Fort in Delhi and the Tag Mahal in Agra do not constitute the symbol, and if the presence in it of the world's largest religious minority does not provide substance of India's composite personality, and if they are unable to avert recurrent religious pogroms, how will the forcible occupation of a Muslim majority area such as Kashmir achieve the goal?

The total number of Kashmiri Muslims in Indian-occupied Kashmir is around 7.5 million, while the total Muslim population in the Indian Union is 120 million. How can the captivity of the less than five percent in a defined areas assure the safety of the remaining 95 percent scattered all over the country?

There were years when because of a state of relative quiescence it was assumed by some that the Muslims of Kashmir were reconciled to their place in India or were at least taking part in Indian political life.

Did attacks on Indian Muslims cease during those periods in the rest of India? They did not; on the contrary, they persisted as before. Nor has the savage repression of the Kashmiri Muslims since 1989, characterized by cold-blooded killings, rape, arson, arbitrary arrests, torture and maiming of human beings satisfied the hate-mongering elements and lessened their frenzy against the larger body of Indian Muslims.

The destruction of the 15th century Babri Mosque in 1991 is an example. If the proven and well-demonstrated loyalty of Indian Muslims since independence does not guarantee their security and well being in India, how will the coerced allegiance of the Kashmiri Muslims do that? India is the only state in the world that demands a price from others for the safety of its own citizens. And with a posture of self-righteousness, to boot.

CHANGE IN THE STATUS OF KASHMIR AND ITS ACCESSION TO PAKISTAN

Nobody has answered this better than the respected Indian statesman, the late Jayaprakash Narayan: "Few things have been said in the course of this controversy more silly than this one. The assumption behind the argument is that the states of India are held together by force and not by a sentiment of a common nationality. It is an assumption that makes a mockery of the Indian nation and a tyrant of the Indian state."

Contrary to the impression that has been created by the defenders of the status quo in Kashmir, it is the non-settlement of the Kashmir dispute, rather than its settlement, that threatens the territorial integrity of India, and it may be added, of Pakistan. A just and fair settlement of the dispute, in whatever form, would give to each country a mutually recognized and secure frontier and thus encourage their respect for each other's territorial integrity. It would strengthen internal cohesion in both countries. The only real safeguard against disintegration is peace and absence of external and internal conflict.

On the question of Kashmir becoming independent - regardless of whether the possibility is practical or theoretical - it has been argued that the emergence of another sovereign entity in the subcontinent would encourage secessionist tendencies in both India and Pakistan and lead to the collapse of their existing federal structures.

What seems to be at work here is the notorious and now discarded falling dominoes theory. No area which is today part of India or Pakistan was dragged into a union against its will; all joined by a volition expressed or confirmed in a popular vote. The only exception is Kashmir, which has never been provided the opportunity to decide its own status or affiliation.

What, therefore, applies to Kashmir does not apply to Assam or Tamil Nadu in India or to Sind in Pakistan. This is also plain from the fact that both countries accepted an international obligation under the auspices of the United Nations regarding Kashmir which neither as a sovereign state would accept regarding any of its constituent units, namely the obligation to withdraw their forces from the territory and let the people decide its status.

The dispute over Kashmir is sue generis. The demilitarization of Kashmir and the holding of a plebiscite in it, in accordance with an international agreement, does not logically justify a bid for secession by other territories nor - what is more important - psychologically encourage it. Moreover another consideration that the Indian contention ignores is that part of Kashmir can emerge as independent and other parts join India or Pakistan. This would mean consolidation and common agreement rather than fission and dispute.

Finally, what is the common sense view of the matter? The Indian contention that the de-annexation of Kashmir would lead to the breakup of the Indian Union implies that the constituent units of that Union are only waiting for an example to be set in Kashmir, which they would follow and splinter off.

The reality, however, is that they are in the Indian Union because (a) they identify themselves as parts of a larger nation, and (b) it is in their perceived interest - economic, social and cultural - to be within the Union rather than face the hazards of a separate, independent existence. If and where the sense of identity and interest is lacking, the unit will secede in course of time regardless of what happens in Kashmir. The danger of the disintegration of the Kashmir dispute is thus only a specter raised to obstruct that settlement.

The late Josef Korbel, who served as chairman of the UN Commission for India and Pakistan (incidentally father of the present United States ambassador to the United Nations, Ms. Madeline Albright), dealt with this Indian argument in an article he wrote for The New Leader, an American magazine, in its issue of 4 March 1957: "This is not true. Pakistan was not expected to withdraw her forces from Kashmir as long as there was no agreed-upon plan for simultaneous Indian withdrawal."

The withdrawal of Indian and Pakistani forces from Kashmir - i.e. demilitarization - as envisaged in UNCIP resolutions would not have been even a presentable proposition if it exposed one side to danger of attack from the other. Accordingly, while the resolution did require Pakistan to begin to withdraw its forces before India would begin the process on its side. They also required that the completion of the process be synchronized and simultaneous on both sides. This obviously required an agreed-upon plan. The Commission prepared such a plan - called the Truce Plan - and presented it to the two governments. India raised several issues. President Truman (US) and Prime Minister Attlee (UK) made a joint appeal to the two governments to accept the arbitration of the Plebiscite Administrator-designate on these points.

Pakistan promptly accepted the proposal, with no if's and but's; India rejected it. Later, two United Nations Representatives, Sir Own Dixon and Frank Graham (US) made intense efforts to secure India's agreement to a rational plan so that the Plebiscite Administrator would be inducted into office and would dispose of all the remaining forces - the residual Indian and the local - as he deemed fit. Sadly, they failed to overcome India's stubborn obstruction. This has been the cause of the stalemate in Kashmir ever since. The solution is there, only India is unwilling to implement it.

7

Kashmir Conflict : Issue and Fight

The bitterness was palpable among the young fighters squatting on the floor of a dingy, cold room in their hideout outside Muzaffarabad. Some of them had just returned from a guerrilla operation on the other side of the Line of Control, dividing the disputed state. They looked frustrated and exhausted with their dishevelled beards and dirty clothes. Some of them were quiet while others talked about their future plans.

It was the most testing of times for the veterans of the 14-year-long guerrilla war after Musharraf had assured India that Pakistani territory would not be used for cross-border operations. Most of them were visibly frustrated and resigned to the fact that their jihad might well be coming to an end. 'We have no choice but to return to our homes,' said 30-year-old Mohammed Ashfaque, in a voice choked with emotion. A resident of Srinagar in Indian-controlled Kashmir, he had left his home and joined the guerrilla struggle some ten years ago after his brother was killed by Indian forces. However, others sounded more defiant and vowed not to lay down their weapons.

Meeting on the sidelines of the South Asian Regional summit in Islamabad, in January 2004, Musharraf and Indian Prime Minister Atal Bihari Vajpayee, had agreed to start a peace process to resolve all outstanding issues, including the Kashmir dispute, through bilateral negotiations. Musharraf was more categorical this time in his pledge to switch off the tap for Kashmiri militants. He had promised to curb the jihadists before, but in the past he had hedged his bets, ordering only a temporary halt, in the hope that India would reciprocate by sitting down for talks.

With India back to the negotiating table and after two assassination attempts on him involving jihadist groups, Musharraf had more reason than ever to crack down on his home-grown militants. He could not allow the militants to take over the country. His tone became increasingly conciliatory towards India and he hinted that he was willing to drop Pakistan's long-standing demand that a plebiscite be held in Kashmir under the 1948 UN resolution to determine its status as long as India was equally forthcoming.

Musharraf's peace overtures had angered the militants, who accused him of having conceded too much ground to India by reversing Pakistan's long-standing aggressive Kashmir policy. The jihadists saw the war in ideological and civilizational terms. Any concession to the 'enemy' was therefore a very serious matter. Many Islamist leaders described the peace process as the beginning of the end of the Kashmir jihad.

Islamabad's policy shift was also driven by external factors. Musharraf's change of tack had also placed him on the horns of a serious dilemma. Islamabad's new role as a key US ally in the war on terror was no longer compatible with Pakistan's use of those proxies, which underscored its Kashmir policy. Yet, while Musharraf was quick to abandon support for the Taliban, he was reluctant to break ties with the militants waging 'a holy war' in Kashmir.

In fact, Musharraf had sought to use his country's broad cooperation with the United States to gain some leeway for continuing Pakistan's proxy war in the disputed Himalayan state. He tried to draw a fine line between what he described as 'freedom fighters' and terrorists. But America was not interested in such distinctions.

For more than half a century, the Kashmir cause had been almost the raison d'e^tre for Pakistan's existence – not to mention for the role of the armed forces in the politics of the state. Musharraf's assumption of power had alarmed India at the time, as he was known for his aggressive stance on Kashmir. Once in power, however, Musharraf displayed the pragmatic tendencies which would later cause him to disappoint fighters like Mohammed Ashfaque so bitterly. The first sign of a thaw came in June 2001, when the two countries agreed to a ceasefire along the 1,000-kilometre Line of Control, dividing the Indian and Pakistani sides of the disputed territory. That helped to ease tensions and cleared the way for the first high level government contact between the two countries. In July 2001, the Indian Prime Minister, Atal Bihari Vajpayee, invited Musharraf for talks after dropping his precondition that Pakistan should first put an end to the infiltration of militants into Kashmir. That put the onus on Musharraf to come up with some offer to defuse tensions.

Musharraf was under tremendous strain when he proceeded to Delhi for talks with the Indian leader. Closely watched by both hardliners and peaceniks, often with contrary agendas, General Musharraf walked a political tightrope. He was under scrutiny, not only by the conservative, militant Islamic groups, but also by the hardline generals. The Jamaat-i-Islami and Islamic militant groups had warned him not to deviate from a single point of the Kashmir agenda. His own future was at stake, and dependent on the outcome of the most crucial diplomatic mission he had ever undertaken. His hardline generals were opposed to any concession on Kashmir. The officers, a number of whom had served in the ISI, argued that it was the 'success of jihad' that had forced India to come to the negotiating table. They wanted Musharraf to continue supporting the Islamic militants fighting the Indian forces.

Although he had appeared stronger with his ascension to the presidency, Musharraf continued to face growing domestic opposition to the perpetuation of military rule. The pressure on Musharraf not to let the talks fail was enormous, as Pakistani leaders had constantly been calling for a negotiated settlement of disputes with India. However, any room to manoeuvre was restricted by the long-standing, thorny Kashmir issue, which was the major cause for the festering conflict in the region.

While the summit was made possible largely because of strong international pressure, it had created its own dynamics. There were strong internal pressures forcing both countries to start a dialogue. For Musharraf, in order to prevent Pakistan from economic collapse, it was important to ease tension with India. A few weeks before his departure to India, in an interview on Pakistan state television, he had declared that Pakistan's economy was not compatible with its defence capability. A de-escalation was necessary, to win the support of the international community and to restart the flow of foreign aid.

On the very first evening of the summit, Musharraf gave a speech which seemed to push all the right buttons: 'The legacy of the past years was not a happy one ... blood has been spilt, precious lives have been lost.we must not allow the past to dictate the future,' he declared in his speech at the Indian President's dinner. Musharraf's call for peace changed the atmosphere and set a positive tone for the summit. The General seemed to have established a good rapport with the ageing Indian Prime Minister. Unlike any other summit, the Agra summit had no prior agreed-upon agenda and most of the meetings were one-on-one. Inevitably though, the summit ended in a stalemate on 16 July 2001, with the two leaders unable to agree on the wording of the declaration. The deadlock did not come as a surprise. The final breakdown came when India refused to accept the centrality of the Kashmir issue and insisted on including the question of 'cross-border terrorism' in the declaration. Pakistan also showed its reservations over the reference to the Agra process as a continuation of the Simla and Lahore declarations. Both sides blamed each other of intransigence, but the reality was that neither leader was prepared to resist pressure from their respective hardliners.

Musharraf's position certainly didn't leave much room for compromise in negotiations. Never before had a Pakistani leader brought Kashmir to the centre of the summit table as forcefully as he did. His blunt talk with the Indian media editors on 16 July, which was televised by several networks, was also used by the Indian hardliners to obstruct an accord. The mood on the Indian side turned visibly bitter when Musharraf declared there should not be any illusion that the main issue confronting the two countries was Kashmir. 'I will keep saying it whether anyone likes it or not,' he said.

All was not lost, however. Musharraf and Vajpayee bade each other goodbye with a promise to meet again and pick up the threads from there. Despite the acrimony and bitterness that marked its closure, the Agra summit had broken the ice and revived the process of dialogue which had frozen after the Kargil conflict in the summer of 1999. The Indian Prime Minister accepted Pakistan's invitation for a return visit to Islamabad. It was also agreed to hold summit meetings between the Indian and Pakistani leaders once a year, and biannual talks at the foreign ministerial level to discuss issues relating to peace, security, confidence-building measures, Kashmir, narcotics and terrorism.

Not surprisingly, the stalemate at Agra was hailed by extremists in both India and Pakistan, who hoped to thrive in an atmosphere of tension. Islamic militant groups like LeT intensified suicide attacks in Kashmir and vowed to extend attacks inside India. Musharraf had provoked the ire of Islamic fundamentalists when he warned them against religious terrorism and militancy and tried to restrict the activities of militant groups, many of whom were fighting in Kashmir. Even more disturbing was the resumption of the exchange of artillery fire along the Line of Control, breaking the eight-month-old ceasefire. With the intensification of guerrilla attacks, India stepped up efforts to get Pakistan branded as a terrorist state. But this attempt to isolate Pakistan received a setback, as Musharraf's decision to support the US-led war in Afghanistan, improved Islamabad's international standing.

The 11 September terrorist attacks and their aftermath had changed the entire regional security scenario and triggered a rapid downslide in India-Pakistan relations. Worried with Pakistan's role as a key US strategic ally, India lost no time in urging Washington not to forget its sufferings from 'Pakistani-backed cross-border terrorism'. New Delhi tried to use the 'war on terror' to its advantage. It portrayed the Kashmir problem purely as a matter of combating terrorism and made the case that it also had the right to pursue militants from Pakistani- controlled Kashmir, exactly as the USA hunted down al-Qaeda and the Taliban in Afghanistan. The tension mounted further in October 2001, following the LeT suicide attack by militants on the Kashmir assembly building in Srinagar which claimed 36 lives. The incident occurred as US forces were in the last stages of preparation to launch an attack on Afghanistan. Indian leaders and military commanders warned of 'hot pursuit', sending troops into Pakistani-controlled Azad Kashmir to destroy militant camps there. Musharraf denounced the attack as an act of terrorism, but that failed to pacify India. Both countries traded accusations, backed by an 'ominous troop build-up' along the border. The situation raised serious concerns in Washington. Fearing that a fire could break out at any time in the base camp of its anti-terror campaign, the USA rushed its Secretary of State, Colin Powell, to India and Pakistan. The Bush administration, which had initially chosen to distance itself from the Kashmir conflict, showed greater enthusiasm to defuse tensions. Powell succeeded in persuading India and Pakistan to exercise restraint, but it was only a matter of time before the situation flared up again. A terrorist attack on the Indian Parliament on 13 December renewed the threat of war.

India quickly blamed two Pakistani-based Islamic militant groups, JeM and LeT, for the attack. This audacious raid on the symbol of Indian power brought the two newly nuclear-powered nations once again to the brink of war. India retaliated by severing diplomatic relations and cut rail and air communications and put Pakistan on notice to rein in the militant groups or face the consequences of war. The gravity of the terrorist attack and the post-9/11 global security environment provided India the excuse to consider military action, to stop what it described, as cross-border terrorism. Meanwhile, India demanded that Pakistan hand over 20 'most wanted terrorists', including Masood Azhar, Ahmed Omar Saeed Sheikh and five other men involved in the December 1999 hijacking of an Indian Airlines plane. The new Bush doctrine of pre-emptive strikes against the source of terrorism and the changes in the international rules of engagement afforded India the chance to engage Pakistan in brinkmanship.

In the third week of December, India launched 'Operation Parakaram' (Valour), which constituted the heaviest Indian troop mobilization since the 1971 war. It was a deliberate move by New Delhi, amidst the war on terror, to threaten Pakistan with military strikes if Islamabad did not stop sponsoring cross-border terrorism. There was every indication that India would not shy away from going to war. With Pakistan's counter-mobilization, nearly one million troops sat eyeball to eyeball across the India-Pakistan border. Both countries moved ballistic missiles and troops close to their shared border. There was a considerable risk of nuclear escalation.

The threat of war, coupled with US pressure, forced Pakistan to take action against the Islamic militant groups. On 12 January 2002, Musharraf banned LeT and JeM, which were blamed by India for the 13 December attack. He promised not to let Pakistani territory be used for cross-border terrorism. Some two thousand activists of banned extremist groups were detained in a nationwide crackdown. Musharraf, however, made it very clear that the measures against the Islamic extremist groups did not change his position on Kashmir. 'Kashmir runs in our blood. No Pakistani can afford to severe links with Kashmir. We will continue to give all diplomatic, political and moral support to the Kashmiris,' he declared.

India reacted positively to Musharraf's 12 January speech and subsequent moves to curb the militants. Nevertheless, it kept its military on high alert and in forward positions. The Indian leaders wanted to see whether Musharraf's pledge was translated into practice. They refused to resume negotiations and normalize relations with Pakistan until all their conditions were met, including their extradition demands. Musharraf's 12 January speech drew domestic as well international, support. But the measures taken by his government were insufficient against the activities of the jihadist groups. The ban was not applied to Pakistani-controlled Kashmir, or the semi-autonomous tribal areas bordering Afghanistan, which enabled militant organizations to shift their infrastructure and cadres to these regions. Hundreds of Islamic militants, returning from Afghanistan after the collapse of the Taliban regime in December 2001, had moved to the Pakistani part of Kashmir and were ready to join the armed struggle on the other side of the border. Most of these militants belonged to the three outlawed Islamic groups.

It became apparent that, while promising to curb Islamic extremism and sectarianism, Musharraf was still not willing to completely de- link Islamabad's connection with the Kashmiri militants. Meanwhile, India's refusal to pull back troops from advance positions and resume negotiations with Pakistan also tied his hands. Cross-border infiltration of militants into Indian-controlled Kashmir slowed down, but never completely stopped. Most of the militants detained following the 12 January declaration, were released. On 20 March 2002, the CIA chief, George Tenet, told the United States Senate Armed Services Committee that the chances of war in the region were the highest since 1971. In the midst of the military stand-off with India, Musharraf decided to hold a referendum to extend his term in the office of President. In his address to the nation in March 2001, Musharraf declared his intent to enter politics and stay at the helm, a far cry from the 'reluctant coup- maker' of October 1999.

With a feeling of de′ja′ vu in the air, Musharraf announced that he was seeking public approval for an extension of his tenure in office, for an additional five years beyond the three-yearperiod stipulated by the Supreme Court. The General also announced plans to introduce a new political formula, which he claimed was in conformity with the country's requirement for progress and stability. He declared that the military would continue to play a dominant role in the new political system, which was to emerge after the parliamentary elections scheduled for October 2002. Predictably, Musharraf received more than 90 per cent of the votes in a highly rigged referendum held in April 2002. The dubious polls not only dented Musharraf's credibility, but also sharpened the political polarization as the country braced for a possible war.

A series of suicide attacks by militants on a bus and in the residential quarters of an Indian army camp in Kaluchak in Kashmir on 14 May 2002 killed 35 people, mainly women and children, and brought the region closer to the nuclear precipice. Free of Islamabad's control, the militants had tried to push the two countries towards a military conflict. India quickly moved its forces to forward positions on war alert. It also expelled Pakistan's ambassador, closing the last line of direct communication with

Islamabad. With missiles and heavy weapons in place, an Indian attack appeared imminent between 29 and 31 May. Nuclear signalling from both sides reminded the world of the gravity of the situation. Some Pakistani leaders openly warned of using nuclear weapons to counter India's overwhelming conventional military superiority. In the third week of May, Pakistan tested a series of nuclear-capable ballistic missiles and stepped up its nuclear weapons programme.

As the world faced perhaps its tensest nuclear stand-off since the Cuban missile crisis in 1962, the USA and Britain launched frantic diplomatic efforts to defuse the situation. President Bush and Colin Powell called the Indian and Pakistani leaders several times, urging them to pull back. On 28 May, the British Foreign Secretary, Jack Straw, visited Islamabad and asked Musharraf to take tougher measures to counter cross-border terrorism. He reminded Pakistan that as a UN member it had the responsibility to bear down 'effectively and consistently on all forms of terrorism, including cross-border terrorism'. In Delhi the next day, Straw called on the Indian leaders to exercise restraint. He also told them that Musharraf had promised to close down 'terrorist camps' operating in Pakistani-administered Kashmir and curb infiltration into India. Serious strains had emerged in relations between Washington and Islamabad after reports that the ISI was still linked with the militant groups. On 31 May, Colin Powell publicly accused Pakistan of continuing infiltration across the Line of Control, despite Musharraf's assurance that it would be halted. The following day, Musharraf told the BBC that he had issued instructions to end the crossing and stop all militant activities. But the statement did not satisfy the Bush administration which had demanded that Pakistan shut down cross- border infiltration permanently. 'When and if, it does stop, it must also stop permanently,' Colin Powell retorted. International patience was clearly running out with Musharraf's game of deception.

Musharraf was firmly wedged between a rock and a hard place. He sincerely wanted to prevent a war, but at the same time did not want to be seen as the leader who gave up his country's 'sacred' cause: Kashmir. He badly needed a face-saving device if he was to take further steps backward to meet the expectations of the international community. Musharraf tried desperately to maintain his balancing act. His 'blow hot, blow cold' posture accurately reflected the difficulties he faced at home, where he was, once again, taking a controversial position on a sensitive issue.

On 1 June, the USA, Britain, France, Canada, Japan, Australia and some other countries, issued travel advisories asking their citizens to leave India immediately and warning others against travelling to the country. Pakistan was already on the 'travel advisory' list after 9/11. The warning led to the exodus of thousands of businessmen, visitors, tourists and diplomatic personnel from India. This threatened the closure of foreign and multinational companies and caused much annoyance in Delhi, which perceived the advisory as an attempt to pressure it against launching an attack on Pakistan.

Once again, intensive US intervention was the key to walking both sides back from the brink. On 6 June, the US Deputy Secretary of State, Richard Armitage, arrived in Islamabad to build on Straw's visit and hammer out a deal between India and Pakistan. A former wrestler and a veteran diplomat, Armitage was known for his blunt talking. He had met Musharraf several times in the past and appeared to have developed a good rapport with the Pakistani military leader. Armitage had one critical objective when he arrived for talks at the sprawling presidential secretariat at the Margala foothills on the afternoon of 6 June: to extract an assurance from Musharraf that would satisfy India and remove the threat of a potential nuclear war.

Musharraf had previously pledged to stop the infiltration of Islamic militants into Kashmir, but Armitage wanted him to go one step further. The talks between the two men had stretched to two hours, when Armitage put the critical question: 'What can I tell the Indians?' he asked. He wanted to know whether Musharraf would agree to a 'permanent end' to the cross-border terrorist activity long accepted by Pakistan. 'Yes,' Musharraf replied. An elated Armitage flew to Delhi the next morning to brief the Indian leaders on his talks with Musharraf. Musharraf's agreement to the word 'permanent', backed by US assurances to India that he would keep his word, immediately led to the easing of tension. It was a hugely significant foreign policy victory for India, which, for more than a decade, had sought an end to the cross-border terrorist attacks. Indeed, Musharraf had no other option, as his refusal to concede would have had disastrous consequences. 'If Pakistan had not agreed to end infiltration, and America had not conveyed that guarantee to India, then war could not have been averted,' Vajpayee told an Indian newspaper a week later.

The Musharraf-Armitage agreement was a turning point in Pakistan's long-standing policy of using militancy as an instrument for its proxy war in Kashmir and paved the way for a new relationship between two nations long divided by a bloody, tense history. In return for his concession, Musharraf received private assurances from US officials that they would stay involved. On 5 June, President Bush had called Musharraf and gave his firm commitment that his administration would remain engaged to resolve the Kashmir conflict. Musharraf told Armitage that he expected an early and substantial response from the Indian side to make his action sustainable.

Within days of Armitage's departure, a thaw was evident. India responded to Musharraf's steps to curb cross-border terrorism by moving its naval fleet back to its base and allowed commercial overflights. It also announced the revival of diplomatic relations with Pakistan. That effectively ended the longest military stand-off between the two countries. Pakistan's military and the ISI had always kept a fairly tight control on their militant clients and the restrictions resulted in an immediate drop in the infiltration of militants into Kashmir. But it never completely stopped. Some militant groups were not prepared to toe the new Pakistani line and continued to send their men into Kashmir. Pakistani officials argued that it was impossible to completely seal the LoC. For Musharraf, the major challenge was how to rein in the powerful militant groups. Predictably, his decision to stop cross-border infiltration, evoked angry reactions from the militant groups who, for more than a decade, had fought Pakistan's proxy war. The atmosphere in the room was grim. A sense of unease gripped the two dozen guerrilla commanders, who had come to meet with a senior ISI officer at an army base in Muzaffarabad in the last week of May. The capital of Pakistani-controlled Azad Kashmir had long been the headquarters of more than a dozen Kashmiri militant groups. Some two hundred kilometres from Islamabad, the city was at an equal distance from Srinagar, the capital of Indian-administered Kashmir. 'We don't have a choice given the tremendous pressure on Pakistan,'

Major-General-Khalid Mahmood told them. 'So, you have to stop all cross-border operations.' Several of the guerrilla commanders leapt to their feet, shouting that Pakistan should not surrender to Indian and American pressure. 'After ditching the Taliban, Musharraf has now betrayed the Kashmiri cause,' said a senior commander belonging to HuM, one of the largest Islamic militant groups involved in the separatist war in Kashmir. 'How can we accept this?' The commanders were bitter and vengeful, and left the meeting declining the officer's invitation to join him for lunch.

This outburst of anger towards Musharraf and his policies appeared logical. Thousands of militants had perished fighting Pakistan's war in Kashmir. Islamic militant leaders, who had depended for over a decade on the active support of Pakistan's army for their cross- border guerrilla actions, viewed Islamabad's move as a betrayal of the Kashmiri freedom struggle. 'We have lost so many friends, brothers and relatives in the Kashmir struggle. What was that for?' asked Amiruddin, a veteran Kashmiri guerrilla fighter. He reflected the sentiments of thousands of jihadist cadres trained and armed by the Pakistani military establishment. 'We are not going to sit quietly.'

The orders came as hundreds of fresh guerrillas were waiting at their base camps in Azad Kashmir to cross the border. It was generally at that time of the year that infiltration took place. 'The volunteers are becoming increasingly upset over the delay. They have not been informed about Pakistan's ban,' said the commander. He complained that the communication link between the guerrilla fighters inside Indian Kashmir and their base on the Pakistani side had been cut off and that training centres inside Azad Kashmir had been closed down. 'Many of our colleagues are stuck across the border without reinforcements and supplies,' he said.

Pakistan's decision to withdraw support had caused a setback to the militancy, but did not bring it to an end. The militant infrastructure remained intact and outlawed groups continued working, either under new banners, or merged into others. Hundreds of Pakistani fighters who were inside Kashmir at that point had continued their jihad, ignoring Pakistan's policy shift. Most militant leaders hoped that the restrictions were temporary and still had faith in the army. 'The army will always be our ally,' a senior militant commander told me. Facing down the jihadists was not going to be an easy task for Musharraf. Since an indigenous insurrection against Indian domination broke out in Kashmir in 1989, some 10,000 fighters had crossed the border to help their Kashmiri brethren.

They were not prepared to give up the cause on Islamabad's orders. As an inevitable consequence of Pakistan's policy of using jihad as an instrument of covert war, some elements within the intelligence agencies had been radicalized by the Islamists. The handlers had become coloured by the ideology of the militants. They were unhappy with Musharraf's decision to support America's war on Afghanistan's Islamic regime, which they had helped install. But even deeper was the resentment on the reversal in Kashmir. There was a strong anti-American feeling in the military ranks. Many officers believed that western countries, particularly the USA, had not come to Pakistan's support when it faced the threat of war from its nuclear rival.

Once again Musharraf was walking a tightrope. His position had become even more tenuous after he ordered his troops to stop the infiltration. He had come to the conclusion that there was now a conflict of interest between the militants and the military. But it was not clear whether other army officers agreed with him. There was a strong feeling in the army that India was trying to humiliate them by dictating terms for peace.

Some hardline retired generals, who had been responsible for organizing the Kashmiri 'jihad', warned Musharraf that there was a limit to how far the army would go along with a policy of using force against those who were seen as fighting for Pakistan's interest in Kashmir. Lt.-General Hamid Gul, a former ISI chief and a fiercely anti-American former commander, accused Musharraf of 'going too far in appeasing the west' and taking a 'step back' on the Kashmir issue. 'By calling those attacking the Indian forces, terrorists, General Musharraf is only echoing the Indian position,' he declared. Despite military de-escalation, there was a wide gap between what the Indian leaders demanded and what Musharraf could deliver. India's mistrust of the Pakistani military leadership had thwarted all moves by the international community to bring the two sides to the negotiating table. It was only after the relatively peaceful polls for the Kashmir state assembly in October 2002, that Delhi and Islamabad opened secret back-channel diplomacy. Beginning in April 2003, Vajpayee's Principal Secretary, Brajesh Mishra, and Musharraf's top aide, Tariq Aziz, held several meetings in London, Dubai and Bangkok exploring avenues to begin a peace process.

A seasoned bureaucrat, Tariq Aziz was a college-mate of Musharraf's and had worked as his principal secretary after the military takeover. A former income tax officer, he was more into political wheeling and dealing and had no experience of diplomacy. However, being Musharraf's closest aide, he was considered the best man for this secret and extremely delicate job. Even the foreign ministry was kept out of the loop. Facilitated by the USA, this was the first senior official contact between the two countries for nearly two years.

Tariq Aziz was later appointed secretary of the National Security Council. In April 2003, the Indian Prime Minister extended a 'hand of friendship' to Pakistan during a public address in Srinagar. Pakistan's Prime Minister, Zafarullah Khan Jamali, responded by speaking to Vajpayee and invited him to visit Islamabad. In yet another highly symbolic gesture, India announced the resumption of bus links with Pakistan. The twice-weekly coach service between Delhi and Lahore had been abruptly suspended 18 months earlier, after Islamic militants had attacked the Indian Parliament in Delhi. The bus service, which started in February 1999, had significant symbolic value. Vajpayee had travelled to

Lahore by the inaugural coach for his historic meeting with Pakistan's then Prime Minister, Nawaz Sharif. Given their deep-rooted mistrust of each other, the process remained a slow diplomatic dance, with the two governments circling one another warily, each making tentative offers. The efforts at that stage were largely aimed at de-escalation and the restoration of the situation that existed prior to the military stand-off, rather than any great leap forward.

Pakistan moved very cautiously, given its traditional suspicion of its much bigger, and militarily powerful, neighbour. It was reluctant to open its airspace to Indian planes and remove all trade barriers. Pakistan feared that lifting the overflight ban could provide India with an opportunity to establish close trade links with, and consolidate its influence in, Afghanistan. There were strong apprehensions in Islamabad that the emerging process could prove to be another false start if India raised the size of the table, rather than picking up the thread from previous talks.

Kashmir remained the thorniest issue as the two countries moved towards a rapprochement. The events of May and June a year before had indicated how quickly the situation could escalate into a fully fledged conflagration, with both countries appearing all too willing to engage in nuclear sabre-rattling. There was no sign of flexibility yet on the Kashmir issue on either side. While India was eager to demonstrate that the Kashmir violence was totally Pakistani sponsored, Pakistan appeared equally adamant to keep up the pressure on Delhi.

Although Musharraf had agreed to clamp down on militant groups, the situation on the ground did not change much. Pakistan's promise of a complete halt to support for the Islamic militants did not seem credible at that stage. Pakistani military officials contend that a total turnaround in Pakistan's policy could not be possible without some reciprocity from India, for example, reduction of troops and an end to human rights violations in the state. 'We will lose all leverage if we just pull out our support to the Kashmiris without any show of flexibility by India,' said a senior Pakistani official. 'In the absence of any light at the end of the Kashmiri tunnel, it would be hard for the government to sell any proposal for peace with India to its own people.' It was quite apparent that the military-backed administration was not ready to put the Kashmir issue on the backburner.

The military officers, who stood by Musharraf when he moved away from Pakistan's long-standing policy of supporting the conservative Taliban regime in Afghanistan and joined the US-led coalition against terrorism, were not likely to maintain their loyalty towards him if he had decided to make a radical shift on the Kashmir issue.

With India agreeing to resume peace talks, Pakistan faced increasing pressure to come down hard on Islamic guerrilla groups and destroy militant infrastructure. A serious international concern was that Pakistan's inability to contain militancy could continue to be a significant obstacle to the normalization of relations between the two countries. While acknowledging that there had been a decrease in infiltration and that the level of violence in Kashmir had declined, Washington was not fully satisfied with the situation.

The situation then took a most dramatic turn in January 2004, when Vajpayee came to Islamabad to attend the seven-nation South Asian regional summit. Few had expected any breakthrough when the aged Indian Prime Minister went to pay a 'courtesy call' on Musharraf at the imposing presidential palace on 5 January. Although there had been hints of a possible meeting, nobody was sure until it actually happened.

The outcome of the 65-minute parley between the two leaders went beyond anybody's expectations. Not only were some significant decisions taken to move the process of normalization forward, but a road map for further interaction was also clearly stated.

Most importantly, Musharraf pledged to prevent the use of the territory under Pakistan's control 'to support terrorism in any manner'. It was the first direct commitment of this nature since the Pakistani- backed armed insurgency in Kashmir began in 1989. The joint statement also declared that both leaders were 'confident' of reaching a peaceful settlement of all bilateral issues, including Kashmir. It was a great leap forward in the relations between the two countries, which had been on the brink of nuclear war just a year before.

The outcome of the Islamabad meeting was not the result of a sudden surge of goodwill. The script was prepared after intensive back-channel diplomacy between Brajesh Mishra and Tariq Aziz. From 1 to 4 January, the two officials were in regular contact. Mishra also met with the ISI chief, Lt.-General Ehsan ul-Haq.

Those interactions remained secret, even from Pakistani foreign ministry officials. Only the President's Chief of Army Staff, General Hamid, and Tariq Aziz were involved in the preparation of the joint communique′. Foreign Secretary, Riaz Khokar, was handed a copy just a few hours before the summit meeting. Musharraf's change of course on the Kashmir policy indicated that the Pakistani military establishment had finally acknowledged that support for militancy could not dislodge India from the disputed land. But there had also been concern that, in the absence of such pressure, India would not agree to a negotiated settlement of the Kashmir dispute. Vajpayee's agreement on a composite dialogue on all bilateral issues, including Kashmir, gave Musharraf some leeway to convince his generals of the need for peace with India.

Musharraf went one step further when he declared his readiness to consider all possible alternatives for the Kashmir solution. In November 2004, he outlined a step-by-step approach towards resolving the decades-old dispute, which involved making some parts of the disputed territory independent or placing them under joint Indian-Pakistani control. Indeed, the suggestion to identify the region, demilitarize it and change its status, signified a radical shift in Pakistan's Kashmir policy.

Though premature, the proposal indicated a significant come-down from Pakistan's traditional hardline position of holding a plebiscite, under the 1948 UN resolution that required Kashmiris alone to decide their political future. For the first time, a Pakistani leader had suggested making the territory a joint protectorate. Finding a solution acceptable to both sides had always been a difficult task, even in the best of circumstances, as Kashmir has been so deeply intertwined with India and Pakistan's perceptions of national security and identity.

Domestic political compulsions had made the issue more complex. What had made securing peace even more difficult was the past baggage of mistrust and suspicion the two nations continued to carry. It had been such an accident-prone relationship that any incident could derail the whole process.

Musharraf's turnaround divided the separatist movement in Indian- administered Kashmir. The moderate elements supported his peace initiatives. For them, militancy could not provide the solution to the festering problem and it was time for the political parties to play their roles for a negotiated settlement of the issue. Once dismissed by the Pakistani military establishment as 'weak links', the moderate Kashmiri leaders became Musharraf's new allies.

Mirwaiz Umar Farooq, a charismatic young Kashmiri leader, remembered his first meeting with Musharraf in New York in September 2001, when the Pakistani military leader accused him of being 'cowardly' for suggesting a non-militant course towards the solution of the Kashmir problem. 'The meeting ended on a bitter note,' Mirwaiz recalled when I met him in his heavily guarded house in Srinagar in April 2005.

The mood had completely changed when the two met again in Holland three years later, following the Indo-Pak rapprochement. 'It was I this time asking him to go slow on the peace process. Musharraf sounded too enthusiastic about the prospect of reaching a settlement,' Mirwaiz said.

The Kashmiri leader was thrown into separatist politics as a teenager after the death of his father, Mirwaiz Maulvi Farooq, in 1989. As a prayer leader at Srinagar's Jamia Masjid, he wielded considerable spiritual and political influence in the disputed state. He led the moderate faction of the All Parties Hurriyat (Freedom) Conference (APHC), a loose coalition of more than 32 organizations, that wanted militancy to give way to political struggle. 'Militancy has played an important role in drawing international attention to the Kashmir issue, but now we should concentrate on a political struggle,' he declared. The moderates were also concerned about the struggle falling into the hands of the extremists.

The resumption of the Indo-Pak talks was fully backed by the moderates, though Musharraf's change of tack shocked the hardliners who had been fighting for the annexation of the entire disputed state with Pakistan. Their bitterness was palpable when the bus service between Srinagar and Muzaffarabad was restored on 7 April 2005, after a 57-year hiatus. It was a momentous occasion when the new Indian Prime Minister, Manmohan Singh, waved off the first bus with its 19 passengers. Described as the mother of all confidence-building measures between India and Pakistan, the bus link reunited divided Kashmiri families. But for the militants it was a betrayal of their cause. In an attempt to derail the peace process, the militants attacked the Tourist Reception Centre in Srinagar, where the passengers of the inaugural bus were kept under strict security.

'This is not what we have sacrificed thousands of lives for,' Syed Ali Shah Geelani, the head of his own faction of APHC, told me when we met at his Srinagar residence, a day after the bus had left for Muzaffarabad.

The 70-year-old, white-bearded Geelani was the chief of Jamaat-i-Islami in Kashmir, and had close links with the Islamic militants fighting Pakistan's proxy war. For his ardent support for Pakistan, he was often described as an ISI agent until Musharraf's turnaround. With Pakistan now betting on the moderates, Geelani felt isolated. But his loyalty to Pakistan was unquestionable. 'Musharraf is destroying Pakistan. Things will change once he is gone,' he said.

"TERRITORIAL DISPUTE" IN KASHMIR DISPUTE

It is a "territorial dispute" only in the sense that the State of Jammu and Kashmir is disputed territory and is so recognized internationally. But the expression can be misleading. For it usually suggested contentious claims of two states to a territory, one party basing its claim on the validity of a de facto or de jure boundary demarcation and the other challenging it. That is why territorial disputes are hardly distinguishable from border disputes, amenable to solution through bilateral agreement, judicial determination or, more often, arbitration.

Kashmir is a case qualitatively different from border disputes. Here the territory involved is a whole country, a country larger than many member states of the United Nations, a country larger the major part of which has existed for more than a millennium as a sovereign political entity on its own, a country whose distinct physical environment, history and culture have shaped its people's individuality. Here the matter is not one of placing a few hundred square miles on one side or the other of an international frontier and thus settling a boundary conflict. It is a matter of the disposition of a country through the same process by which the two contestants, the Indian Union and Pakistan themselves emerged as independent states - the process of establishing sovereignties on the basis of popular consent. As long as the Kashmir dispute remains unresolved, the agenda of the independence of the South Asian subcontinent remains unfinished.

If this support had really rested on, and reflected, popular sentiment, then the history of the Kashmir dispute would have been entirely different. In that case, India would have been not merely willing but eager to have the United Nations conduct a plebiscite in Kashmir so that the accession would be speedily ratified and India's position vindicated for good. All that India would have required would have been sufficient safeguards against a breach of the Ceasefire Line or eruption of violence during the period of the plebiscite. These would have been easily obtained. Indeed, they were provided for in the plan drawn by the United Nations Commission for India and Pakistan (UNCIP). With a Plebiscite Administrator appointed by the United Nations and inducted into office, the freedom of the voters from coercion and intimidation would have been assured. Pakistan would have had no means to exert any pressure whatsoever on the voters nor would it have chosen to draw overwhelming international censure for disrupting the plebiscite process. If there has been popular support in Kashmir for joining India, the dispute over Kashmir would have lasted for a year or so at most. It would have dissolved long ago.

Let us here contrast the cases of Hyderabad, Junagarh and Goa - three areas that India annexed through what it called (a phrase reminiscent of Nazi ideology) "police action". In none of these cases did India have to bring in the resounding names of a local political organization or leader to justify the annexations. Yet, leader or no leader, organization or no organization, the overwhelming majority of the people in these areas wished to be part of the Indian nation and, though a certain arrogance on India's part raised some eyebrows, world opinion recognized the fact and the incorporation of the these areas in India met with international acquiescence. Pakistan's complaints in the cases of Hyderabad and Junagarh and the protest of the United States over the invasion of Goa were storms of the teacup variety; the controversies subsided in short time.

The presentation by India of Sheikh Abdullah and his National Conference as the embodiment of mass approval for the entry of Indian troops into Kashmir has itself provided an eloquent commentary on the nature of India's claim to Kashmir. The same Sheikh Abdullah was dismissed as Prime Minister in 1953, kept in prison for years and charged with treason because he insisted on complete autonomy for the State and stressed repeatedly that the accession was provisional. At one time, in 1957, he sent a hand-written letter from jail t the Security Council denouncing the Indian position. The National Conference formed what was called the Plebiscite Front, which demanded that the issue of accession be referred to the people's vote. The fact that later in 1975 Sheikh Abdullah turned a somersault and, signing on the dotted line, became Chief Minister again is an indicator more of his personal character than of the strength or consistency of India's political position in Kashmir.

A glimpse into Kashmir's political history might be apposite here. Kashmir was unique among all the Princely States of India in organizing a political movement on its own in opposition to autocracy.

This took the form of a mass agitation in 1931, which a year later, gave birth to the Muslim Conference. Sheikh Abdullah was undoubtedly the hero the agitation and no one equalled his appeal to huge Kashmiri gatherings. He was at the peak of his popularity from 1931 to 1933. As early as 1934, however, a streak of opportunism in him became visible when he stayed away from an agitation directed by his more steadfast and less theatrical colleague, Ghulam Abbas, against the limitation of the franchise for the legislative assembly and the restriction of the assembly's powers. From that time onwards, although he retained his unsurpassed capacity to arouse the emotions of the masses, his political position zigzagged and his popularity began to wane. When he succeeded in converting the Muslim Conference into the National Conference, he attracted the patronage of Jawaharlal Nehru, enlisted the support of the great propaganda machine run by the Indian Congress, gained some glitter in non-Kashmiri eyes but lost the cohesiveness of his Kashmiri following. Within a short period, the co-architect of the National Conference, Prem Nath Bazaz (Hindu) and the former President of Muslim Conference - both expressed disillusionment about Abdullah's integrity. The former established his own party and the latter revived the Muslim Conference. Non-Muslims regarded Abdullah as a Muslim chauvinist (what is called 'communalist' in India) and Muslims suspected that he had struck some kind of a deal with the Dogra regime despite its practice of open discrimination against the Muslims. Both were right not because Abdullah was taking the middle position but because he easily swung from one extreme to the other.

Two other things affected Abdullah's public standing. First, he betrayed pronounced fascist proclivities and frequently resorted to strong-arm methods in bullying his opponents. This became a scandal in the late 1930s and the early 1940s; he had to suffer physical reprisal for his hooliganism in places like Poonch and Rajauri. Second, while still employing his emotive rhetoric, he veered more and more towards cooperation with the Maharaja's autocratic regime. As if this was not enough, he broke the pledge he had made that he would not side with the Indian Congress against the Muslim League (the two major parties in British India).

In an attempt to recapture his following among Muslims, especially the intelligentsia, Abdullah joined prominently in the jubilant reception accorded to M.A. Jinnah on his visit to Kashmir in 1944. Jinnah tried to reconcile Abdullah and Abbas and put the question squarely to Abdullah. "How much significant support have you obtained from Hindus for the objectives of the National Conference?" When Abdullah could cite only the names of a few individuals, Jinnah queried, "The what is the point of dividing the Muslims into two camps, the Muslim Conference and the National Conference?" Abdullah thought he had a answer to that. "But the National Conference is in reality the Muslim Conference in a better guise," he said. Came back the forthright rebuke, "That means you are committing a fraud on Hindus." This left Abdullah only with one course: vituperative speeches against "outsiders" like Jinnah. (In private remarks, he, however, disowned the speeches.) This was the nadir of Abdullah's position in Kashmir.

When he felt the ground slipping from under his feet, Abdullah sought the counsel of a group of very able communists from Lahore. They drafted the manifesto called 'New Kashmir' for him in 1944 and then produced a most impressive declaration about the sale deed miscalled the Treaty of Amritsar to which the Maharaja owed his title to Kashmir. Armed with this and a stirring slogan, Abdullah launched his 'Quit Kashmir' campaign against the Maharaja in May 1946. He was jailed on a charge of sedition and Jawaharlal Nehru felt impelled to enter the fray. Considerable publicity was generated as a result, but apart from small groups (mostly the cadres of the National Conference, better-trained than those of the Muslim Conference) the masses, both Muslim and Hindu, stood aloof. The Maharaja demonstrated his triumph by arranging to be driven in a spectacular motorcade through the main street of Srinagar on his birthday in September. It was not the respect and sympathy for the Maharaja on the part of the great Muslim majority but the distrust of Sheikh Abdullah that made this possible. The wrong medium had eclipsed the right message.

After the partition of British India in August 1947, Abdullah wrote letters to his friends from jail recommending Kashmir's accession to India, making sure that the letters would be seen by the Maharaja's officials. This reinforced the assurances that the Maharaja had received from the leaders of the Indian Congress, including Mohandas Gandhi, that Abdullah would help him to join India. Abdullah was granted "royal clemency" and released from jail in return for colluding with the Maharaja in maneuvering accession to India. He flew immediately to Delhi to confer with the Indian leaders, as did the Maharaja's courtiers. Abbas, the leader of the Muslim Conference, languished in jail.

At the time, Abdullah's constituency in Kashmir, in the estimate of impartial observers, had shrunk to a few districts of Srinagar. That, in essence, was the reality of the popular backing for India establishing sovereignty over Kashmir. The estimate, of course, was not shared by Jawaharlal Nehru, nor perhaps by Gandhi, but when doubts began to grow in Delhi whether Abdullah's presumed popularity would swing the vote in India's favour, did India begin to wriggle out of its pledge to a plebiscite. The doubts about success turned to certainty of defeat when Abdullah, had to be ousted as Prime Minister and jailed in 1953. From that time, Indian policy was set dead against any ascertainment of the wishes of the people of Kashmir on the accession issue. Nehru did make a promise to the Prime Minister of Pakistan to cooperate in the holding of a plebiscite by April 1954 but, as the ensuing correspondence between the two showed, it was done only to palliate an aroused public opinion in both Kashmir and Pakistan.

No invasion of one country by another encounters an immediate insurrection. There were no popular uprisings in the capitals of Western Europe when they witnessed the victorious march of the Nazi troops. Nor did the Soviet forces when they were triumphant, face mass upheavals and defiance in Eastern Europe. There was no immediate revolt in Kabul against the Soviet invasion of Afghanistan. Resistance against foreign occupation requires organization and takes time to develop.

If in Kashmir, India did succeed in dampening the sentiment of revolt for a number of years by co-opting the section of the people represented by the National Conference which was joined by a whole lot to careerists, it nor more belies the claim of popular loathing of Indian occupation than the existence of the Vichy regime belied French resistance to Nazi occupation. If Sheikh Abdullah who in 1947 supported India taking over Kashmir by force had been at one time the most popular leader in Kashmir, Marshall Petain, who capitulated before Hitler and cooperated with him, had been the most respected war hero of France. All occupation regimes find collaborationists in the occupied countries; there are Quislings and Lavals and Najibs in every society. Kashmir could not be in exception. There were some added circumstances in Kashmir.

First, simultaneously with sending its troops into Kashmir, India made a solemn declaration that the accession of Kashmir was provisional and subject to the people's verdict. She gave this solemn assurance to the people of Kashmir, to Pakistan, to Britain and to "the whole world", in Jawaharlal Nehru's words. This created the reasonable expectation in the mass mind that India's annexation of Kashmir was a temporary affair and would be reversed by a peaceful process. Arzi Ilhaq (temporary accession) became a common expression. A mass uprising seemed unnecessary.

Second, at the time of the entry of Indian troops, the leaders of the Muslim Conference were in jail or in exile from the Vale. The organizing force of resistance was dispersed.

Third, fighting ensued between the Indian army and the Azad Kashmir forces in extensive parts of the State. Though vastly outnumbered, ill equipped and poorly organized, and hence unable to reach Srinagar and Jammu, the two capitals, the Azad forces did hold some ground and, even before Pakistan provided them regular military support, they had prevented India from overrunning the whole State. Newspapers in India itself at the time reported a number of incidents of a few guerrillas holding at bay large companies of Indian troops with all their armour and air support. This along with the proceedings of the Security Council and the dispatch of a United Nations Commission in 1948, created the kind of expectancy that inhibits a people's revolt.

First, it is open to question who in Pakistan count on an insurgency in the Vale of Kashmir at the time. There are different versions, none wholly plausible. However, if anyone in authority did, his thinking must have been at the adolescent level. He must have thought that insurgencies are made like instant coffee; he must have lacked education in rebellions. Uprisings, as distinguished from acts of sabotage, rarely go with inter-state wars; when they do, they end in disaster. Of the first of these two lessons, the Vietnam War provides a good illustration: throughout that war, no uprising took place in Saigon. Of the second, the genuine Shiite uprising in Iraq at the time of the Persian Gulf War in 1991 has been another graphic example. Even when Saddam Hussein's retreating troops, waving white flags, were being bulldozed with the earth, he still had the means to reduce the rebellion to cinders.

If a state at war defeated but not yet admitting defeat, does not make a suitable target for rebellion, far less does an undefeated state. Indian troops would have to be forced by Pakistan's military offensive to begin a retreat from Karachi before a civilian uprising against the remnants of Indian authority and welcoming the entry of Pakistani forces could take place. This had nothing to do with passivity or docility in the Kashmiri character - that myth has been shattered now. It has everything to do with the dynamism of popular uprisings. They need their own impulse and are sustained by their own strategy; they abort if they lack native political guidance. To ignore this principle is to plan for failure.

Second, the situation in Kashmir in 1964-65 has been misrepresented in both Pakistan and India for opposite psychological reasons. India feels the compulsion to prove Kashmiri acquiescence in Indian occupation, Pakistan to account for the miscarriage of its plans. Neither acknowledges the fact that Kashmiris did rise on their own against Indian rule in 1964. When Jawaharlal Nehru sent a senior intelligence official who was his confidant to Srinagar to make a report on the situation, the man returned and candidly said to him, "Prime Minister, from what I have seen, Kashmir is not a part of India." Even Lal Bahadur Shastri, who had not yet become Prime Minister, remarked significantly after his visit to Kashmir that the situation would have to be resolved ultimately in accordance with the people's wishes. The agitation was intelligently directed by the indigenous Committee of Action set up in Srinagar. There is evidence that Nehru had accepted the need "radical rethinking" about India's policy with regard to both Kashmir and Pakistan. Nehru's death at that delicate point, Sheikh Abdullah's trip abroad during which he met some world leaders, including Zhou En-Lai, his consequent re-imprisonment, Shastri's political inferiority when stepping into Nehru's shoes, the frequent military probing and exchanges across the Ceasefire Line, the worsening of Indian forces by Pakistani troops in the Rann of Kutch (distant from Kashmir), the crescendo of belligerency on both sides, and finally the entry of commandos from Azad Kashmir and Pakistan uncoordinated with a native plan for a guerrilla campaign - all tangled the plot and arrested its denouement.

Nevertheless, besides rendering help to commandos wherever physically possible in August 1965, Kashmiris hardly showed themselves as resigned to Indian occupation since the world media had their attention riveted on the fighting between India and Pakistan, non-military happenings in the Vale of Kashmir itself went rather unnoticed. Still, a number of major western newspapers, including the New York Times carried stories about what was called "the children's revolt": young boys and girls showing defiance of Indian authority. It was then that the slogan (unacceptably abusive but betraying the people's exasperation) "Indian dogs, go home" gained currency in Srinagar and was blazoned by the letters I.D.G.O. painted on walls and pavements. There was not - there could not be, as we have seen - an organized revolt. Nor was there the quiescence that Indians like to believe and Pakistanis prefer to complain about.

It is no more unrealistic that it was to expect Algeria to cease to be a department of France, Namibia to be detached from South Africa or Estonia or Lithuania to become independent of the Soviet Union. France had ruled Algeria, South Africa had held Namibia and the Soviet Union had annexed Estonia and Lithuania for longer periods than the Indian Union has occupied Kashmir. What belongs to a State and cannot be pried loose from it is what feels itself to be part of that State, some discontent notwithstanding. Kashmir never felt itself to be part of India before 1947 and feels even less so after its forcible seizure by the Indian troops. The de-annexation process is inevitable in the post-colonial age. The only question is whether it is accomplished by armed struggle, resulting in a spiral of violence and counter-violence or through negotiation and/or other means of peaceful settlement. The choice always lies with the occupying power. Until now, India has pre-empted negotiation by its adamant assertion that the status of Kashmir is not negotiable.

Is this adamancy an insuperable obstacle, considering that it is backed by the military power of the Indian Union, one of the most formidable in the world? The question invites reflection. Even as recently as the mid-1980s, the idea of the liberation of Estonia and Lithuania was regarded as a pipe dream. So was the institution of majority rule in South Africa. The military and technological arsenal at the disposal of the Soviet Union was mightier than what the Indian Union possesses. The same could be said of the apartheid regime proportionately in the context of the South African subcontinent. Yet military power did not bring political strength to the Soviet Union nor immunize South African because the rest of the world did not bend its knee to it. It is the deference down by the West to India's military power that reinforces India's obduracy. It also weakens the liberal section of Indian opinion that would prefer a sensible and human policy with respect to Kashmir. Unwittingly, the West contributes to the depletion of the already small but the most promising resource in India's political society, the resource of self-criticism, and to the encouragement of that sanctimoniousness which the more thoughtful Indians regard as a bane of their country's attitudes in international affairs.

We have spoken of countries that were liberated from the Soviet Union. Since their release was followed immediately by the collapse of the Soviet Union itself, the suggestion might seem to lurk that Kashmir's freedom is envisaged in the prospective context of the disintegration of the Indian Union. Quite the contrary. It has been brought out elsewhere in these pages that the liberation of Kashmir would strengthen the cohesion and solidity of the Indian Union. It would cure India of what was called "a frontier sore" by Lord Ismay who advised Lord Mountbatten, one of the men chiefly responsible for the invasion of Kashmir by India.

The impression is not groundless but, on a more serious examination, it turns out to be superficial. For some years now, Pakistan's leaders have not displayed qualities or care and sensitivity in certain statements they have made on Kashmir. A couple of these statements, blithely citing the Indian Independence Act passed by the British Parliament in 1947, directly contradict the position clarified by the Founder of Pakistan himself who, besides being the redoubtable constitutionalist that he was, had vetted the Act before it was adopted (the Indian Congress leaders had done the same). In his characteristically straightforward manner, he published his view that the British government or Parliament had "no power or sanction" to restrict the freedom of the Princely States to remain independent, if they so desired. It must be noted, in passing, that he spoke of 'States' not of 'Princes'. The viability of independence, of course, was a separate issue; it could not be judged by legal criteria and it could not be regarded as the same in all cases.

But occasional crude utterances by Pakistan's present-day spokesmen do not affect the validity of Pakistan's traditional position in the Kashmir dispute. The dispute is on the agenda of the world organization as the India-Pakistan question. Pakistan cannot in fairness be expected to relinquish its position as a party to the dispute and assume instead the lesser role of a supporter of Kashmir in the India-Kashmir conflict. The military occupation of Kashmir by India violates not only Kashmir's self-determination but of Pakistan's as well. For Pakistan came into being as the successor state of the British Indian empire comprising Muslim-majority areas as India did comprising Hindu-majority areas. This happened on the basis of a tripartite agreement arrived at by Britain, the Indian Congress and the Muslim League. It followed from the agreement that, unless the State of Jammu and Kashmir chose to remain independent, its Muslim-majority area would be incorporated in Pakistan exactly as the Muslim-majority area of the province of Punjab was. In fairness and in accordance with the principle of the settlement to which both the Indian Union and Pakistan owe their independence, there were only two options for Muslim-majority Kashmir: either to remain independent or to join Pakistan.

The pre-emption of both these options by India's military action had made Pakistan as much the wronged, aggrieved party as Kashmir itself. In Pakistan's eyes, Kashmir is not just another country whose self-determination is to be promoted in the way Pakistan championed the cause of the freedom of Morocco or Tunisia (in the early 1950s), for example, or of other peoples under colonial rule. Kashmir is potentially a part of Pakistan and its society is intertwined with Pakistan's. If matters had been allowed to take a straight course in 1947, Kashmir would have been one of the provinces of Pakistan (the sentiment for Kashmir's independence at that time was very weak). This is not Pakistan's self-view. Not to speak of all impartial observers, even Lord Mountbatten, who played a crucial role in engineering India's annexation of Kashmir, has conceded that but for a certain "basic mistake" by Pakistan, "Kashmir might well have eventually acceded to Pakistan, either with or without a plebiscite or might conceivably have been peacefully partitioned between India an Pakistan". The "basic mistake" he mentions is questionable but even if it were admitted, neither Pakistan nor Kashmir would merit permanent punishment for it in the form of a an unnatural disposition of the State. Mountbatten's statement recognizes Kashmir's place in Pakistan.

Seen in this light, Pakistan's position would be changed radically were it to come forward as a proponent of independence for Kashmir. It would imply that Pakistan is gratuitously demoting its locus standi and renouncing a claim, which has been made stronger by Pakistan's unquestioned willingness to submit it to the verdict of the people of Kashmir impartially ascertained. Pakistan is acting within its rights and conforming to its obligation in disallowing that kind of a stance for itself.

However, there is a marked difference between not becoming a proponent of Kashmir's independence and becoming an opponent of it. The former is consistent with Pakistan's involvement and interest in the dispute; the latter is entailed by India's standpoint. One would expect persons charged with responsibility for handling delicate issues of law or diplomacy to perceive the difference.

Let us thrash out the question a little. India is asserting a primordial or proprietary right with respect to Kashmir; its rejection of the proposition of independence for Kashmir follows as logically as does its irate reaction to the proposal of a referendum or plebiscite to determine a solution. Pakistan, in contrast, is asserting a claim to Kashmir which, though in justice immeasurably superior to India's, Pakistan is not holding to be self-validated; Pakistan is demanding that both claims - its own and India's - be referred to the democratic decision of the people of Kashmir. The demand was originally accepted by India and the common ground of both parties was the basis of the plan of settlement laid down in the resolutions of the United Nations. This aspect of the issue has been fully brought out in the voluminous debates at the United Nations. What still needs to be made clear is that neither Pakistan's demand nor its original acceptance by India nor its endorsement by the United Nations encompasses the whole area of the right involved. For overriding the contesting claims of India and Pakistan and the putative right of one or the other is the right of the people of Kashmir to decide the issue according to their own will. That the two claims of India and Pakistan be submitted to the people of Kashmir makes them subjects of legitimate consideration but it does not exclude the exercise of a different option by the people of Kashmir. The exclusion is inherent in India's position, not in Pakistan's. Enlightened opinion in Pakistan fully appreciates the point and is far ahead of the country's official spokesmen.

The statement that "Kashmir has been historically a part of India" is true precisely in the same sense as the statement, for example, that Belgium or Norway has been historically a part of Europe. All through the ages, the word "India" has been like Europe, the name of a region, a subcontinent, not of a state. It has been a geographical, not a political, term. The great empires of the past - the Maurya (3rd century BC), the Mughal (16th to 18th century) - which more or less unified the subcontinent did not have uniform boundaries; the included variously what today are the states of Afghanistan, Pakistan, India, Nepal, Bangladesh and Myanmar, as well as Kashmir. Even under the British, "India" was not a compact political entity: there was what was called "British India" and "Indian or Princely India".

In the sense currently employed, India is as much a new state as Pakistan; both were established in August 1947; both came into existence on the basis of the agreed two-fold principle that (a) Hindu-majority areas in British India would constitute India and Muslim-majority areas form Pakistan and (b) the territories not directly administered by British (i.e. Princely India) would be incorporated in one of the other (i.e. India or Pakistan) according to geographical contiguity and the composition of the population or they could remain independent, if their people so wished.

Kashmir was the largest of the territories not directly ruled by the British. It is a Muslim-majority area, contiguous to Pakistan, sharing the largest part of its border with Pakistan. Its territorial highways led into Pakistan or Central Asia; its rivers flow into Pakistan; its commerce was conducted through what is now Pakistan; from 14th century onwards, it drew its cultural stimulus exactly from the same sources as Pakistan. Politically, it has maintained an independent, sovereign existence through the preponderant part of its history.

From whatever standpoint one looks at it - geographical, historical, cultural or economic - Kashmir's inclusion in India is as irrational as it has been shown to be contrary to its popular will. The mere circumstance that the state, which has its capital in Delhi, appropriated the name of a region to itself - a gigantic advertising gimmick - does not provide it with an historical claim or entitlement to Kashmir. Incidentally, India's native name inscribed in its constitution is Bharat but it fights shy of using that expression; indeed, it has uses a word which does not exist in any of its dozen main languages. It is the only country in the world which has borrowed its own name from others. As historically "India" meant the land of the Indus, it is Pakistan that has a title to the description, not the state that has arrogated it.

All movements of resistance against foreign occupation which embrace a whole society draw in all its elements - the extremists, religious or secular, at one end and the criminal-minded, at the other, with sincere freedom fighters in the middle, constituting the bulk. The resistance in France against Nazi occupation had the active participation of communists; could it on that account be regarded as a communist movement? No insurgency - particularly against a regime, which has become incapable of civilized administration - remains uncontaminated by extremism, crime of corruption: this had been historically true even in the most sophisticated societies. Such contamination, however, does not affect the purity of its object viz. liberation from an alien, brutal regime; restoration of human rights and assertion of the popular will. This holds in the case of Kashmir as it would in all similar cases.

Speaking of fundamentalism, there is a marked difference between Pakistan and India. The extremist religious forces in Pakistan have never been able to muster popular electoral support and they operate to the extent that they do and meet with resistance within Muslim society itself. In India, in contrast, the fundamentalist frenzy is directed against the Muslim population. The barbarities inflicted on the Muslims of Kashmir are to a great extent actuated by Hindu hatred against Muslims. Communal hatred and intolerance. No attempt is underway to establish a theocratic state in Kashmir. However, it is only natural that, under the unbearable stress of the kind faced by Kashmiris, people should try to draw spiritual strength and sustenance from the faith they follow. A powerful ingredient of the Kashmiri psyche in both normalcy and crisis is the consciousness of their Islamic affiliation. But the fact is writ large on Kashmir's history since the 14th century that this consciousness has harmonized with amity between Muslims and Hindus.

The mass exodus of Kashmiri Pandits from the Vale of Kashmir has been cited as a glaring example of the extremism of the Resistance movement. Any impartial investigation will show that the exodus was encouraged and facilitated by the Government of India, represented at the time in the person of the notorious Governor, Jagmohan, to clear the field for the actions that had been planned against the Kashmiri Muslims. The total breakdown of the administration in Kashmir was also an important contributing factor. When there is anarchy, people flee. In any uprising, those who collaborate with the oppressors become targets. However, more Kashmiri Muslims have been targeted than Pandits. It is not a question of religion: it is a question of what side you are on? The popular uprising or the imposed regime?

Moreover, if the international community continues to look the other way while Kashmir burns and a repulsive military machine massacres its people, then desperation will set in. In such an environment, fundamentalism becomes the face of frustration. Extreme repression, accompanied by little relief and meager sympathy from the supporters of human freedom, can so traumatize a people as to pervert their psychology and disfigure their movement.

India's uses the pejorative term "fundamentalist" in order to exploit the fear and prejudice associated with this phenomenon, real or perceived, and thus undermine support for the cause of Kashmir's freedom. India's use of the label "terrorist" is similarly motivated. The aim is to divert the sympathy and compassion that would be felt at the plight of the Kashmiri people to concerns felt in other contexts.

KEY ASPECTS OF KASHMIR DISPUTE

Before we discuss the various proposed options, it is important to first understand the nature of the dispute between India and Pakistan, which provides the backdrop to the official statements and positions taken by both governments in the post-1947-48 period, when India first took the Kashmir case to the United Nations. The following are the key aspects of this long-standing dispute.

Legacy of the Partition of the Sub-continent in 1947: The sub-continent was partitioned on the agreed principle that contiguous Muslim majority areas were to be separated from the contiguous non-Muslim majority areas, to form the two independent states of Pakistan and India. There were about 562 Princely States, which existed under the overall paramountcy of the British Crown. The Cabinet Mission, in its statement of May 16, 1946, clarified that 'Paramountcy could neither be retained by the British Crown nor transferred to the new Government'. Also, in Section 7 of the Indian Independence Act, 1947, it was stated that ' the suzerainty of His Majesty over the Indian States lapses.' Thus, legally the Princely States became independent. However, the last British Viceroy Lord Mountbatten, during his address to the Chamber of

Princes on July 25, 1947, asserted that 'the rulers were technically at liberty to link with either of the dominion (India or Pakistan)'. As regards the criteria to be followed, he held that 'normally geographical situation and communal interests and so forth will be the factors to be considered.' On various occasions between June and July 1947, Quaid-e-Azam, the Governor General-designate of the new State of Pakistan, stated, 'The legal position is that with the lapse of Paramountcy on the transfer of power by the British all Indian States would automatically regain their full sovereign and independent status.

They are, therefore, free to join either of the two Dominions or to remain independent. The Muslim League recognises the right of each State to choose its destiny. It has no intention of coercing any State into adopting any particular course of action.' By August 15, 1947, the majority of the Princely States, owing to their geographical contiguity and Hindu population, joined India while only ten joined Pakistan. However, disputes over independence arose with India in the case of three Princely States, namely Junagadh, Hyderabad and Jammu and Kashmir.

Junagadh, a maritime state in Kathiawar, with a Muslim ruler and a Hindu majority population, decided to accede to Pakistan on August 15, 1947. By middle of September 1947 Pakistan accepted the accession. India reacted by criticising Pakistan's acceptance as ' in utter violation of the principles on which Pakistan was agreed upon and effected.'

On September 17, India deployed troops around Junagadh and by November 1947 India had militarily annexed the State, as its first expansionist act after the partition of 1947. It is to be noted that this happened when Pakistan had no defence structure of any sort. Pakistan's complaint, claiming Junagadh as its territory, is still pending before the Security Council. Similarly, Hyderabad, also with a Muslim ruler and a majority Hindu population, despite Indian pressures, decided to remain independent and in fact executed a Standstill Agreement with India in November 1947, which India duly signed. However, India continued to increase pressure on Hyderabad and by the middle of 1948 had imposed an economic blockade as well as carried out border raids. During a parliamentary debate, on July 30, 1948, the then British Prime Minister, Winston Churchill referred to a speech by Pandit Nehru made in the last week of July, 1947, in which he had declared, 'If and when we consider it necessary we will start military operations against Hyderabad.' Commenting on this remark, Winston Churchill said 'It seems to me that this is the sort of thing which might have been said by Hitler before the devouring of Austria.' On August 24, 1948, Hyderabad filed a complaint before the Security Council, but before the case was heard before the Council, Hyderabad was militarily annexed by India on September 13, 1948.

While India laid claim on the other two Princely States on the basis of them being Hindu majority areas, as well as geographically contiguous to India, and that the partition of the sub-continent was agreed to on these principles, it did not apply the same principle to the Jammu and Kashmir State, which had a Muslim majority population, under a Hindu ruler who was in favour of remaining independent. During the previous hundred years, the subjects of the Jammu and Kashmir State had been in a state of ongoing series of revolts against the Dogra rulers.

When Partition took place, the Muslim majority population of Jammu and Kashmir was in favour of joining Pakistan, whereas the Hindu Maharaja was reluctant, hoping that he would retain his independence. Internally, there were already tensions due to repressive measures of the Maharaja against the Muslims. The situation further deteriorated when, towards the end of July 1947, the Maharaja ordered the Muslims to surrender their arms to the police, and communal violence erupted.

In the Jammu province, hundreds of Muslims were massacred by the Hindus and Sikhs, who attacked Muslim villages. The massacre was one of the first attempts of ethnic cleansing, which, in fact, had begun even before independence, with the connivance of the local administration comprising units of the Maharaja's Army and Police. In August 1947, on the eve of Partition, Poonch revolted against the Maharaja's rule and in September 1947, the Muslim population liberated the area from the State Police. According to some estimates, between August-October 1947, in the State of Jammu and Kashmir out of the Muslim population of 500,000 about 200,000 just disappeared, presumably were killed, and many Muslims from among the rest fled to the neighbouring West Pakistan (now Pakistan).

SIGNIFICANT DEVELOPMENT

Another significant development of the time was that on August 12, 1947, the then Prime Minister of Jammu and Kashmir, Janak Singh, proposed a 'Standstill Agreement' to both India and Pakistan. This was agreed to and signed by Pakistan on August 15, but India was reluctant and suggested further discussions, keeping matters pending. Eventually no discussion took place and, thus, the 'Standstill Agreement' was never signed by the Indian government with the Maharaja of Kashmir even though it had signed a Standstill Agreement on November 29, 1947, with Hyderabad, since Prime Minister Nehru had other plans to annex the State of Jammu and Kashmir.

In October 1947, there was a revolt by the Muslim population against the Maharaja. He fled from the capital Srinagar to Jammu on October 26, 1947, and appealed to India for help. India claims that the Maharaja signed the 'Instrument of Accession' on October 26, following which the Indian forces landed in the State supposedly on October 27, 1947.

Regarding the signing of the Instrument of Accession, its timing, terms and conditions, and the timing of the landing of Indian troops, are all controversial. The study of historical events shows that initially the Maharaja sent the Deputy Prime Minister, R. L. Batra, to New Delhi, on October 24, with a 'letter of accession to India' which could not be signed. Mr. Batra, in New Delhi, held discussions with 'who would listen to him; but his mission was fruitless.' According to British historian, Alastair Lamb, this was 'certainly no blanket unconditional Instrument of Accession but rather a statement of the terms upon which an association between the State of Jammu and Kashmir and the Indian Dominion might be negotiated in return for military assistance. The Indian side have been careful to avoid specific reference to this particular document in their descriptions of the State of Jammu and Kashmir's plea for assistance. It is probable that it involved no more than a token diminution of the State's sovereignty. It certainly did not provide for an administration in the State of Jammu and Kashmir presided over by Sheikh Abdullah.'

Moreover, research also shows that Indian leaders were not in favour of signing the Instrument of Accession before any military help was provided to the Maharaja. The Maharaja was not in favour of unconditional surrender of sovereignty. Pandit Nehru, however, was of the view that what was required was *'not so much the formalities of accession as some pragmatic arrangement whereby the Maharaja's government might be obliged to collaborate politically with Sheikh Abdullah and his National Conference, bolstered in power by Indian arms.'* Also, during the Indian Defence Committee meeting on October 25, 1947, which discussed the situation in Jammu and Kashmir, V. P. Menon stressed, *'it would technically be quite proper for India to send its forces to the State of Jammu and Kashmir without its prior accession to India, be it definitive or provisional.'*

Subsequent research has also thrown doubts on the official Indian version, which claims that its intervention was legal, basing it on the signing of the so-called 'Instrument of Accession' signed by Maharaja Hari Singh. According to the British historian Alastair Lamb, the Maharaja was forced to sign a conditional Instrument of Accession *after* the Indian troops had landed at Srinagar. As the International Law expert Dr. Ijaz Hussain points out, article 49 of the Vienna Convention on the Law of Treaties states, 'A treaty is invalid if its conclusion is procured by the threat or use of force in violation of the principles of the Charter of the United Nations.' Therefore, the fact that the Instrument of Accession was signed under duress in the presence of Indian troops 'points to the use of force in obtaining consent of the Maharaja to the said Instrument. This makes it patently defective.'

THE INSURGENCY AND POLITICAL SYSTEM

Contrary to the popular view that the insurgents picked up their guns in response to an undemocratic political system, in no way was the movement fighting for greater democratic rights. In fact, as already shown, they had already picked up their guns prior to the election. Their cause was religiously and ideologically fuelled. In many ways, the ruling National Conference party had encouraged this atmosphere through a range of propaganda campaigns. Even as far back as the 1984 election, Farooq Abdullah and the National Conference deliberately tried to create revulsion against India for their own political ends. These Propaganda ads tried to demonstrate that India's iron fist was bleeding Kashmir. There is little evidence of Indian repression in this period, and it seems likely that the National Conference was trying to use this as a way to hide the poor and corrupt performance of the State Government. Indeed, perhaps if India had done more to intervene in State affairs, it could have abated the insurgency that followed.

The Role of Pakistan

Having failed to take Kashmir by force, and unable to win the hearts of the Kashmiris by offering them a democracy when they themselves had a military dictatorship, Pakistan had to woo the Kashmiris by its ideology of communalism.

Before the insurgency in Kashmir began, there was an insurgency movement in neighboring Punjab, which had also been split between India and Pakistan in 1947. That died out by the late 1980s, when the Sikhs that had taken up arms against India had realized they were being used by their Pakistani sponsors and gave up arms. And so Pakistan's attention turned to Kashmir. One major reason Pakistan needed to sponsor insurgency in India was to gain intelligence on India, and its army. After suffering three consecutive defeats, each time after attacking India unprovoked and by surprise, Pakistan was fearful India would be tempted to launch a pre-emptive strike against Pakistan to destroy its army to ensure Pakistan never again attempted to invade India.

The Pakistani view is that they are providing moral support to the Kashmiri People in their fight for freedom against the brutal Indian Army who commit excessive humans rights abuses on the oppressed Muslims living in India, a non-Muslim country. The Indian perspective is that they are dealing with a proxy war by Pakistan who have never accepted the Kashmiri's democratic reaffirmation of their accession to India. The Kashmiris themselves are split between supporting Pakistan, India and independence.

But while the Pakistanis and Indians live in relative peace, it is the Kashmiri who suffers the most while the issue remains unresolved.

The slogans: "Pakistan se kya rishta? La ilaha ilallah" (What is the relation with Pakistan? There is no God but God.) followed by "Azaadi ka matlab kya? La ilaha ilallah" (What is the meaning of freedom? There is no God but God.) indicate that Pakistan for Kashmiris meant Islam, and freedom for Kashmiris meant Pakistan. Those who coined and floated these slogans went on to form the Jammu Kashmir Liberation Force (JKLF). The JKLF wanted to liberate Kashmir. In fact its founder, Hashim Qureshi, later fled to Western Europe for asylum after the Pakistanis hijacked his organization and used its members to fight India as part of a religious struggle rather than for the independence he had desired.

In 1990 a report showed that almost a thousand of the elite Kashmiri Muslims were on the payroll of the ISI. In 1993, with pro-independence insurgents separating from the pro-Pakistan factions, Pakistani border troops shot and killed some thirty Kashmiri youth on their way to POK for training. Slowly but surely the ties between Pakistan and the Kashmiri youth were being severed.

Republic Day

In addition to the Afghan War, local Kashmiris also watched on TV as mass movements against authoritarianism arose in East Europe and Central Asia. The most significant of these was in Romania, where on Christmas Day 1989, dictator Nicolae Ceausescu was executed. Less than a month later was to be Kashmir's turn.

Perhaps the most significant event was the insurgents successful kidnapping of India's Home Minister. In December 1989, there was a change in the Federal Government in India, with Rajiv Gandhi losing to VP Singh's Government. Singh's deputy, the Home Minister, was Mufti Mohammed Sayeed, the current Chief Minister of Jammu & Kashmir. Just weeks after being sworn in, his daughter was kidnapped near Srinagar by insurgents who demanded the release of their colleagues from prison. Mufti, holding the third highest office in India behind the President and Prime Minister, broke India's policy of non-negotiation with terrorists and released the captured insurgents and his daughter was released. The whole episode has subsequently been referred to by insurgents as a key moment when they were able to show their Kashmiri people that India could be brought to its knees.

These incidents gave the Kashmiris fighting for independence a great deal of confidence, unlike the early years when dreams of independence were always viewed as a practical impossibility. Many Kashmiris felt that independence was imminent after the fall of the communist era, and some locals remarked that they thought the reality of independence was only a matter of weeks away.

Kashmiri Independence Day

January 20, 1990 was to be Kashmiri Independence Day. This date was chosen a few weeks prior as the day the masses would take to the streets and take power from India, effectively their army, for the Kashmiri people (and they would subsequently become a Republic and/or join Pakistan). Most Kashmiris were convinced that this would occur, and in fact the largest exodus of Kashmiri Pandits occurred on January 19. Despite the fact that the masses were limited to Srinagar, and not regions of the State such as Ladakh and Jammu did not mean it was not a very real threat. There were reportedly between January 1 and January 19, 1990, 319 violent acts - 21 armed attacks, 114 bomb blasts, 112 arsons, and 72 incidents of mob violence. In fact the Indian Government was so desperate they sent Jagmohan, the former Governor of the State, on the night of 18th January to make a last ditch effort to save the Kashmir Valley. He was able to organize a last minute blockade that stopped people from leaving their local neighborhoods so they could not reach the main streets and mobilize into a large crowd. The momentum of the masses was soon lost, and such a mass protest was never attempted again.

Exodus of Pandits

One reason why Kashmiris were uncomfortable in joining Pakistan was its large non-Muslim minority, who would have no place in Islamic Pakistan. Hence by resorting to the systematic killings of Hindus, as well as spreading fear amongst them through newspaper ads and pamphlets ordering them to leave or face death, Pakistan was able to overcome this major obstacle.

With most of the Hindus gone by January 1990, and the secular minded Muslims powerless to help them return, Pakistan was able to strengthen its claim on Kashmir. There was religious indoctrination, by misusing mosques and other available platforms, in a bid to frighten the secular Muslims.

Kashmiri Pandits

The crimes against humanity perpetrated against the Kashmiri Pandits were tragic. While genocide occurred on a small scale, it is more likely that the objective was to drive them away rather than wipe them out. The dozens of killings and rapes were always followed by warnings for Pandits to get out, which suggest that the attacks were more as a statement rather than intent for mass genocide. But what was most surprising to Pandits was how there were large demonstrations in several Kashmiri cities by common Kashmiris with the slogan: "Asi gachi Pakistan, batni rosin batta gatssin." In Kashmiri this means: We will become a part of Pakistan, Pandit women can stay with us but Pandit men must leave." They could understand why the extremists wanted them to leave, but were shocked when the masses joined in.

The Momentum Dies

The list of innocent persons who fell prey to the bullets of terrorists is again illustrative of the Islamization drive. The victims included prominent educationists and subscribers to secular ideals. Not only Pandits, but Muslims such as Professor Mushir-ul-Haq, Vice Chancellor, Kashmir University, and Maulana Mohammad Syed Masoodi, a renowned Muslim scholar were among such victims at the hands of the terrorists. Libraries of Universities were destroyed for having unislamic books, and freedom of speech was suspended. It was clear the movement was not against India, but all things unislamic in their eyes.

While comparisons to Nazi Germany are fraught with danger, it does seem the population were caught in a mass hysteria that they now admit was a mistake. I have heard many anecdotal stories from others who have met with Kashmiri Muslims in Kashmir who have shown much resentment in not doing anything to stop the fundamentalists. It is difficult to determine if they genuinely wanted an Islamic State of Kashmir, or if they merely followed the trend as if it were a fad.

THE RISE OF KASHMIRI SECESSIONISM IN INDIA

While the post-1947 political history of Kashmir was at times turbulent and a separate ethno-national consciousness among the Kashmiri Muslims remained consistently strong, it was only in the late 1980s that widespread frustration among the Kashmiri Muslims against some of their own leaders and the policies pursued by New Delhi erupted into a full-blown secessionist movement against India.

The rise of secessionism in Kashmir is attributable to certain fundamental changes that took place in the state in the 1980s. As a result of demographic changes and the spread of modernisation and communications, a younger, more educated and more politically conscious generation emerged in Kashmir in the 1980s. Economic development and employment opportunities did not expand commensurately, however, leading to a rise in unemployment among the educated poor. Moreover, starting from the early 1980s, the Congress government at the centre indulged in vote fraud and subversion of the electoral process in Kashmir in order to further the interests of the Congress Party in the state. This first led to the dismissal of the legitimately elected National Conference government of Farooq Abdullah, the son of Sheikh Abdullah, in the state in 1984. Subsequently, the Congress Party led by Rajiv Gandhi and Farooq Abdullah's National Conference entered into an electoral alliance and blatantly rigged the state elections of 1987. This blatant electoral abuse encouraged by the Congress and Farooq's 'betrayal' led to widespread resentment among the Kashmiri Muslims against the Indian government and the National Conference.

In the early 1990s, the secessionist movement in Kashmir split into two main branches. In the first branch were those who advocated the creation of an 'independent' state of Kashmir to be achieved by the secession of Kashmir from India and the POK from Pakistan followed by the merger of these areas. The main secessionist organization espousing this view is the Jammu and Kashmir Liberation Front (JKLF) which wants a sovereign, secular and democratic Kashmir that would include all Kashmiris irrespective of their religious affiliation.

The JKLF position is unacceptable to the Hindu and Buddhist minorities in Kashmir since both these communities fear that in an independent Kashmir, the Muslims would dominate due to their substantial numerical majority. The Hindus of Jammu and the Buddhists of Ladakh have, therefore, called upon the Indian government to protect their status in Kashmir. These communities have made it clear that if Kashmir secedes from India, then only the Valley should secede since it is predominantly Muslim. But this view is unacceptable to the JKLF which claims to represent the whole of Kashmir.

The second current of Kashmiri secessionism was represented by the Muslim fundamentalist groups and religious elites in the Valley who wanted to make Kashmir either a part of Pakistan or, at the very least, an independent Islamic state with close ties with Pakistan. The principal insurgent groups that advocate this kind of religious nationalism and pro-Pakistan sentiments are the Harqat ul-Ansar and the Hibz ul- Mujahideen. Pro-Pakistani sentiments are also demonstrated by the All-Party Hurriyat Conference, an umbrella organisation of various political parties in Kashmir. These fundamentalist organisations regard Kashmir as a region which legitimately should be under the control of Muslims. Hence, they look upon the Hindu and Buddhist minorities as 'outsiders' and resort to violence against them.

In the initial years of the secessionist movement, nearly all Hindu families were driven out by the insurgents from the Valley. Politically motivated violence against Hindus in the Jammu region (mainly with the aim to alter the demographic balance of the Jammu province) was also carried out. Further, Buddhists in Ladakh were targeted for violence and intimidation leading to a Buddhist counter-mobilisation.

In this climate of spiraling political violence and 'ethnic cleansing', the pro-India leaders among the Kashmiri Muslims became sidelined or were eliminated by the insurgents for being 'soft' on India. Violence also broke out within the ranks of the insurgents over ideology and strategy. The insurgents did not even spare the members of their own community from intimidation and violence in order to maintain a strong hold over them.

The Onset of the Indo-Pakistan 'Proxy War' Over Kashmir With the outbreak of insurgency in Kashmir, a 'proxy war' erupted between India and Pakistan which is still ongoing. This proxy war is being fought on three different planes.

International Diplomacy

Since 1989, India and Pakistan have carried out an international diplomatic tug-of-war over Kashmir. Since the outbreak of the insurgency, Pakistan has tried to 'internationalise' the Kashmir dispute by highlighting in international forums the human rights abuses carried out by the Indian military in Kashmir and asking for international mediation in the dispute and the holding of UN-sponsored plebiscite to ascertain the wishes of the Kashmiri people regarding the state's future political status.

The strategy worked initially. Under intense Pakistani lobbying, the Organisation of Islamic Countries (OIC) voted for sanctions against India for human rights violations in Kashmir in May 1993. In Britain, the Labour Party raised the Kashmir issue in the Parliament and called on the British government to put pressure on India to honour the Kashmiris' right to self-determination under UN supervision. In the United States, the Clinton Administration also criticised India for human rights violations in Kashmir leading to strains in India-US ties.

However, as the conflict dragged on, Pakistan's diplomatic initiatives failed to bring about international pressure on India to hold a plebiscite in Kashmir for a number of reasons. First, reacting to the international outcry over human rights abuses, the Indian military reformed its operating methods in Kashmir. Emboldened by this development, the Indian government started encouraging foreign dignitaries to visit Kashmir to see firsthand the destruction and massacres caused by the Kashmiri insurgents and foreign 'volunteers' who were armed and trained by Pakistan. Indian diplomats also presented this 'evidence' in international forums and foreign capitals. The Indian government further argued that the 'real problem' in Kashmir is one of 'cross-border terrorism' directed at India by Pakistan, and called upon the western states to brand Pakistan as a sponsor of terrorism in Kashmir. India also categorically ruled out any international mediation in Kashmir by moving a unanimous resolution in a joint sitting of the two houses of Parliament which stated that Kashmir is an inalienable part of the Republic of India.

Secondly, the US placed more stress on curbing the conventional and nuclear weapons proliferation in the subcontinent and undertaking confidence building measures (CBMs) between India and Pakistan than pressing for a plebiscite in Kashmir. The end of the Afghan war and the collapse of the Soviet Union also downgraded Pakistan's importance to US national security interests. Further, the rise of Islamic fundamentalist forces in West Asia and Pakistan's strong links with fundamentalist groups in Afghanistan and Kashmir did not go down well with the Clinton administration. Additionally, the US concern over Pakistan's clandestine nuclear weapons programme resulted in the suspension of US military aid under the Pressler Amendment.

Thirdly, in spite of the presence of several 'irritants', Indo-US relations witnessed an upswing in the 1990s, attributable mainly to the convergence of politico-economic and security interests between the two states and the reduction in India's apprehensions about a possible US hegemonic role in world politics after the Gulf War. Indicating the growing cooperation between the US and India, a number of high-ranking American officials visited India in the 1990s to discuss trade and security issues. The two countries held several joint military exercises. India's market-oriented economic reforms have also found favour in Washington. The evolving friendship between India and the US further eroded Pakistan's appeal to the West on behalf of the Kashmiri secessionists.

Fourthly, Pakistan's diplomatic effort to garner support from the Islamic world for its position on Kashmir also received setbacks.

To be sure, the Islamic countries voiced their concern about the plight of the Kashmiri Muslims and the highhanded measures undertaken by the Indian army~ yet they stopped short of endorsing Kashmir's independence or accession to Pakistan due to India's patient diplomacy in the Islamic world.

India established a working relationship with the Rabbani Government in Afghanistan and secured a promise of Afghan neutrality on the Kashmir dispute. Prime Minister Rao visited Uzbekistan and Kazakhstan in May 1993 where he secured support for India's position that the Kashmir dispute must be settled bilaterally within the framework of the Shimla Agreement. India was also able to procure the backing of Iran for its position on Kashmir. Under pressure from Iran (and China), Pakistan had to withdraw a resolution it had tabled in the International Conference of the Human Rights Commission at Geneva in March 1994 denouncing India for violating human rights in Kashmir.

Finally, Pakistan's position on Kashmir evoked considerable opposition from China. Beijing is particularly concerned about the 'demonstration effects' of Kashmir's independence on the Xinjiang autonomous region.

In 1993, Chinese troops had to quell an armed uprising in Xinjiang and the continued army presence may well engender further resentment and separatist sentiments among the region's 10 million Muslims. Signs of orthodox Sunni practice are steadily increasing in Xinjiang, and developments in Kashmir and Central Asia are being watched closely, feeding hopes for a successful independence movement. Secessionists in Xinjiang could also influence other separatists among China's Tibetan and Mongol populations and threaten China's hold on the Tarim Basin, an oil producing area essential for the PRC's economy. Acting on these fears, China indicated to Pakistan that while it would like to see a negotiated solution to the Kashmir dispute, it would not accept any form of independence for Kashmir. Thus, in spite of the international concern about the plight of the Kashmiris, Pakistan's diplomatic efforts to win international support for a UN-sponsored plebiscite in Kashmir proved to be unsuccessful. This was a major setback for Pakistan's Kashmir policy.

Insurgency and Counter-Insurgency

The outbreak of secessionist sentiments in Kashmir in 1989 provided Pakistan with a golden opportunity to loosen India's hold over the region by providing military and financial help to the various insurgent groups that sprang up. In implementing this policy, Pakistan benefited immensely from the Afghan war.

During the height of the Afghan war, the United States trained and equipped the Afghan mujahideen (freedom fighters) and 'volunteers' from neighbouring Muslim countries for guerrilla operations against the occupying Soviet forces and government troops.

These operations were run by the Pakistani military's Inter Services Intelligence (ISI) directorate under the supervision of the US Central Intelligence Agency (CIA) officials from bases in the border regions of the North-West Frontier Province in Pakistan. As a result, the ISI developed an expertise in unconventional warfare and established close ties with the Afghan *mujahideen.*

Once the 'proxy war' between the US and USSR ended in Afghanistan in 1989, the ISI turned its attention towards Kashmir. Initially, the ISI provided covert military support and training to the pro-independent JKLF.

Most of the ISI-run training centers for Kashmiri insurgents were located in Azad Kashmir and along the Pakistan-Afghanistan border. Further, large quantities of sophisticated weapons, including Stinger antiaircraft missiles and automatic rifles, which the US had brought into Pakistan to be used by the Afghan *mujahideen,* were diverted to the Kashmiri insurgents. By 1992-93, with the emergence of strong pro-Pakistan secessionist groups such as the Hizb-ul-Mujahideen and Harqat ul-Ansar, the ISI stopped supporting and funding the JKLF. The Pakistan government also cracked down on JKLF's leaders and sympathisers in Azad Kashmir. Along with the training and support that it provided to the Kashmiri insurgents, the ISI also encouraged veteran guerrillas of the Afghan war, who were left aimless after the Soviets withdrew from Afghanistan, to infiltrate into Kashmir to carry out a *jihad* (Holy War) against India.

New Delhi responded to the insurgency by dismissing the local government and declaring president's rule (direct rule by the central government) in Kashmir. India also responded to the insurgents through a massive show of force.

As the secessionist movement grew in strength in the early 1990s, India's military presence in Kashmir escalated simultaneously. Numerous reports of the Indian army's highhanded and repressive behaviour towards the Kashmiri Muslims started to filter out and the army operation in Kashmir drew heavy fire from human rights groups and activists in India and abroad.

It also led to the widespread alienation of the Kashmiri Muslims from the Indian state. As the stalemate in Kashmir continued in the 1990s, India's approach towards taming the insurgency centred on doing several things.

The main requirement was to win back the confidence of the Kashmiri civilians by clamping down hard on the insurgents who were regularly infiltrating the LoC from the POK. One way the Indian military attempted to do this was to raise, train and arm small anti-insurgency forces composed of former Kashmiri insurgents who were captured by the Indian security forces and were 'persuaded' to give up the secessionist struggle.

Another policy which was strictly implemented was to exercise tighter control over the behaviour of the regular security forces in order to reduce the instances of human rights abuses by the security personnel. It was felt that when the security environment of Kashmir improves, regular military personnel could be gradually withdrawn leaving charge to the paramilitary forces.

The Indian government was also keen to re-start the political process in Kashmir as and when the security environment improved. For this purpose, the government kept open the lines of communication with several Kashmiri Muslim groups, including the All Party Hurriyat Conference and the Jammu and Kashmir Democratic Liberation Front (JKDLF). Improving the security environment and the re-starting of the political process in Kashmir were the stepping stones for holding state elections, which was viewed by New Delhi as the only way to erase secessionist sentiments from the minds of the Kashmiri Muslims.

Throughout 1995 and early 1996 the Indian government prepared the ground for elections in Kashmir. In May 1996, elections for the Indian national parliament were held and the people of Kashmir voted for the first time after 1989.

In spite of the call for poll boycott by the insurgent groups, voter turnout in Kashmir during the national parliamentary election was around 35-45%, although many voters claimed that they were forced to vote by the Indian troops stationed in Kashmir. The national election of May 1996 was followed by state elections in Kashmir in September 1996.

This election was widely publicised by India as a "rejection of the insurgency" by the Kashmiri people. Voter turnout was around 53%, not much less than the 56.7% for India as a whole in the general election in May. With many pro-independence and pro-Pakistan groups boycotting this poll, the National Conference led by Farooq Abdullah won easily and formed the government.

In the aftermath of the 1996 state elections, there was quiet optimism in New Delhi that a new beginning has been made in Kashmir. While there was no denying that the reconstruction of Kashmir was an enormous task, the return of Farooq Abdullah to Kashmiri politics after a gap of seven years was seen by many experts as an opportunity for moderate Kashmiris, who were sidelined during the armed insurgency, to re-enter Kashmiri politics.

Critics further felt that Farooq Abdullah's re-entry into Kashmir politics offered India a chance to win back the loyalty of the Kashmiris~ however, it would all depend upon how quickly the National Conference government could bring 'genuine' democracy to Kashmir and jump-start Kashmir's devastated economy. Political freedom and economic opportunity were thus seen as the key to solving the insurgency in Kashmir.

Low-Intensity Border Skirmish

Since the late 1980s, as tensions between India and Pakistan flared up, the two sides appeared to be on the brink of war on at least three different occasions~ incredibly, they moved back from the brink all three times. The lack of war, however, did not imply that the LoC was quiet. On the contrary, throughout the 1990s, Pakistani troops stationed along the LoC and on the Siachen Glacier, the world's highest battlefield, have periodically resorted to firing and shelling of Indian 'forward positions' and border villages.

It is generally believed in India that these unprovoked firings serve two purposes for the Pakistani military: one, to infiltrate armed insurgents into Kashmir under cover of gunfire from across the LoC and, secondly, to scuttle any initiatives for the resumption of bilateral dialogue between the two states. On almost every occasion, the Indians returned the fire.

There are compelling financial, political and strategic reasons for the existence of simmering 'low-intensity' tension across the LoC and the Siachen, rather than open warfare. First, a conventional war (let alone a nuclear one) between India and Pakistan today will be economically and financially ruinous for both states given the astronomical rise in the cost of warfare and the state of their respective domestic economies. A short conventional war between India and Pakistan would cost some US$2.5 billion, twelve times more than the cost of the last India-Pakistan war in 1971. Some Pakistani estimates put Pakistan's cost of fighting a conventional war with India today at US$350 million per day. Similar studies done for India place the figure at US$400 million per day. Given the state of the Indian and Pakistani economies today, such exorbitant expenses would be difficult to meet.

Secondly, the 'political cost' that India and Pakistan would have to pay domestically as well as internationally for initiating a war today would be astronomical given that both states possess nuclear weapons.

Finally, Pakistan's conventional military capabilities, in spite of the substantial modernisation it has undergone in the last decade, still remains weak compared to India. Its armed forces have also been badly hit by the stoppage in American military aid since 1990. On the other hand, the modernisation of the Indian armed forces and the maintenance of a steady supply of ammunition, equipment and spares for its Soviet- made inventory have been badly hit by the demise of the Soviet Union. The prolonged use of the military in domestic political problems and foreign misadventures has also generated battle fatigue and affected morale within the armed forces. As a result, neither side today would be capable of inflicting an overwhelming defeat on the other side in a conventional war.

This is precisely the sort of scenario in which, if a conventional war is waged, both India and Pakistan might be inclined to carry out a nuclear 'first strike' against the other to break the military (and political) deadlock once and for all. To prevent even an inadvertent escalation of a conventional war to a nuclear showdown with catastrophic consequences, both sides need to ensure that a conventional war between them does not erupt in the first place and that the "logic of deterrence" works.

8

Major Disputes between India and Pakistan

Consequently boundary has been marred by a number of disputes and hostile activities from both the countries ever since it came into being.

THE RANN OF KACHCHH DISPUTE

Rann of Kachchh boundary was well defined according to Radcliffe award but Pakistan advocated that it was not properly delineated. That country argued that the Rann was not a marsh but a land-locked sea or lake and as such it should be equally divided between India and Pakistan. India countered Pakistani claim by presenting documentary proof that the Rann was a marsh which always remained a part of the Kachchh state. As this state merged with India after independence, the entire Rann of Kachchh should be given to India.

Pakistan claimed about 9,065 sq km out of a total area of 20,720 sq km of the Rann of Kachchh. During the 1965 Indo-Pakistan war, the Pakistan troops invaded this area and reached inside the Indian Territory.

The matter was referred to a boundary tribunal constituted by the International Court of Justice which awarded 906.5 sq km area of the Kachchh to Pakistan. After a number of protests and representations both India and Pakistan accepted the award and the demarcation of the boundary was completed in June 1969.

THE KASHMIR PROBLEM

The former princely state (more precisely the state of Jammu and Kashmir), is undoubtedly the most complex and serious problem between India and Pakistan and is major stumbling block in normalising the relations between the two countries.

The Kashmir problem has led to bloody wars between the two countries in 1948, 1965, 1971 and more recently in 1999. Besides there had been skirmishes adding to bitterness between the two countries. Both countries have large political, economic and strategic stakes in Kashmir and this state has become a symbol of national prestige and honour for either of the two countries. With an area of 2,22,236 sq km Jammu and Kashmir is the sixth largest state of India and represents heterogametic character with regard to geographic, economic, cultural and linguistic elements. The whole state of Jammu and Kashmir can be treated as conglomeration of six distinctive regions.

These regions (excepting for Hunza-Gilgit and Nagar) were brought as a united political unit by Maharaja Gulab Singh, who entered into a subsidiary alliance with the British within the Indian empire in 1849. The first is the beautiful Kashmir Valley.

It is the most important centre of tourist attraction and politically the seat of central authority. Until recent time, it was accessible from India by a single road. This road remained snowbound until the introduction of snowplows in 1948. A few roads connect it with Pakistan.

The nucleus of dispute in this valley is its overwhelmingly Muslim population. The minority of Kashmiri Brahmans have been holding high positions of economic, social and political significance, whereas the Muslim peasantry remained very poor.

The second is the Jammu region which lies in the southern part of the state. It covers only one-seventh of the total area of the state and is predominantly a Hindu region. More than half of the population of this region consists of Hindus. Jammu is the winter capital of the state and home of state's former rulers—the Dogra Rajputs.

The Third region is Gilgit. It lies in the northern part of the state. This region is marked by high mountains and is almost entirely inhabited by Muslims. Previously it used to be reached from Srinagar by crossing high mountains, plateaus and glaciers. Now it is well linked to Pakistan through Karakoram highway built by China-Pakistan in 1970.

The fourth region is that of Baltistan which lies in the extreme northern part of the state. Like Gilgit, it contains high mountains and is not easily accessible. It is reached by road along the Indus River in Pakistan. It is an overwhelmingly Muslim area.

The fifth region is that of Punch which lies to the north of the Jammu region and in the west of the Kashmir valley. It is near the Pakistan border and is inhabited by Muslims. Pakistan has easy access to this region.

The sixth is the Ladakh region which is also known as 'Little Tibet'. It lies in eastern part of the state and covers about one-third territory of the state. It is a vast, barren, high plateau which resembles Tibet in many respects.

As mentioned earlier, the state was ruled by a Hindu whereas about 77 per cent of the population of the consisted of Muslims before partition of the country. It is an extremely important state from the strategic point of view because of its contiguity to India, Pakistan, China and Afghanistan and proximity to Tajikistan (formerly a part of the U.S.S.R.).

The state was sought by Pakistan on the basis of its Muslim majority status. Moreover, major rivers of Pakistan namely Ravi, Chenab, Jhelum and Indus flow through Kashmir. Unlike most of the rulers of princely states who had acceded to either India or Pakistan before August 15, 1947, ruler of Kashmir did not make up his mind.

The Maharaja thought that any decision to accede to India or Pakistan may spark off chain reactions and disturb the peace of the state. Pakistan cut off the communications and stopped the supply of essentials to coerce Kashmir to accede to Pakistan. On October 22, 1947, fully armed tribesmen, supported by Pakistani armed forces, invaded Kashmir.

They indulged in large scale killing of Hindus and Muslims and committed large scale looting and arson. This forced the ruler to make a desperate appeal to the Indian government for military help. India promised to help the ruler but only after he decided to accede to the Indian Union.

The ruler agreed to this condition and the instrument of accession of Kashmir was signed by Maharaja Hari Singh on October 26, 1947. The accession was accepted by the Governor General of India on October 27, 1947. Thus, Kashmir became legally and constitutionally an integral part of the Indian Union.

Pakistan described the Maharaja's accession to India as based upon "fraud, deceit and Violence", and maintained that it was totally against the wishes of its long oppressed Muslim subject. Soon after, Pakistan rushed its own troops to support the invading tribesmen. India quickly moved its troops to halt the invaders and Indo-Pakistan war broke out in 1948.

India could have done much better, had it flushed out the invaders from the entire state. Instead, India took the case of aggression from Pakistan to the United Nations which immediately appointed a commission to investigate the dispute.

The United Nations commission on India and Pakistan (UNCIP) proposed a plebiscite to ascertain the wishes of the people of the state. It also called on India and Pakistan to agree on a cease-fire line. A cease-fire line was delimited with areas of high altitude left un-delimited. The line was accepted by both India and Pakistan on January 1, 1949.

The cease-fire line left India in possession of two-thirds of the state including the Kashmir valley, lying south-east of the line, and one-third area in the north and west of the line remained under Pakistan's control.

The area is administered through the so-called Azad Kashmir government. The cease-fire line (adjusted under Shimla Agreement as Line of Actual Control) has crystallized into de facto boundary between areas controlled by India and Pakistan respectively.

Right from the beginning Pakistan has been insisting on plebiscite in the entire state in the hope that such an exercise will give clear mandate in its favour. That country argues that plebiscite has been recommended by the United Nations. India, on the other hand, held the position that Kashmir's accession had given India sovereignty over Kashmir.

Initially agreeing to the proposal of plebiscite, India rejected it on the ground that Pakistan had not withdrawn its invading forces from Kashmir. This condition was stipulated by the United Nation resolution, but had never been realised on the ground. India has been regularly stressing upon the illegality of Pakistani support of the raiders and the Azad Kashmir government.

Pakistan blames India for failing to withdraw its forces from the Indian- controlled territory, and for supporting a regime prejudicial to holding of a plebiscite. Since then the issue has been listing in the U.N. Security Council and the Cease Fire line or Line of Actual Control divides Kashmir between Indian and Pakistani occupied areas.

Ever since Kashmir's accession to India, the Kashmir government in Srinagar has maintained a close relationship with the Indian Union, and in 1952, negotiated a pact which has given it a special status within India. In 1956, arrangements were made for establishing an elected constituent assembly for Kashmir which voted to make it a regular state within India. Since then, India has treated Kashmir as a constituent unit of the country and the state is no longer open to a plebiscite.

Two major considerations have guided India's policy about Kashmir problem. First, India is secular state and surrender of Kashmir to Pakistan on religious grounds would amount to denial of the nation's essential principles.

Second, the strategic location of Kashmir is of great importance to India. China's occupation of Tibet and part of Ladakh and building a road through Aksai Chin to serve Tibet and Sinkiang, and full scale aggression on India in 1962 further lent urgency to the strategic aspect of Kashmir's location.

China helped Pakistan in building a new road across its occupied area to Sinkiang and Pakistan, in turn, ceded a large territory of 5,180 sq km to China.

This move by Pakistan has been termed as illegal; because India claimed that the entire state including the territory controlled by Pakistan, annexed by China and ceded by Pakistan to China belonged to India. Thus, out of a total area of 2, 22,236, a territory of 78,114 sq km is under illegal occupation of Pakistan, and 5,180 sq km illegally handed over by Pakistan to China and 37,555 sq km under illegal occupation of China in Ladakh district. Pakistan has so far made four abortive attempts to conquer Kashmir. Its forces had to trace back in 1947-48 war when Kashmir was legally acceded to India. Pakistan again invaded in 1965 and it was badly mauled by the Indian forces.

The 1971 India-Pakistan conflict led to the liberation of East Pakistan and emergence of a new country by the name of Bangladesh. This left Pakistan a truncated country and added much to already increasing bitterness between India and Pakistan.

In 1999, Pakistani troops stealthily occupied certain positions in the Kargil sector for which India had to use strong force. Unable to beat India in regular warfare, its forces are launching proxy war in Kashmir and sending foreign mercenaries and terrorists to disturb law and order in and incite communal tension in the state. Due to its link with Islamic terrorist organisations and ISI, Pakistan has become the hot- bad of international terrorism and is posing a serious threat to world peace. Even after about six decades of Kashmir's accession to India, there seems no sign of resolving the Kashmir problem as both sides stick to their respective positions.

India is taking no chance to safeguard the integrity and sovereignty of the country, particularly of Jammu and Kashmir. There are an estimated 1,00,000 Indian troops ranged along 188 km International Border, the 788 km Line of Control (LoC) and 150 km Actual Ground Position Line (AGPL).

THE SIACHIN GLACIER DISPUTE

Siachin glacier is about 75 km long and 2 to 8 km wide. This glacier has the distinction of being the largest glacier outside the Polar or sub-Polar regions. It covers an area of about 450 sq km at an altitude of about 5,800 metre above sea level in Ladakh region near Karakoram Range.

The Karakoram highway between China and Pakistan is very close which enhances its strategic value. India occupies about two-third area of the glacier in its south-eastern part. Here Nubra river emerges from Karakoram glacier and meets the Shyok river which is a tributary of the Indus river. Indian troops use the Nubra valley to reach the glacier. The glacier has four passes. Of these Gasherbrum, Saltoro and Vilafondala are in India and Gyongla is in Pakistan.

It is worth mentioning that LoC demarcated in 1972 after the Shimla agreement stopped dead at the grid reference NJ. 9842, with no indication as to how it would run along the 70-odd km left to the Chinese border in the north.

While Pakistan decided to extend this line eastward to Karakoram Pass, thus claiming an area two-thirds the size of Sikkim, India's decision was to go by the wording of 1949 Karachi agreement that was superseded by LoC of 1972 which spoke of line "thence northwards joining the glaciers". Further, India wants Pakistan to officially recognise the Actual Ground Position Line (AGPL) begin NJ. 9892 grid point as a pre-requisite to de-militarisation of the Siachin glacier.

Pakistani troops established an observation post on Saltoro range. To counter this, India launched Operation Meghdoot on April 13, 1984. Since then both the countries are maintaining troops in this inhospitable environment at a very high altitude. A number of skirmishes have taken place making it the highest battlefield in the world.

Sending men and material in such an area is a very expensive affair. On an average India spends about Rs. 4 crore per day for maintaining troops in this hostile area. Pakistan also spends about Rs. 1 crore for the same purpose. Casualties on both sides of the border are also very high.

Even in normal circumstances, Indian troops suffer one casualty every second day while Pakistani troops suffer one casualty every fourth day. Besides there are psychological disorders, frostbite, high altitude pulmonary and cerebral edema and snow blindness. Such heavy losses can be avoided if both the countries start living in peace as friendly neighbouring countries.

SIR CREEK

Sir Creek forms the boundary between Gujarat state of India and Sind Province of Pakistan. This creek is extremely rich in marine life and both the countries desire to include it in their respective territories. While India claims that the middle point of Sir Creek should be demarcated as the international boundary, Pakistan wants the eastern bank of the Creek as the border between India and Pakistan.

As such Sir Creek has become a contentious issue between the two countries as Pakistan has been claiming a 40 km region inside India's territory.

Pakistan has responded positively to the goodwill gesture initiated by India since early 2004 to ease tension on the border. This can lead to friendly relations between the two countries if the concerned countries take necessary positive steps for normalisation of relations.

Some of the steps taken/proposed are:

(i) Srinagar-Muzaffrabad has survice.

(ii) Kargil-Skardu bus link and routes into Poonch-Rajouri sector.

(iii) Amritsar-Lahore bus and rail link.

(iv) Meeting points for divided families across LoC at Poonch, Mendhar,

(v) Suchetgarh, Uri, Tangdar and Kargil.

(vi) Rail link between Munnabao (Rajasthan) and Khokrapar (Sind).

(vii) Link between Ferozpur and Sahiwal.

(viii) Trade across the LoC/border.

(ix) Mechanisms to permit two-way religious pilgrims.

(x) Promotion of cultural interaction and cooperation.

(xi) Joint efforts to promote tourism.

PAKISTAN RESOLUTION IN RETROSPECT

Pakistan owes her emergence to four outstanding leaders – Sir Syed Ahmad Khan (1817-98), Maulana Muhammad Ali (1878-1931), Muhammad Ali Jinnah (1876-1948), and Allama Muhammad Iqbal (1877-1938). These leaders provided intellectual and political leadership to Indian Muslims during the ninety years (1858-1947) of the British imperial dominance.

Surprisingly though, all of them were thorough-bred nationalists at one time or another. But, betimes, they got disillusioned and shied away willy-nilly from their Hindu compatriots, either because of Hindu ethnocentrism in the late 19th century or Congress's rather exclusive, unitary nationalism in the 1920s and 1930s. That makes Pakistan, in part, a product of these Hindu, myopic approaches, asymmetrical with the prime dictates of the ground realities in a multi-nation and multi-cultured subcontinent. In part it was, of course, a product of the Muslims' quest for an equitable share in power, a quest designed primarily to organise their society on the basis of their pristine value structure.

Interestingly, three of these four leaders – Sir Syed, Iqbal and Jinnah – had initially started out as full blooded nationalists, but were obliged to end up, finally, at threshold of Muslim "separatism". And that, of course, after a good deal of traumatised reappraisals. So did Maulana Muhammad Ali, who joined mainstream nationalist politics midway through his career. But he was the foremost "nationalist" leader along with Gandhi during the Khilafat and Non-Cooperation Movement (1920-22), and he also presided over the subsequent Cocanada Congress session (1923), a unique honour for a Muslim, an honour that was inexplicably denied to Jinnah, though he occupied the top echelon of Congress leadership for several years and was considered the embodied symbol of Hindu-Muslim unity. Yet, within seven years, Muhammad Ali would vehemently denounce Gandhi's much-trumpeted Civil Disobedience Movement, launched in April 1930. In his presidential address to the All India Muslim Conference at Bombay on April 23, 1930, he declared, "We refuse to join Mr Gandhi, because his movement is not a movement for the complete independence of India but for making the seventy millions of

Indian Musalmans dependents of the Hindu Mahasabha". And he was cheered by over 20,000 Muslims that had gathered on the occasion.

Jinnah's postures and predilections during his long political life (1904-48) were a microcosm of Muslim India's during the period. For some seventeen years (1904-20), he had stood on the Congress's platform, pleading the Congress cause and envisioning a truly nationalist destiny for India. For another sixteen years (1921-37), though out of Congress for good, he was still working for a nationalist destiny; he was still striving for a Hindu-Muslim settlement and he was still collaborating with the Congress and its leadership. In pursuit of his mission, he devised several constitutional formulae, but all to no avail. At the Congress-sponsored All Parties National Convention at Calcutta in December 1928, called to consider and ratify the Nehru Report (1928) as the blueprint of India's future constitution, Jinnah had put forward the six minimum Muslim demands for acceptance. But all of them were outvoted one by one. In vain did Jinnah argue: "... what we want is that the Hindus and Muslims should march together until our object is obtained... I want you... to rise to that statesmanship which Sir Tej Bahadur describes. Minorities cannot give anything to the majority... If they are small points, why not concede? It is up to the majority and majority alone can give."

In aggregate terms, the most acrimonious and acerbic controversy in Indian politics in the late 1920s (since the Nehru Report) and all through the 1930s had hinged around the basic issue of Hindu "Unitarianism" vs Muslim Federalism. The difference in the approaches was sharply reflected in the formation of ministries in the Hindu and Muslim majority provinces in mid 1937. While the Muslim provinces went for coalition governments, the Hindu provinces under the Congress's aegis opted for exclusive, one party government.

Till early 1937, however, Jinnah was still his "nationalist" self; preaching his credo eloquently; trying to unite Hindus, Muslims and Sikhs. But, alas, Jinnah came to be caught on the wrong wicket. For one thing, at about this time, Pandit Nehru, the Congress Rashtrapathi (1936-38), began expounding his controversial "two-forces" formula, which counted Muslims out of India's politic body as a religio-political entity. He fired his first salvo in that direction on September 18, 1936, saying that "... the real contest is between two forces-the Congress representing the will for freedom of the nation and the British Government in India and its supporters who oppose this urge and try to suppress it. Intermediate groups, whatever virtue they may possess, fade out or line up with one of the principal forces. The issue for India is that of independence. He who is for it must be with the Congress and if he talks in terms of communalism he is not keen on independence."

To this formula Nehru returned, on January 10, 1937. Shorn of its sophistry and anti-imperialist tone, this represented a challenge to Muslim individuality in Indian politics, an individuality which they had nurtured and claimed since the times of Sir Syed Ahmad Khan. It also represented not only a challenge to the continued existence of the Muslim League (AIML), but also a moment of truth for Jinnah who had led that body continuously since 1919, except for his three years of self-exile (1931-34) in England.

Yet Jinnah's response was surprisingly conciliatory, if only because he still hoped for a rapprochement with the Congress. In his speech at Calcutta's Muhammad Ali Park, on January 4, 1937, he said "I refuse to line up with the Congress. I refuse to accept this proposition. There is a third party in this country and that is Muslim India.... We are not going to be camp followers of any party". (Italics for emphasis) Despite this timely rebuttal, he held out the olive branch, saying, "We are willing as equal partners to come to a settlement with our sister communities in the interest of India." And Jinnah reaffirmed this stance repeatedly for the next six months.

The deep divergence that characterised the Hindu-Muslim, Congress-League, thinking in 1937 stemmed from the basic dichotomy between Hindu "Unitarianism", a la the Nehru Report, and Muslim federalism, a la Jinnah's Fourteen Points (1929). In essence, it centred on the issue that whether India was uni-national or bi-national, whether it was uni-cultured or bi-cultured. In denying the "intermediate groups" the right to existence and in denying "all third parties' in the historical sense, Nehru was not only denying the AIML the right to exist or its due importance; more important: he was denying the Muslims the right to organize themselves politically on a platform of their own or on a platform other than that of the Congress. In other words, he was denying them their distinct individuality in India's body politic as a religio-political entity.

Jinnah, as opposed to this, felt that India was multinational and multi-cultured; that Muslims had the right to maintain their separate entity; that Muslim India represented the "third party" in India's body politic; that they should refuse to be "camp followers of any party" and that, above all, Muslims should organise themselves politically to make the third party claim a fait accompli. As a corollary to this claim, he demanded equality of status for Muslims. Of course, he repeatedly offered to coalesce with the Congress in the struggle for freedom, but only if the Muslims were "assured of their political freedom".

Thus, he told a meeting at the residence of Syed Ali Zaheer, presided over by the pro-Congress Syed Wazir Hasan, on May 9, 1937, "While we shall not knock at the Government House, we shall not also bow before Anand Bhawan", the Congress headquarters at Allahabad. Six weeks earlier, in late March 1937, he had told the AIML Council in categorical terms why he considered the Muslims' merger with the Hindus, and the AIML's with the Congress, almost impossible. It was impossible for Muslims to merge with Hindus because "their language, culture and civilization are quite different", he argued. National self-government, he said, was his creed; but Muslims "must unite as a nation and then live or die as a nation" (italics for emphasis).

The Muslims were considered a minority at this stage of India's political evolution. But "minorities", argued Jinnah in the Indian Legislative Assembly on February 7, 1935, while speaking on the Report of the Joint Parliamentary Committee on Indian Constitutional Reforms, "means a combination of things. It may be that a minority has a different religion from the other citizens of a country. Their language may be different, their race may be different, their culture may be different, and the combination of all these various elements – religion, culture, race, language, arts, music, and so forth – makes the minority a separate entity in the State, and the separate entity as an entity wants safeguards. Surely, therefore, we must face this question as a political problem; we must solve it and not evade it..."

Thus, what was at issue in the Congress-League, Nehru-Jinnah, controversy was, above all, the status of Muslims in Indian politics. Their status, in turn, depended upon whether India was uni-national or bi-national. The Congress's political conduct in 1937, remarked Penderel Moon in his Divide and Quit, meant that "there would be no room on the throne of India, save for Congress and Congress stooges". The developing Congress's policy, thus, gave Muslims a foretaste of what the Hindu un-remitted centralism and homogenic ambitions meant. Under the sort of nationalist dispensation envisaged by the Congress, Muslims would surely be relegated to a back seat.

Their values would be at a discount, their cultural identity in jeopardy. Above all, they would have no hope of shaping their spiritual, social, and cultural life according to their own ethos. All this meant culturicide, pure and simple. The Congress's conduct and rule were thus, in gross violation of 'minority' rights, civil society, and of adequate, if not good, governance – issues which, under the prevalent Westphalian Model (1648), with its overriding credo of the sovereignty of 'nations' and the 'sanctity' of borders, had not acquired the measure of importance and criticality which they have had since the demise of the Soviet Union (1991), the prime anti-Human Rights paradigm in the twentieth century. All this obviously posed a new and serious challenge to Muslims as a religio-cultural entity.

In immediate terms, it was this situation, at once despairing and agonising, that turned Muslim thinking towards Pakistan. If the Islamic way of life could not be preserved in an all-India set up, it should be saved wherever it was possible. Pakistan, or more accurately the demand for it, was thus a last-ditch attempt: an attempt to centralise, to quote Iqbal, "the life of Islam as a cultural force" in a specified territory, so that "the most living portion of the Muslims of India" could develop to the fullest in that territory, their "spiritual, cultural, economic and social life according to their own genius", to quote Jinnah, – a development which was practically impossible under the sort of dispensation envisaged by the Hindu-dominated Congress. Such, in short, were the urges and motivations that, in immediate terms, led to the formulation of the demand for Pakistan.

At another level, with the grim prospect of having been denied a place on the throne of India, what alternative did the Muslims have except for forging a throne for themselves in their majority provinces? And Pakistan simply meant only that much-and nothing more. Hence, in 1940, Muslims had no choice but to go to the Pakistan platform – unless they were prepared to be decimated as a religio-political entity in India's body politic.

AN EXERCISE REPLETE WITH CONSTANT AMENDMENTS

One of the most delicate issues faced by the British Government in India attributed to complex communal problems; the different communities residing in the vast continent of India, professing diverse faiths, inherited district social and political traditions, divided by the regional and geographical areas, always created a difficult task for the policy makers in their efforts to unite the people on a common platform. During the 20th century the British Government initiated efforts to establish a legal framework order to streamline the aims and objectives of different communities.

The Acts of 1909 and 1919 were designed to meet the ever-increasing needs of the educated Indians, who demanded substantial share in the management of public institutions. Imbibed with national spirit and driven by the dream of freedom from the foreign yoke, the Indian leaders, irrespective of their political affiliation, pressurised the British Government to introduce reforms in the public institutions of India. Realising the growing discontent among the Indian people, the British Government invited the prominent persons, representing various interests and classes, to England to participate in the Round Table Conferences held in 1930-32. The delegates deliberated on the basic issues and tried to evolve a viable constitution, catering to the needs of the rulers as well as the ruled. It was a unique exercise in the history of constitutional development. The British parliament passed the Government of India Act on August 2, 1935, providing a framework for the future development of a popular constitution. The Act was amended by the British parliament on July 18, 1947, as the Indian Independence Act, setting up in India, two Independent Dominions.

On August 14, 1947 Pakistan came into being as an independent country. The preparations for the constitution of the new dominion were commenced with the election of the Quaid-i-Azam Muhammad Ali Jinnah as the first president of the Constituent Assembly of Pakistan on August 11, 1947; it was a historic occasion. Addressing the Constituent Assembly the Quaid said, "The Constituent Assembly has got two main functions to perform. The first is the very onerous and responsible task of framing our future constitution of Pakistan and the second of functioning as a full and complete Sovereign body as the Federal Legislature of Pakistan."

Identifying the major problems to be confronted by the Legislature he pointed out, "The first observation that I would like to make is this: You will no doubt agree with me that the first duty of the government is to maintain law and order, so that the life, property and religious beliefs of its subjects are fully protected by the State. The second thing that occurs to me is this: One of the biggest curses from which India is suffering-I do not say that other countries are free from it, but, I think our condition is much worse-is bribery and corruption. (Hear, hear). That really is a poison. We must put that down with an iron hand and I hope that you will take adequate measures as soon as it is possible for this Assembly to do so."

Condemning the evil of black-marketing, he categorically stated, "A citizen who does black-marketing commits, I think, a greater crime than the biggest and most grievous of crimes. These black-marketers are really knowing, intelligent and ordinary responsible people, and when they are indulged in black-marketing, I think they ought to be very severely punished."

Another evil he described and which needed to be crushed in the new state was nepotism and jobbery. He declared, "I want to make it quite clear that I shall never tolerate any kind of jobbery, nepotism or any influence, directly or indirectly, brought to bear upon me. Wherever I find that such a practice is in vogue, or is continuing anywhere, low or high, I shall certainly not countenance it".

In this speech he laid down important guiding principles to be followed by the lawmakers and administrators. He briefly stated his ideas about the duties of the future state. Rejecting the criticism against the creation of Pakistan, he referred to the prevailing situation. He said, "Any idea of a United India could never have worked and in my judgment it would have led us to terrific disaster. Maybe that view is correct; maybe it is not; that remains to be seen."

The question of minorities remained a core issue in any political adjustment. In spite of countless efforts, both individual and collective and private and official, Hindu-Muslim unity became a dream, never to be realised. The partition of India conclusively decided the fate of the minorities in each dominion. The minority issue acquired a new dimension in parameters of Pakistan. In spite of the prevailing hatred and discontent, the Quaid assured the minorities that their rights and interests would be safeguarded. He laid down the noble principle for the posterity of Pakistan, "Now if we want to make this great State of Pakistan happy and prosperous we should wholly and solely concentrate on the well-being of the people, and especially of the masses and the poor. If you will work in cooperation, forgetting the past, burying the hatchet, you are bound to succeed.

If you change your past and work together in a spirit that every one of you, no mater to what community he belongs, no matter what relations he had with you in the past, no matter what is his colour, caste or creed, is first, second and last a citizen of this State with equal rights, privileges and obligations, there will be no end to the progress you will make."

Pakistan, being an ideological state, was demanded to establish an Islamic State which created fears in the mind of the minorities about the safety of their own religion and culture. To remove this misconception the Quaid declared: "You are free: you are free to go to your temples; you are free to go to your mosques or to any other places of worship in this State of Pakistan. You may belong to any religion or caste or creed—that has nothing to do with the business of the State." He further stated that "in course of time Hindus would cease to be Hindus and Muslims would cease to be Muslims, not in the religious sense, because that is the personal faith of each individual, but in the political sense as citizens of the State."

Concluding his historic address, he pronounced his policy, reflecting his noble sentiments, "I shall always be guided by the principles of justice and fairplay without any, as is put in the political language, prejudice or ill-will, in other words, partiality or favouritism. My guiding principle will be justice and complete impartiality, and I am sure that with your support and cooperation, I can look forward to Pakistan becoming one of the greatest Nations of the world." The Quaid's speech was appreciated worldwide; even his opponents admired the liberal and secular ideas expressed in the speech. However, questions were repeatedly asked about the pattern of the constitution, which he articulated in his broadcast speech to the people of the USA in February, 1948.

"The constitution of Pakistan has yet to be framed by the Pakistan Constituent Assembly. I do not know what the ultimate shape of this constitution is going to be, but I am sure that it will be of a democratic type, embodying the essential principles of Islam. Today, they are as applicable in actual life as they were 1,300 years ago. Islam and its idealism have taught us democracy. It has taught equality of man, justice and fair play to everybody. We are the inheritors of these glorious traditions and are fully alive to our responsibilities and obligations as framers of the future constitution of Pakistan. In any case Pakistan is not going to be a theocratic state-to be ruled by priests with a divine mission. We have many non-Muslims-Hindus, Christians and Parsis-but they are all Pakistanis. They will enjoy the same rights and privileges as any other citizens and will play their rightful part in the affairs of Pakistan."

After his death Prime Minister Liaquat Ali Khan, inspite of the critical situation faced by the country, devoted his energies for the preparation of the constitution. On March 7, 1949 he moved in the Constituent Assembly, the Objective Resolution, embodying the main principles on which the constitution of Pakistan was to be based. The objective resolution became preamble of future constitutions.

"In the name of Allah, the Beneficent, the Merciful; Whereas sovereignty over the entire Universe belongs to God Almighty alone and the authority which He has delegated to the State of Pakistan through its people for being exercised within the limits prescribed by Him is a sacred trust;

This Constituent Assembly, representing the people of Pakistan, resolves to frame a constitution for the sovereign independent State of Pakistan. Wherein the State shall exercise its powers and authority through the chosen representatives of the people;

Wherein the principles of democracy, freedom, equality, tolerance and social justice as enunciated by Islam, shall be fully observed.

Wherein the Muslims shall be enabled to order their lives in the individual and collective spheres in accord with the teachings and requirements of Islam, as set out in the Holy Quran and the Sunnah; Wherein adequate provision shall be made for the minorities freely to profess and practise their religions and develop their cultures;

Whereby the territories now included in, or in accession with, Pakistan and such other territories as may be hereafter be included in or accede to Pakistan shall form a Federation wherein the Units will be autonomous with such boundaries and limitation on their powers and authority as may be prescribed;

Wherein shall be guaranteed fundamental rights including equality of status, of opportunity and before law, social, economic and political justice, and freedom of thought, expression, belief, faith, worship and association, subject to law and public morality;

Wherein adequate provision shall be made to safeguard the legitimate interests of minorities and backward and depressed classes;

Wherein the independence of the judiciary shall be fully

secured; Wherein the integrity of the territories of the Federation, its independence and all its rights including its sovereign on land, sea and air shall be safeguarded; So that the people of Pakistan may prosper and attain their rightful and honoured place amongst the nations of the world and make their full contribution towards international peace and progress and happiness of humanity. The first constitution of Pakistan was prepared in eight years. The Constant Assembly was dissolved by Governor General Ghulam Muhmmad in October, 1954. A new Assembly tackled the task vigorously and on February 29, 1956, presented the first constitution which was promulgated on 23rd of March, 1956 as the constitution of the Islamic Republic of Pakistan. However, its life was very brief and on October 7, 1958, the first Martial Law was imposed in Pakistan and the constitution was abrogated. The Martial Law regime appointed a Constitution Commission which produced its report in 1961 and a new constitution was promulgated by President Ayub Khan based on the basic democracies and presidential system. This constitution was also abrogated by General Yahya Khan when he imposed Martial Law in 1969. The nation remained without a constitution till 1973 when a new Constituent Assembly adopted the present constitution unanimously.

The Constitution is considered a sacred document to be preserved and protected. It signifies the aspirations of a nation. However, in the case of Pakistan, the constitution was neither respected nor implemented in letter and spirit. The present constitution was amended on a number of occasions to serve the needs of the rulers. God knows how long the country would face this situation which is becoming alarming every day. God save Pakistan. (Ameen)

ANALYSIS OF TERRORISM IN KASHMIR AND THE INDIA-PAKISTAN DISPUTE

All these reasons have caused numerous wars and untold death and destruction for both India and Pakistan. However, the biggest fallout of the above factors has been rampant terrorism and the related proxy war between Pakistan and India since 1988. Terrorism has ravaged the valley and its people. This terrorism is not aimed at directly gaining any strategic advantage or territory from India. Rather, it is aimed at terrorizing and exterminating innocent and moderate Kashmiris to convert Kashmir into a radical Islamist region· Such a region would automatically be at odds with a secular, passive and Hindu dominated country like India. The region would therefore, naturally secede from India and possibly join Pakistan. This proxy war which employs the technique of terrorism rather than direct military action has completely changed the face of the Kashmir problem. It has converted the territorial dispute into a multifaceted social, economic, political, military and religious problem that must be resolved before Kashmir can ever experience peace and security.

This war is far more sophisticated and organized than the genocide in Congo and conflict in the Gaza strip. During the late eighties and early nineties, the Pakistani government and army, through the I.S.I. (Inter Services Intelligence), helped set up an entire terrorist network in Kashmir. Reports suggest that the I.S.I. had setup a war council consisting of approximately seventy hardcore terrorists· The I.S.I. has worked in conjunction with this terrorist network to achieve two major objectives. The first objective is the removal of all non-Muslims from the Kashmir valley, and the severing of all connections to the central government. By doing so, it hopes to change the demographics of Kashmir to make it more natural for Kashmir to become a part of Pakistan. In essence, they want to convert Kashmir from being a part of secular India into an Islamic nation. The second objective is to neutralize a large part of the Indian military forces by keeping them occupied and making them less potent in the event of a confrontation with Pakistan.

Many techniques have been employed to achieve these two objectives. The most important of these techniques is the establishment of a network of religious schools in the valley. These religious schools reject secularism and the secular, scientific syllabus prescribed by the government. Instead, these schools implant religious bigotry, communal hatred and radical religious fundamentalism in thousands of impressionable young minds throughout the valley· A network of hundreds of such schools has been established by the terrorist organizations throughout the valley. They have also destroyed many regular schools in the valley to force children to go to the religious schools or remain uneducated. They have also established a network of mosques throughout the valley. These mosques are instrumental in spreading religious fundamentalism. Together, these mosques and schools act as centres through which fundamentalism and violence have spread throughout Kashmir. These structures also act as important places for terrorist organizations to recruit people. These recruits, after being thoroughly indoctrinated and trained in terrorist training camps, add to the religious hatred brewing in the valley. Simultaneously, terrorists are also destroying Hindu temples and systematically exterminating Hindus to erase any link between Muslims and Hindus in the valley. This has further increased the communal tension in the valley.

Behind the scenes, the I.S.I. and the Pakistani army are supervising, controlling and supporting these terrorist organizations. They have armed the terrorists with the latest weapons and provide cover fire to help them infiltrate the L.O.C. into India. The I.S.I. coordinates between different terrorist organizations to effectively spread violence and create communal tension throughout the valley. The terrorists, with help from Pakistan, have created training camps in Kashmir, Pakistan and Afghanistan to indoctrinate and further train recruits. It was estimated that there were as many as 5,000 terrorists in various camps located in Pakistani Punjab and the North West Frontier Province.

The local government and administration are also deeply involved in the proxy war in the valley. In the early 1980's the local administration began to be penetrated by fundamentalists, some from terrorist organizations. Simultaneously, moderates in senior posts in the local government were systematically exterminated. As a result, organizations like the Jamaat were able to organize black outs and major protests to bring the entire state to a standstill. Religious fundamentalists in high government positions also used government resources to provide logistical and monetary support to terrorists.

These fundamentalists discriminate against non Muslims in Kashmir, even denying them emergency medical aid or simple amenities like electricity and water.

It is interesting to note that on multiple occasions, security forces have uncovered evidence linking these terrorists with Pakistan and the Pakistani Army. In 1999, Security Forces recovered pay books and I.D. cards establishing the militants and 'freedom fighters' as regular soldiers in the Pakistani Army, specifically, the Northern Light Infantry. It has become clear that Pakistan, through organizations like the I.S.I. covertly supported terrorism in Kashmir. This fact is further supported by the Centre for Contemporary Conflict in the U.S. which published an analysis of the Kargil conflict in 1999. The extent of Pakistan's involvement in the current situation in Kashmir is also evident in the sudden fall of Kashmiri groups that support an independent Kashmir like the JKLF (Jammu and Kashmir Liberation Front). The JKLF comprised largely of radical Kashmiris and unlike today's terrorist groups in the valley had few foreigners. However, as it became clear that the group did not support secession of the state to Pakistan, the group was suddenly marginalized and replaced by groups which supported secession to Pakistan· Clearly, the situation in Kashmir has become a Pakistan supported proxy war from an indigenous struggle for self-determination.

OTHER FACTORS SUPPORTING THE RISE OF TERRORISM IN KASHMIR

External factors, especially bad administration by the Indian government and gross violations of human rights by Indian security forces, have also created an environment conducive to terrorism in Kashmir. The biggest such factor has been the apathy of the central and state governments of the time with regard to Kashmir. The public infrastructure in Kashmir is almost non-existent and corruption and religious fundamentalism plague the public administrative machinery. During the beginning of the proxy war, the state and central governments did little to help the people of Kashmir. The ineffectiveness of the Janata Dal government, in power in 1989, only worsened the situation. The Indian central government displayed its weakness as it nearly collapsed when terrorists kidnapped the daughter of the Home Minister. In exchange for her safety, the government readily exchanged five captured militants. This near collapse of the Central Government, coupled with the government's general apathy and ineptitude with regards to terrorism has only encouraged the terrorists in Kashmir. Such apathy and ineffectiveness have also created a sense of alienation and neglect for the Muslims in Kashmir. This sense of alienation only adds to the hatred against Hindus and India for the Muslims in the valley, thus, supporting communal tension in the area. Furthermore, this sense of alienation also encourages the terrorists to continue their activities.

Global politics have also played an important role in the proxy war in Kashmir. Kashmir has often been used as a strategic tool in the region. Pakistan has always desired greater international and western involvement in the issue. Such involvement is important as it keeps the issue alive and centre stage. When the international community began to stress that the Kashmiri people had become alienated, Pakistan began the proxy war in Kashmir while consistently maintaining that the terrorists were freedom fighters. This created an impression in the international community that the people of Kashmir indeed wanted to accede from India. However, towards the end of the Clinton administration, the west, led by the United States began to follow a policy of non interference that supported a bilateral resolution of the dispute as preferred by India. This was extremely detrimental to Pakistan. As a result, Pakistan began to project Kashmir as a major humanitarian disaster like Kosovo. It claimed that the people of Kashmir had been completely alienated by the rest of the country. During this period, attacks against innocent civilians were stepped up and India was projected as performing gross civil rights abuses in Kashmir. However, during the same period terrorists were systematically eliminating non Muslims in the valley. They were spreading terror throughout the state to create the impression of a purely Muslim region in a Hindu country where human civil rights abuses were rampant. This was done primarily to force the west to become more involved in Kashmir as it did in Kosovo and Bosnia. Direct western military involvement would be extremely beneficial to

Pakistani interests as the valley is still mostly in Indian possession. Thus, in a sense, the current proxy war in Kashmir is also influenced by global politics.

IMPACT OF TERRORISM AND THE PROXY WAR

In the beginning, only high ranking Indian officials like the Inspector General of Police and a Colonel in the army were targeted. However, militants eventually began to kill innocent Hindu Pandits and Sikhs. They began to perform religious genocide and caused a mass exodus of Hindus and Sikhs from the region. Several hundred thousand of them live in refugee camps outside Delhi today·

The proxy war and terrorism have largely ruined the state. Today Kashmir is compared to some of the worst global genocides in terms of the terror and atrocities faced by the people in the area. According to official statistics nearly 66,000 people have been killed in Kashmir since 1990· Terrorists have subjected innocent Kashmiris (Hindus, Sikhs and moderate Muslims) to intimidation, panic, rape, murder and assault with a view to removing such people from Kashmir. Targets were labeled not only as political but also as religious opponents. Some of these people were killed because they were identified as 'informers' and 'agents of India'. These people were often moderates and the intelligentsia including doctors, teachers, lawyers and poets· They were looted and their valuables were used to further finance the activities of the terrorists. The terrorists grossly violated the universally accepted charter of Human Rights and other international laws as they debased and dehumanizes moderate Kashmiris· Their goals included the dismemberment of the state from India for the establishment of a new political order based on religion. Anybody identified as opposed to this campaign was subject to severe torture and persecution. Such people, often Sikhs and Hindus, were dismembered, bled to death, strangulated by steel wires, burnt alive, hung, impaled, and even had their eye balls gouged out· Such violence and brutality has caused the mass exodus of nearly 350,000 Kashmiri Pundits from the region· Since 1988 this destruction has shown no sign of letting up.

As a result of terrorism, Kashmir has also become one of the most militarized regions in the world. There are nearly 180,000 to 350,000 troops stationed in Kashmir· Roadblocks and checkpoints have isolated the region and make movement nearly impossible. Normal life has been grossly interrupted and people are forced to live in constant fear of both terrorists and Indian security forces. In fact, Indian security forces have been known to commit severe human rights violations in Kashmir. An Amnesty International report says that "Security forces continued to enjoy virtual impunity for human rights abuses as a result of provisions contained in special security laws, including POTA, as well as in the Protection of Human Rights Act." Indian security forces have been known to commit rape, perform extrajudicial executions and detain people without proper trial or treatment. Such gross violations of Human Rights further add to communal tension in the valley and worsen the situation.

In this manner, the proxy war waged by Pakistan has been largely successful in achieving its objectives. It has mostly erased secularism in the valley thus destroying all commitment to a united and multi-religious India. It has also damaged the impression of the government at the centre as it has been unable to do much about the situation in Kashmir. In addition, it has destroyed any remnants identifying the state with India thus creating a sense of alienation for the people. The liquidation and exodus of the Hindu population has made the predominantly Sufi Muslims in the valley more susceptible to religious fundamentalism. Most importantly, a Muslim rather than secular Kashmiri identity for the state has been created. The terrorists have thus effectively taken a major step towards making Kashmir a part of the fundamentalist part of the Islamic world rather than a secular state in the Indian union.

POTENTIAL STEPS TOWARDS A PEACEFUL SOLUTION

It is quite evident that the Kashmir issue has evolved over time. I t has changed from a relatively simple territorial dispute to a far more complex cultural, religious and political issue having global implications. Any solution simply resolving the territorial dispute would be inadequate. Therefore, it is necessary that the problem also be dealt with on its religious, cultural and social fronts if there is to be any hope of peace in the valley.

The first step to a solution must involve the cessation of violence in Kashmir. In order to achieve this, there has to be action by all parties. On the Pakistani side there must be an end to all support for terrorism in Kashmir. To achieve this, international pressure is very important as it could put an end to the training camps and monetary assistance that terrorist organizations have ample access to in Pakistan. There must also be a change in the local mood in Pakistan and Kashmir that is seeking the establishment of Islamic rule in Kashmir and the destruction of India rather than the betterment of the people of Kashmir. This would restrict the popularity of these groups in Pakistan and would be instrumental in putting an end to violence in Kashmir. This can only be brought about by promoting education and secularism in Kashmir and in Pakistan. These concepts are sadly quite contrary to the reality that governs Pakistan today.

Similarly, there must also be a change in Indian foreign policy. India must attempt to resolve border disputes, and develop a friendly relationship with China before it can set about resolving the Kashmir issue. As long as Pakistan and China remain allies and have India as their common adversary, the strategic importance of Kashmir will not allow any solution to the issue.

Simultaneously, the Indian government must also display greater involvement in the state. It must consider the needs and wants of the Kashmiri people to make the people feel recognized and a part of India. This would go a long way towards ending the sense of alienation and neglect that looms over most people in the valley. This can be achieved by sending greater humanitarian assistance to people in the valley, ending corruption, injustice and inefficiency in the local administration. Investment in Kashmiri infrastructure, in general, would improve the life of the people and would lead to less resentment against India. The government must also bring the wanton abuse of Human rights by Indian security forces into check. Such violations not only add to the communal tension but also create distrust against the security forces trying to protect the people. Furthermore, the Indian government has vehemently opposed and prevented any plebiscite or even unofficial polls regarding the desire of the people to accede to Pakistan. This creates an impression of illegal occupation of the region by Indian forces. India must change this policy and keep an open mind towards a plebiscite in Kashmir.

India must also try to end the small but resilient pockets of discrimination against Muslims in the rest of India. Recently, there were riots against Muslims in the western state of Gujarat. These riots, which lead to the death of thousands of Muslims, inflamed communal tensions in the rest of the country, especially in Kashmir. This adds to the hatred between the communities and also leads to an increase in terrorism related violence in the valley. As a result, India must also take steps to promote secularism in the country, especially in Kashmir.

Steps must be taken to resume normalcy in Kashmir. This would be greatly facilitated by withdrawing security forces from the state if violence in the region decreases. Furthermore, the Hindu population displaced from Kashmir should be resettled into their original homes. This is very important as this would breed religious tolerance and also greatly contribute to the economy of Kashmir.

Furthermore, the territorial dispute should also be resolved. This is important as it would lend a sense of identity to the people of Kashmir. These people sorely lack a sense of identity which adds to feeling of resentment and hatred against India. There are many proposed approaches to achieve each of the above steps. However, every option must be reviewed carefully and an amicable solution between both countries must be found.

Latest developments

Recently, there has been remarkable progress towards peace in Kashmir. The U.S. led 'war on terror' has been a blessing in disguise. It has provided Pakistan with an opportunity to sever all links with terrorist organizations. Additionally, the global pressure on terrorism has started limiting the access to financial and logistical support for terrorists. In an unprecedented move, the Pakistani president, General Pervez Musharraf has proposed a possible solution to the territorial dispute. His proposal for the demilitarization of Kashmir and the division of territory between the two countries, though not perfect, is being hailed worldwide as the first step towards a peaceful resolution to the half century old dispute between India and Pakistan. His proposal includes the identification of areas around the LoC that are either to be jointly controlled or given independent status or be put under U.N. mandate·

Furthermore, the Indian and Pakistani premiers met for the first time in two and a half years. They have promised further talks. There is also going to be expansion of, track II diplomacy, confidence building measures and transportation and communication links between the two countries. In reciprocation, India has withdrawn some of its troops from the valley All these steps promise a great deal of potential for a resolution to the issue. However, no concrete steps directly dealing with the problem have been undertaken, and until such steps become visible progress will be impossible.

9

Indo-Pakistan Wars

The summer vacation was coming to an end and the Cricket World Cup was still on. Breaking all this was the news from India's borders with Pakistan. Pakistan had shot down two IAF fighter jets and taken a flight captain as a prisoner of war. A new war had begun.

Since the brutal partition in August 1947, India and Pakistan had fought three wars. After the period of relative peace for about 28 years, a new war beckoned Indian soldiers.

Most of the Indo-Pak disputes centre around Kashmir. When the nation was partitioned, India's last Viceroy Lord Mountbatten allegedly ensured that there would be road access to Kashmir from both India and Pakistan, by providing a chunk of the district of Gurudaspur in Punjab to India (only road access to Kashmir valley from the rest of India). Although the claim is unproven, it makes sense as the Viceroy wanted to ensure the economic survival of the state as well as provide it a choice between India and Pakistan. Most of the state of Kashmir was taken over by India, and since then, Pakistan has been eyeing the Indian part of Kashmir.

1948 WAR

The first war with Pakistan was over Kashmir. Pakistan wanted to force the Maharaja of Kashmir's hand and set off a year-long war with India. At the end of it, both armies were exhausted, and the cease-fire line (called the Line of Control, or LoC) at the end of the war is used to this day as the unofficial border in Kashmir.

In August 1951, over the objections of the UN, India conducted polls to elect a Constituent Assembly for Jammu & Kashmir. The Constituent Assembly created a new Constitution for Kashmir and also ratified the accession of the state to India. Since then India has considered the state people's verdict as the official proof for the accession's legitimacy. Pakistan didn't accept this.

1965 WAR

In 1965, a second war was started after Pakistan started patrolling in India's territorial claims in the Great Rann of Kutch (in Gujarat and 1000 kilometers away from Kashmir). The Great Rann (Rann means desert in Sanskrit) is among the world's largest salt marshes and is practically barren. India had started controlling the territory in 1956. As Pakistan started patrolling in India's claims in the first week of April 1965, tensions started. In June, British Prime Minister Harold Wilson brokered a peace deal that gave Pakistan 350 square miles of the Rann.

Buoyed by the success of this venture and emboldened by the defeat of India in the 1962 Sino-India war, General Ayub Khan of Pakistan kick-started Operation Gibraltar that sent the Pakistan army to infiltrate Jammu & Kashmir and foment extremists there. Nehru was already dead and the General thought it was time to test India's strength under the new leader. Also, the most famous political leader in Kashmir - Sheikh Abdullah - had just visited Pakistan, and it was alleged that he had talked about the growing unrest in the valley.

On August 5 1965, days before the 18th independence celebrations of both the nations, between 26000 and 33000 Pakistani soldiers entered Kashmir. The local population, instead of rising in revolution as Pakistan expected, tipped off the Indian Army [the same happened in each war]. In the next one month, both nations fiercely fought, with India taking over 1800sq km of fertile Pakistani territory in Punjab and Kashmir and Pakistan taking over 550 sq km of desert in Gujarat and Rajasthan. India lost 3000 soldiers and Pakistan 3800. A daring commando mission by Pakistan failed miserably with most of the commandos ending up as prisoners of war.

While India held advantage over land, Pakistan had a better success in the air, with its US-bought aircraft. The Indian Air Force was forced to keep several aircrafts in the east front to keep a possible Chinese attack at bay and therefore was not able to sufficiently hit back Pakistan's Air Force. The Indian Navy was also not very successful with the sole aircraft carrier, INS Vikrant, locked up in Bombay harbor fearing submarine attacks and the Pakistan Navy raiding the coastal town of Dwarka.

Both nations claimed victory, but felt that they didn't have enough ammunitions to go on. Pakistan was on the brink of defeat on land, having also lost more territory, and thus was eager for a ceasefire. India had already fought a war with China just three years before this and feared a possible attack from the Red army. It was also weakened by massive inflation and poor economic conditions. Moreover, its navy and air force were both exposed to much superior weapons. Thus, India was ready for ceasefire too. Both nations were pressured by the US and the USSR to end their business.

India and Pakistan ceased fire on September 23, and both nations met in Taskhent in USSR then (currently a part of Uzbekistan) in January 1966. On the last day of the conference, the Indian Prime Minister mysteriously died of a heart attack. Both nations went to the pre-war borders.

THE 1965 INDO PAKISTAN WAR

Preamble

The analyses of all wars and all naval operations invariably reveal facets which caused confusion and facets of great achievement. From the records presently available of events in 1965, two general features stand out prominently:-

(a) 1965 was the first time after independence in 1947 that the Cabinet, the Ministry of Defence, the Chiefs of Staff Committee and the Services Headquarters came face to face with the procedural realities of war and its international implications. Every single personage and institution had to carefully feel the way forward. There were no precedents to go by. Expectedly, there was considerable confusion. Had the war been longer, many grey areas would have progressively clarified. Instead, its short duration permitted achievements to be exaggerated and shortcomings to be subsumed.

(b) The second feature was the clear determination of both the Indian and Pakistan Governments to localise the war, to desist from attacks on cities and non-military targets and to anticipate reciprocity in not sinking each others merchant ships. This too created confusion.

In the doctrines prevalent at that time, the Armed Forces were trained to go all out in war. They were not accustomed to the political niceties of only one or two Services fighting and the third service being confined to defensive action within geographical limits.

The media on both sides were sensationalising the achievements of their respective Armed Forces. For all practical purposes India and Pakistan were actually at war with each other. Indeed in his broadcast on 6 September, President Ayub Khan of Pakistan stated that Pakistan was at war. But neither the Government of India nor of Pakistan formally "declared war", thereby increasing the confusion.

With hindsight, it is clear that the interplay of factors was complex. India wanted to treat events as a local dispute over Kashmir and hence an internal affair. Pakistan wanted to internationalise the Kashmir issue. Then there was the dilemma of two members of the same British Commonwealth being at war with one another. In fact Britain, America and Canada declared on embargo on 14 September on all supplies of military equipment and stores to both India and Pakistan. Soon thereafter, France and Sweden imposed a similar embargo. In a wider perspective, declaration of war could have invited Great Power involvement and United Nations intervention.

For the Navy, the events of 1965 yielded invaluable lessons. Many of the shortcomings were remedied before the 1971 war. Many of the inherent contradictions of "being at war without formally declaring war" re-surfaced during naval operations in 1971.

THE DRAMATIS PERSONAE IN THE 1965 WAR

General J N Chaudhuri was the Chief of the Army Staff and Chairman of the Chiefs of Staff Committee. Vice Admiral B S Soman was the Chief of the Naval Staff. Air Marshal Arjan Singh was the Chief of the Air Staff. Rear Admiral BA Samson was the Flag Officer Commanding Indian Fleet (FOCIF).

Mr Lal Bahadur Shastri was the Prime Minister. Mr Y B Chavan was the Defence Minister. Mr Swaran Singh was the Foreign Minister.

In the Ministry of Defence, Mr P V R Rao was the Defence Secretary, Mr HC Sarin was the Secretary Defence Production Mr GL Sheth was the Additional Secretary and Mr DD Sathe was a Joint Secretary. Mr LK Jha was the Principal Secretary to the Prime Minister. Mr CP Srivastava, the Private Secretary to the Prime Minister, published his memoirs "Lal Bahadur Shastri" in 1996. Mr RD Pradhan, the Private Secretary to the Defence Minister, published his memoirs "Debacle to Revival" in 1998.

Pakistan's Plan

The picture that emerges from published Pakistani sources and memoirs is of an aggressive plan comprising three major operations named Desert Hawk, Gibraltar and Grand Slam.

The first phase, Operation Desert Hawk, to be launched in early 1965, was a probing encounter to claim territory in the Rann of Kutch, where the boundary had not yet been demarcated. This operation was meant to serve several purposes. First to assess India's responses. Next to draw India's military forces southward to Kutch, away from the Punjab. Thirdly to give Pakistani military forces a dress rehearsal for a full scale invasion of India later in the year, initially in Kashmir and thereafter in Punjab. Fourthly to test how far America was serious in enforcing its ban on the use of American supplied Patton tanks and other military equipment for an attack on India.

Concurrently with this first phase, the training was to be started of about 30,000 men in guerrilla and sabotage activities. These men were to be formed in ten 'Gibraltar' forces, each commanded by a Pakistani Army officer and comprising six units of five companies of 110 men per company. Each company comprised regular troops of the Azad Kashmir Army, which was part of the Pakistan Army, along with Mujahid (volunteers for a jehad) and Razakar (defenders of the faith) irregulars. The Gibraltar Forces were placed under the command of a Major General of the Pakistan Army who was also commanding a division of regular troops.

The second phase, Operation Gibraltar was to commence in early August 1965 and envisioned several stages. Infiltrators would penetrate sixty locations throughout Kashmir and at each location initiate terror, arson, murder, destroy bridges, communications and government property.

After a few days of large scale damage, it would be announced over a new radio station called 'Voice of Kashmir' that the people of Kashmir had risen in revolt.

In due course, after describing the success of the people's uprising, the radio station would announce the formation of a National Government. Concurrently the Pakistan Government would deny the Indian Government's allegations of infiltration and label as aggression the Indian Army's crossing the Cease Fire Line into Pakistan Occupied Kashmir to stop further infiltration.

Towards end August, the Pakistan Army would launch the third phase Operation Grand Slam. This would be a large scale attack across the India - Pakistan international boundary into the Chamb area in order to capture Akhnoor and cut India's only road link with Kashmir.

Pakistan would allege that this was a response to India's aggression across the cease fire line. After the successful launch of the thrust to Akhnoor, the Pakistan Army would launch a massive attack with Patton tanks on Punjab to capture Amritsar and as much Indian territory as possible for eventual exchange after the cease fire.

Since none of the foregoing was known to India at the time, India's responses to these unfolding events provide insights into the why's and wherefore's of the Indian Navy's actions in 1965.

THE INTRUSION IN KUTCH - OPERATION DESERT HAWK - APRIL 1965

The Rann of Kutch is a marshy area about 300 miles long and 50 miles wide on the western seaboard of India. The incident started in January 1965 with Pakistan claiming the entire Rann of Kutch on the grounds that Sind, one of Pakistan's provinces, used to exercise administrative control over the area during the British period. This was one of the many undemarcated areas pending since partition in 1947. Pakistan was keen to have at least the northern portion of the Rann, which it had earmarked for offshore drilling with the help of an American oil company. India asserted that Kanjarkot, Chadbet and Biarbet, which Pakistan claimed, belonged to India and not to Pakistan.

Operation Desert Hawk started with skirmishes between Indian police patrols and Pakistani border guards about an eighteen mile track, a mile and a half inside Indian territory where Pakistani forces established two posts. By early April, the fighting had spread to within 10 miles of the fort at Kanjarkot. On 9 April, Pakistan forces in brigade strength attacked the Central Reserve Police manned Sardar post near the old ruined fort of Kanjarkot. The CRPF contingent was forced to withdraw. The task of sanitising the area was then taken over by the Army. The Indian Army asked the Pakistan Army to vacate Kanjarkot. The Pakistan Army refused. On 16 April, Pakistan claimed Kanjarkot to be Pakistan territory. On 24 April, Pakistan launched a division size attack, using Patton tanks and field guns. The attack was contained with considerable casualties on both sides. When the incident had started, the British Prime Minister initiated moves to secure a cease-fire. During the Commonwealth Heads of Government conference in London, he succeeded in his efforts. A simple cease fire was declared on 29 April. On 15 June fighting erupted again. On 30 June, a formal cease fire was signed in London restoring India's police control over the disputed areas while allowing the Pakistan police the use of the disputed track.

Both the national and the international press commented adversely on the performance of the Indian troops. Though the Army did nor fare as badly as Pakistan claimed, Pakistan did make local gains. Logistics favoured Pakistan. It had an airfield at Badin where it had deployed F 86 Sabre fighter aircraft. And Pakistan had deployed its Army in force - an infantry division and two regiments of tanks, including the Patton tanks recently received from America. India protested to America against the use of these American supplied arms and America protested to Pakistan. Nothing much happened.

On the naval side, no encounter occurred. Early in 1965, the Indian Fleet had visited Bahrein and Kuwait as planned. The aircraft carrier VIKRANT had carried out a routine cooperation exercise with the Army in the Kutch area. When the skirmish occurred, some ships were on routine assignments on both coasts and in the Andamans. Most ships were in Bombay undergoing maintenance in preparation for the annual exercises in the Bay of Bengal for the duration of the southwest monsoon. The aircraft carrier had disembarked her air squadrons and was on her way back to Bombay for docking. When Pakistan intruded in Kutch, she was ordered to sail back and reembark her aircraft. By the time she had done so, the cease fire had been declared. This delay in her docking was to result in the carrier not being available for operations later in the year.

The official history of the Pakistan Navy titled 'Story Of The Pakistan Navy 1947 - 1972' states:

"In March 1965 the Indian Navy, having completed a series of exercises off Bombay and Cochin, sent their aircraft carrier and a number of destroyers and frigates on a goodwill visit to the Gulf ports. On their return they joined up with other units from Bombay and carried out extensive exercises off Kutch. These exercises included anti submarine, anti aircraft, strike and photo recce missions by carrier borne aircraft. This appears to have been a prelude to the Kutch operations in which the aircraft carrier played an important role in transporting men and material to the port of Kandla, which was being used as a support base for operations in the area.

"In Karachi, COMPAK arrived suddenly one afternoon and enquired how soon ships could proceed to sea. All available ships were made ready and proceeded to sea a few days later for the

Rann of Kutch operations which was a prelude to the September 1965 War.

"A notable feature of the 1965 war was that both its genesis and its outcome have remained largely unstated, but it was caused by frictions generated by the gradual change in India's stance over the Kashmir issue. In Pakistan it was becoming increasingly evident that India wanted to do a volte face on its commitment to a plebiscite in Kashmir. This was clear from the pronouncement of its leaders and by the practical steps initiated for the incorporation of the disputed territory in the Indian Union. The predominant view in Pakistan was that if nothing was done to thwart India's efforts, she would be emboldened to proceed ahead with her plans for the assimilation of the state into its territory. Lack of any response on Pakistan's part, it was feared, would enable the Indians to strengthen their claim over the State as time passed."

In June, a formal cease fire agreement was arrived at, effective from 1 July. It provided for ministerial level talks which, if they did not produce a compromise, would be followed by reference of the Kutch issue to a tribunal to demarcate the boundary. The ministerial meeting never took place - Pakistan did not reply to India's communications -so a tribunal was appointed. The tribunal upheld by 2 to 1 Pakistan's claim to the northern half of the Rann and awarded 10 percent of the disputed territory to Pakistan.

Mr Pradhan's memoirs state:

"After the cease-fire on the Rann of Kutch the Indian army had started moving troops to their battle locations with the object of restraining any Pakistani adventure in the Punjab or in Jammu and Kashmir. However for want of intelligence assessment the movement was considerably slow. During March and April 1965, the Kashmir valley was simmering with anti-India propaganda. In May 1965 the Indian government was forced to rearrest Sheikh Abdullah. There were pretests and agitations and the Pakistani hawks decided that the time was ripe to launch a guerrilla type operation in Jammu and Kashmir named `Operation Gibraltar'."

Pakistan's incursion into Kutch roused strong feelings amongst the people of India. They had vivid memories of the humiliation India had suffered at the hands of the Chinese in 1962. The opposition parties alleged that Prime Minister Shastri had not acted firmly enough. Several considerations appear to have weighed with the Prime Minister in handling the Kutch crisis. Mr C P Srivastava was the Private Secretary to the Prime Minister in 1965. His memoirs "Lal Bahadur Shastri", state:

"At the back of his mind was always the firm advice of the Army Chief that an escalation of fighting in the Rann of Kutch area was, tactically, not in the country's interest and that if there had to be a trial of strength between India and Pakistan, it should be elsewhere."

Mr L K Jha, the Principal Secretary to the Prime Minister in 1965, recalls:

"I was involved with some of the overall considerations which were guiding the war effort and meetings of the Emergency Committee of the Cabinet as`well as the Secretaries where some aspects were viewed largely from the political point of view but equally from an operational point of view.

"Now, first of all, the attempt on our part was to keep the whole thing confined, territorially as well as otherwise, to a local conflict, rather than allow it to assume the character of an Indo -Pak War. This was the prime objective of our policy - it had been in the past also. But at the same time, we had come to realise that fighting on terrain chosen by the enemy would always leave you at a disadvantage. This came out very, very vividly during the Rann of Kutch affair when Pakistan had all the logistic advantage and we had a tremendous problem in getting men, material and supplies moving to the front.

"At that very time, a political decision had been taken that we would not fight with our hands tied behind our backs and therefore a plan for opening a second front in the Punjab by marching into Lahore had been drawn up and perfected. But it was not launched because a cease fire came into existence, and we naturally hoped that some peaceful way of resolving the Rann of Kutch dispute would be evolved and in fact it went to an international body to settle.

"But even when there was the state of uncertainty, a kind of simple cease fire without any formal agreement, the

Commonwealth Prime Minister's Conference was taking place in London. Shastriji went to London and I went with him. And when going, there was concern - supposing things hotted up in our absence, should the operation to march into Lahore be launched or not? The arrangement I made with Shri Y B Chavan, who was then the Defence Minister, was that if such a contingency arose, he would send me a message indicating the date by which the Prime Minister must get back because we were about to move forward. However the contingency did not arise.

"In fact I recall, and it might be useful for the record, a meeting between Prime Minister Shastri and President Ayub during the Commonwealth Conference session. It was a private meeting and I was there. Ayub said somewhat patronisingly " You know, your chaps tried to commit aggression on our territory, our chaps gave them a few knocks and they began to flee". Then Shastriji said "Mr President, you are a General. I have no military knowledge or experience. But do you think if I had to attack Pakistan, I would choose a terrain where we have no logistic support and you have all the advantages? Do you think I would make such a mistake or any of my Generals would allow me to make that mistake?" And one could see from the face of President Ayub that this thought startled him. Because quite obviously he had been led to believe, in my judgment by Bhutto, that the Indians had attacked in the Rann of Kutch. And he was firmly of that view until this question was posed by Shastriji. I could see him visibly pause and not pursue the point any further".

Mr C P Srivastava's memoirs state:

"Why was air power not deployed in the Rann of Kutch conflict? Air Chief Marshal Arjan Singh told me the reason. He said that soon after the commencement of hostilities in the Rann of Kutch region, he received a telephone call from Air Marshal Asghar Khan, his counterpart in Pakistan, suggesting an informal agreement that neither side should employ the Air Force in the conflict. Arjan Singh himself agreed on the wisdom of this proposal but he confirmed the arrangement after receiving political clearance from the Defence Minister and the Prime Minister. Arjan Singh was also of the opinion that the Rann of Kutch was not a suitable area for large-scale operations by India". "Shastri was a man of peace and he was determined to go to the farthest extent possible, consistent with national security and honour, to maintain peace with Pakistan."

Another consideration seems to have been Prime Minister Shastri's belief that it would be easier to make up with Pakistan, the people of which were of the same stock as Indians, than to make up with China. He was in favour of peace. And if war was forced upon India then, whilst reacting in whatever manner India thought fit, the conflict should be localised as far as possible.

Yet another consideration seems to have been the international political climate. After Russia's open clash with China, Russia began to be more friendly with her neighbors Turkey, Iran and Pakistan, who were still members of American led military alliances directed against Russia. In trying to woo Pakistan, Russia appears to have been influenced by the prospect of Pakistan getting closer to China. Russia invited President Ayub Khan. He visited Moscow in April 1965 during the Rann of Kutch conflict and India noticed that Russia tended to take a neutral position in the conflict. It was reluctant to say anything in public when it was trying to woo Pakistan. India also came to know that Russia was considering President Ayub Khan's request for arms. Prime Minister Shastri visited Russia soon after President Ayub Khan. Russian leaders reassured him that they were trying to wean Pakistan away from military pacts as well as from China and if they were successful, India would benefit more than Russia.

There was also the lurking threat from China. After the Sino Pakistan border treaty in 1963, China's Prime Minister Chou En Lai had made a state visit to Pakistan in 1964. This was followed by a state visit by President Ayub Khan to China in March 1965.

And there was Indonesia, whose relations with India had deteriorated after the Bandung Conference of 1955. The Communist Party of Indonesia had come to power and had close links with Communist China. In the end 1950's, the strength of the Indonesian Navy had increased substantially. Between 1959 and 1965, Russia gave Indonesia one cruiser, fourteen destroyers, fourteen submarines, eight anti submarine patrol vessels, twenty missile boats and several motor torpedo boats and gunboats. Indonesia had arrived at a mutual defence arrangement with Pakistan. Indonesian leaders started voicing claims to Great Nicobar which was closest to Sumatra and wanting the Indian Ocean to be renamed as the Indonesian Ocean. After China's attack on India's northern frontiers in 1962, the Army's hands were more than full and the Indian Navy had been charged with the garrisoning of the Andaman and Nicobar islands. In 1965, the Navy was responsible for the defence of these islands.

Not the least of Prime Minister Shastri's worries was the internal situation - the likelihood of Hindu - Muslim riots, the differences of opinion, between political parties and within the Cabinet, on how to deal with Pakistan's bellicosity and the no - confidence motions in Parliament at a time when there was a pressing need for greater unity.

NAVAL MOVEMENTS BETWEEN MAY AND AUGUST 1965

The 'Story of the Pakistan Navy' states:- "After the Rann of Kutch operations, the Pakistan Navy's ships went to sea frequently and carried out intensive maneuvers. Changes of formation from surface to anti aircraft disposition were carried out while long periods were spent patrolling off Karachi. Exercises continued throughout the monsoons. In August, all leave was stopped in the fleet and preparations were made for possible hostilities".

The 'Indian Navy's History 1951 - 1965' states:-

"The Indian Fleet sailed for the Bay of Bengal in end June. No directive had been received from Government to prepare for war. It had been arranged for a British submarine to be available off Madras in July for anti submarine training, after which it was planned that ships of the Fleet visit the Andamans, Calcutta and Visakhapatnam".

THE INTRUSIONS IN KASHMIR - OPERATION GIBRALTAR - AUGUST 1965

It is clear from Pakistani published sources that in mid May,six weeks before signing the formal cease fire in London, President

Ayub Khan was given a military presentation on Operation Gibraltar. During the presentation, at his behest, the assault on Akhnoor was included in Operation Grand Slam. He accorded approval for Operation Gibraltar to be launched. In end July, he addressed the Force Commanders of Operation Gibraltar.

The first infiltration across the Cease Fire Line (CFL) started on 1 August over a 700 kilometer front from Kargil to Chhamb. The Indians as well as the local Kashmiris were taken by surprise.

Operation Gibraltar commenced on 5 August. Sixty companies of Pakistani armed personnel in disguise, armed with modern weapons and explosives, infiltrated across the cease fire line to blow up strategic bridges, raid supply dumps, kill VIP's and cause arson. On 5 August itself, some infiltrators were apprehended.

In his foreword to Air Marshal Asghar Khan's book 'The First Round', Mr Altaf Gauhar, then Pakistan's Secretary of Information and Broadcasting states: (Page xii)

"The truth is that the first four volunteers who were captured by the Indians described the whole plan in a broadcast on All India Radio on 8 August 1965, nearly a month before India crossed the international boundary".

On hearing these broadcasts, Pakistan realised that their secret plan was now open knowledge.

Mr C P Srivastava's memoirs state:

"It was only on 8 August 1965 that more detailed information about extensive infiltration by armed men from Pakistan was provided to Prime Minister Shastri. He immediately summoned a meeting of the Emergency Committee of the Cabinet. The Chief of Army Staff attended this meeting. He assured the Prime Minister that the Army and the police were in control of the situation, the raiders were being rounded up but further sabotage could still occur by the raiders not yet captured. The Prime Minister asked the Chief of Army Staff to take whatever action he considered necessary to prevent new infiltrations."

"On 9 August, as per its pre-arranged plan, Pakistan announced a rebellion in Kashmir and the heroic exploits of the freedom fighters who were helping them. It also reported receiving a broadcast, by a secret radio station calling itself as the 'Voice of Kashmir', of the setting up of a Revolutionary Council to take over all authority in Kashmir. Within days however, it became clear to the world that this was a propaganda hoax. Soon even Pakistani newspapers ceased further propaganda. By 11 August, the Pakistan Army realised that Operation Gibraltar had flopped. From 15 August onwards, the Pakistan Army stepped up its violation of the cease fire line on the Srinagar - Leh road".

Mr PVR Rao, the Defence Secretary in 1965, stated in his 1972 USI Lecture:

"The firm decision that the Army should cross the Cease Fire Line to root out the infiltrator's bases and, in case Pakistan regular forces intervened, our forces should be free to retaliate at any suitable place of their choice was taken on the night of the 13th August by the Prime Minister, when the Defence Minister and certain officials, including the Chief of the Army Staff were present. These decisions were taken on the request of the Chief of the Army Staff that to check infiltration, the infiltrators' bases should be destroyed and in any fight between regular forces, the Services should not be restricted. Shri Lal Bahadur Shastri was anxious to avoid any extension of the conflict but was determined that measures to liquidate infiltrators should be pursued vigorously. The Prime Minister gave expression publicly to the decision taken at his speech from the Red Fort on the 15th August, when he declared that ``resort to the sword will be met with the sword'. And even as the speech was being made, our troops occupied certain posts across the Cease Fire Line near Kargil and, in the following days, occupied various places across the Cease Fire Line, including Haji Pir and destroyed the infiltrators' hideouts. After giving the broad directive on the 13th August, the Prime Minister did not concern himself with the details of the operations. He left all operational decisions to be supervised by the Defence Minister, but I used to report to the Prime Minister at his residence every evening the progress of the operations".

In Naval Headquarters in Delhi, the situation had become quite vexed. With all the operational ships of the Indian Fleet away in the East, the resources available in Bombay were meagre. The frigate TALWAR, which had been carrying out essential maintenance was hurriedly boxed up and sent for investigating the presence of possible enemy vessels in the Kori Creek, a few miles southwest of the Indo Pakistan border in the Gulf of Kutch.Her first patrol was for 5 days from 12 to 16 August, then again from 24th to 28 August. No encounter occurred.

From the East, the Flag Officer Commanding the Indian Fleet (FOCIF), Rear Admiral B A Samson, reading of the increasing tension in Kashmir, rang up the Chief of the Naval Staff (CNS), Vice Admiral Soman, on more than one occasion and suggested that the Fleet return to Bombay. He was told that the Fleet should adhere to its programme of visiting the Andamans and Calcutta.

OPERATION GRAND SLAM - SEPTEMBER 1965

Mr Pradhan's book states:

"By the first week of August, the infiltrators had not achieved their objective. In order to raise the guerrilla's morale and spark the support of the local population, Pakistan undertook a limited offensive against Chhamb in the Jammu area. As a counter offensive, in the northern sector, Indian troops crossed the CFL and captured Kargil Heights thus securing the safety of the Leh-Srinagar road. Further, in order to hit the infiltrators' bases, India decided to cross the CFL on the western sector and capture two strategic areas in POK the Hajipur Bulge and the Kishanganga Bulge. The operations began on 23 August and four days later, an Indian column led by Major Ranjit Singh Dayal (later Lieutenant General) made a final heroic assault and captured the 18,600 feet high Hajipur pass. The Pakistanis were ill-prepared to defend these strategic areas in POK and the Indian offensive unnerved them. By the end of August, Pakistan had failed to achieve any success and President Ayub was under pressure to do something to check the loss of further territory and avoid military humiliation.

"Pakistan had limited options of regaining the initiative in Jammu and Kashmir except perhaps by crossing the CFL from the west in the Chhamb area. It offered many advantages. It was contiguous to Pakistani territory and was well connected to Pakistan's rail and road network and the nearby cantonments of

Sialkot, Kharian and Jhelum. The plains sector of Chhamb-Akhnur, being suited to the use of armour, Pakistan could threaten the Akhnur bridge over the Chenab. All communications between India and its garrisons in Chhamb, Naushera, Rajauri and Poonch passed over this bridge. If Pakistan succeeded in capturing the bridge, it could cut off the logistic requirements of the Indian troops west of the Chenab and the valley itself".

When Pakistan Army Headquarters found that the tide was turning against them, pressure began to build up to retrieve the situation by launching the third phase - Operation Grand Slam - to capture Akhnoor and Amritsar. One major problem, which could only be resolved with the approval of President Ayub Khan, was that this operation would require the Pakistan Army to move across the international frontier between Sialkot and Jammu. President Ayub gave his approval on 29 August. On 1 September, after heavy preparatory artillery fire, a column of seventy tanks and two brigades of troops drove towards Akhnoor bridge to cut off the supply line from Punjab to Kashmir.

THE DEVELOPMENTS IN DELHI

Mr Pradhan's memoirs state:

"On 30 August, General Chaudhuri went to Srinagar for an on-the-spot assessment. He was due to return to Delhi on 1 September. That very morning at 3.45 am, Pakistan started the bombardment of India's front positions. The blitzkiieg offensive was planned to exploit Pakistani superiority in armour and heavy artillery. `Operation Grand Slam' caught the Indian commanders by surprise - a full scale war had erupted".

"In the morning meeting on Wednesday, 1 September 1965, General Kumarmangalam said 16-days is the least (period) before Pak should retaliate.

"The VCOAS's assessment that sixteen days would be the minimum period before Pakistan launched an attack showed how faulty both military assessment and intelligence were".

Air Chief Marshal Arjan Singh recalls:

"In the Air Force, we were aware of the seriousness of what

was happening. We had thought it out. In my opinion and the Army may not accept it, the attack on Chamb Jaurian took the Army by surprise. It was a very strong attack by the Pakistan Army. As far as I know, we only had a Brigade plus. The main purpose of the Pakistan Army was to capture Akhnoor Bridge, the vital link between Jammu, Rajouri and Poonch. If the Pakistanis had captured or destroyed Akhnoor Bridge, they would have cut the LOC and then there was no way of supplying that area except by air. That was their main aim initially. After that, probably their attempt would have been to cut the Jammu, Udhampur and Srinagar road or interrupt the road traffic to the valley.

"It was a big attack and our Army was quite overwhelmed by it. The Pakistanis kept advancing the whole day. General Chaudhuri came to me first and said that he would like the Air Force to participate. I said "We have discussed it. We will participate but I cannot do it unless it is a decision of the Government. Once you use the Air Force, then it widens the scope of war and that means all out war". Then he and I went to Mr Chavan. At that time it was perhaps an hour and a half before sunset. Things were getting bad there and the Army were very concerned that during the night, Pakistan might do much damage and advance further and probably even capture Akhnoor. I must also say that I was very keen and the Air Force was very keen that we should participate, otherwise, we felt, why have an Air Force? And I must say to his credit, Mr Chavan did not take more than five minutes to tell me to go ahead. He did not say what should be done but he said "I leave it to you, you do it the way you like. Attack where you like, the way the Army wants it".

"We had only one air station at Pathankot which was nearest to Chamb-Jaurian, the scene of fighting, and we put up everything we had readily available over there, about 20 aircraft or so. We lost four aircraft, all Vampires. Vampires were a bit out of date. However, though I felt sorry to have lost them, but I thought the air attack was worth it because otherwise the Pakistan Army's attack would not have been halted. It is recognised by the Army also that from the time we attacked, the Pakistan troops did not move forward. We probably did not do extensive damage, but it put the fear of God into them, that they were attacked from the air and probably would be again attacked at night. We were not very good in attacking at night, but PAF may have thought it otherwise. That attack was absolutely essential and very useful in the whole operation because it stopped the Pakistan Army advancing on to Akhnoor and cutting the only LOC to the Northern area.

"It was at about that time that we decided to react at a place of our choice. Pakistan has been always keen to fight a war at places of its choice. That is obviously the right thing to do. Everybody wants to fight a war at his own safest choice. Pakistan's endeavour has always been to get the Army involved in a big way in Kashmir, in the Valley and in the mountains. They have the advantage over there. Our endeavour has been, and it had been clearly and openly stated even before 1965 that any attack by the Pakistan Army on Jammu and Kashmir will be considered as an attack on India. This was repeated by Prime Minister Shastri even during August when attacks were going on in J&K. Somehow the Pakistan Army did not quite take it seriously. They thought that because they had attacked Chamb Jaurian which was a part of Jammu and Kashmir, India's reaction will be only there and not somewhere else. But even for our own sake, thank God we decided that Pakistan should be attacked somewhere else and not in Jammu and Kashmir. You cannot tie the Army in a limited and difficult maintenance area and fight the war against Pakistan at places which are more favourable to them. Chamb Jaurian is near Gujranwala and Gurdaspur and not far from Rawalpindi and Lahore. All the forces kept there could help the Pakistan thrust. In our case all our troops were sitting around Pathankot, Amritsar, Ferozpur and Ambala. They were involved in Kargil area and other high places, and could not be withdrawn easily. So that is how the decision to attack on the Lahore and Sialkot front was taken".

In his 1972 USI National Security Lecture 1972, Mr PVR Rao states:

"The attack by Pakistan at Chamb on the morning of the 1st September came as a surprise in its exact location and intensity.

From about the 26th August, there were heavy Pak troop movements in this area under our continuous observation, but the Army had concluded that the attack would come further north. Because of this, though there was already a clearance for use of the Air Force, there were no coordinated plans. When the Pak attack came through, Gen Chaudhuri was in Srinagar. He returned to Delhi at about 4.30 p.m. and came straight to the Defence Minister's room, where a meeting was in progress. As he walked in, the General asked for immediate air support, stating that he had just come from Pathankot and the Air Officer there was having the aircraft ready. Air Marshal Arjan Singh agreed without hesitation to go to army support, only pointing out that in attacks launched without adequate preparation, losses must be accepted and that pilots may make mistakes between friend and foe. The Defence Minister agreed that the attack may go in forthwith".

Mr C P Srivastava's memoirs state:

"Shastri received information about the Pakistani invasion by about midday over the telephone from General Chaudhuri, who was then in Srinagar and immediately convened a meeting of the Emergency Committee of the Cabinet. While the Cabinet Committee was considering the situation, General Chaudhuri reached New Delhi with the latest information and made an important proposal for the Prime Minister's approval. General Chaudhuri reported that although available Indian forces were putting up resistance, the Pakistan Army, which had Patton tanks, was pushing ahead. Indian units did not have matching armour and were thus not in a position to stop the invasion. He said the situation was hazardous and requested immediate support from the Air Force.

"A similar situation had arisen in 1962 at the time of the Chinese invasion, when the question of the use of the Air Force had been considered in order to halt the forward rush of the Chinese Army. At that time the Government had decided against the use of the Air Force. On this occasion however, Prime Minister Shastri decided that the Air Force should immediately go into action. He was conscious of the danger that the Pakistan Air Force might bomb Indian cities or vital installations but this was a danger that had to be faced. The Cabinet Committee concurred. Defence Minister Y B Chavan conveyed the decision to the Chief of the Air Staff, Air Marshal Arjan Singh, who replied that the Indian Air Force was ready".

Air Chief Marshal P C Lal was the Vice Chief of the Air Staff in 1965. His memoirs "My Years with the IAF" state:

"The IAF was kept informed of what was happening and was more or less ready for ground support but they could not give it till asked to do so by the Government and by the Army. Vampire aircraft had been moved up from Poona to Pathankot on the Air Force's own initiative on 30 August. On the afternoon of 1 September, the Army Chief, General Chaudhuri, asked the Defence Minister to request the Indian Air Force for ground support. The DM's request came at 4 p m. By 5.19 p m the Vampires at Pathankot were airborne".

Intense air battles took place over the next few days between India's Vampire, Mystere and Gnat aircraft and Pakistan's American supplied Sabre and Starfighter aircraft. The Pakistan Army had achieved initial surprise at Chamb. By 2 September they had occupied areas up to a depth of five miles. By 5 September, they were at a village called Jaurian, only 20 miles from Jammu, on their way to the crucial Akhnoor bridge over the River Chenab. The Air Force halted the Pakistani columns at Jaurian.

Regarding the developments on 4 September, Mr Pradhan's book states:

"The loss of Akhnur would be a major disaster and Chavan decided to go ahead with an operation that had been planned after the Rann of Kutch incident. On 20 April, Shastri had declared before Parliament "If Pakistan continues to disregard reason and persists in its aggressive activities, our Army will defend the country and decide its own strategy and employment of its manpower and equipment in the manner it deems best." General Chaudhuri with the approval of the Defence Minister had worked out a plan code-named `Operation Riddle' to launch an offensive action to secure the eastern bank of the Ichhogil Canal. It was felt that the mere presence of the Indian troops on the canal opposite Lahore would draw Pakistani forces from Sialkot and other area and thus reduce its offensive capabilities in other sectors. Moreover, if India could establish a bridgehead over the canal, the Pakistan army would be forced to fight there and that would lead to the attrition of her smaller army. By basing the defence line along the canal, India would confine the war to Pakistani territory in addition to acquiring a large chunk of Pakistani territory. Operation `Riddle' was planned to meet an eventuality like the one the Indian's were facing on 4 September".

The Entry in Defence Minister Chavan's diary on Tuesday, 7 September 1965 reads:

"Morning Meeting-Army is doing well according to plans. CAS gave further bad news of losses at Kulaikunda and over a base in West Pakistan.

"Bombing by both sides in East Pakistan has created a problem. I told CAS to hold his hand in East Pakistan. We do not want any wasteful escalation there. Politically also, it would be unwise to do anything which might provoke China at this moment. He (CAS) agreed".

Mr Pradhan's amplifying note states:

"A difficult situation had arisen when the Pakistan Air Force attacked Kulaikunda in West Bengal. They also dropped some paratroops between Gauhati and Shillong in Assam. All of them were captured.

"Chavan did not want any escalation in the east and had advised CAS not to initiate any action on that side. However due to some misunderstanding, the same day Canberras of the Eastern Air Command attacked Chittagong and Dacca airfields. In retaliation, the Pakistan Air Force attacked Indian bases at Kulaikunda, Bagdogra and Calcutta hitting a number of aircraft on the ground".

Mr L K Jha recalls:

"When the conflict started in the Jammu area of Kashmir and their tanks came into our territory where our tanks could not easily go because the bridges were not strong enough, there was a real dilemna. Air Marshal Arjan Singh and General Chaudhuri were present at a meeting to discuss things where we all turned to Arjan and asked him whether he could take on the Pak tanks from the air. Now there was a great deal of hesitation, again on the basic policy of keeping the conflict as narrow-based as possible and in not involving the Air Force. Whether to bring in the Air Force was a matter where a very crucial decision was involved but there seemed to be no other alternative. Arjan agreed to take the Pak tanks on at very short notice without any prior preparation and even in the late afternoon.

"It was still being thought of as a local battle. But we realised that the terrain where we were fighting was one where we were much more vulnerable and communication depended on a couple of bridges - if they were blown up, we just would be completely cut off. And therefore thought turned to using the plan which had been earlier evolved for marching into Lahore. But even then it was a very firm decision that we would not allow things to escalate into a full scale war - I mean war in the legal sense - between India and Pakistan.

"Admiral Soman had in the meantime - ever since the involvement of the Air Force - been straining at the leash, saying 'look, let me go into action'. But again the same consideration which was acting as a restraint - on using the Air Force or going into Lahore - prevailed. It was felt that if we now opened up another front off Karachi, it would become a major engagement and would no longer be a matter of localised conflict. So the decision was taken that the operation to march into Lahore would be launched but that the Navy would not be involved.

"The Indian Army crossed the international border at Wagah on the morning of 6 December and headed for Lahore. President Ayub went on the air. It was a very, very strong and angry broadcast. Admiral Soman thought that the opening of the Lahore front meant that a no holds barred situation had come and he, I think, issued a signal that we were at war with Pakistan. This signal had to be countermanded, because we did not want to go to that stage so soon. But still we realised that the Navy had the capability and if the events so necessitated, I don't think there would have been too long a hesitation to use it. But the feeling was strong that if we could contain the Pakistani forces and hold them on land, then perhaps it would be wiser not to get the Navy involved. I knew that the Navy was not happy with this decision because they were very anxious to go into action."

Admiral Soman recalls the details of the constraint placed on the Navy and what he did about it:

"One morning, I received a file signed by HC Sarin, ICS, (then Secretary Defence Production) saying "the Navy is not to operate north of the latitude of Porbandar, and is also not to take or initiate offensive action at sea against Pakistan unless forced to do so by offensive action by the Pak forces.' If I remember correctly, both the Defence Secretary, Shri P V R Rao, ICS, and the Defence Minister, Shri Y B Chavan, were out of Delhi at that time. I rang up Sarin and told him that I could not accept that order and was seeing the Defence Minister as soon as he returned, which was the very next day.

"When I saw Chavan he said that he was sorry that even after the Chinese debacle in 1962, the Navy had continued to be overlooked and as such it would perhaps be better if the Navy did not go looking for trouble. I said that while I was most grateful to him for having appreciated that we were at that time the stepchild of the Government, non participation by us in an aggressive manner in this war would not only adversely affect the morale of the service but the Navy's image in the public would go down the drain. He mentioned the fact of the aircraft carrier being in the dock and the responsibilities assigned to the Navy for the defence of the Andaman and Nicobar Islands from a possible and probable attack from Indonesia which, in the Government's order of priorities, was more crucial than naval operations against Pakistan.

"I assured him that I was fully aware of these implications of the Navy's operations and responsibilities. MYSORE had already been deployed in that area and all that I was asking for was to leave the Navy to plan and do what it can in an active manner instead of remaining passive. Finally the Defence Minister said that even the Prime Minister, Shri Lal Bahadur Shastri, did not want the conflict to escalate at sea and that was that. I requested him for permission to see the Prime Minister so that I could convince him of what I felt strongly about and he readily agreed.

"When I called on the Prime Minister, he brought up the same two points - the Navy had not been strengthened since the Sino Indian conflict and its responsibilities in the Andaman and Nicobar area were more important than in the Arabian Sea. I told him that it was wrong in principle to tie down one arm of the Defence Services to passive action in a war situation. It should have the freedom to act offensively so long as it did not bite off more than it could chew. When he brought up the question of the undesirability of any escalation of the war at sea, I reminded him of what happened to Germany on a few occasions in the two World Wars when they kept their fleets bottled up. I added that I was sure that had they used their Navy fully, from the start of the wars, the history of the world would have been different, however much the rest of the world disliked this possibility. On this he seemed to be annoyed and told me ' You have no choice '. I then asked him whether he had any objection to my seeing the Supreme Commander of the Armed Forces meaning the President. He smiled and politely said " No, you do not have to see him".

Mr PVR Rao, the Defence Secretary, recalls:-

"I was Secretary at the time and have not signed any such order. The Additional Secretary was not concerned with operational matters. What the Admiral has stated was substantially the Government decision. It was communicated in writing at best in the minutes of the Defence Minister's morning meeting, which were issued by Shri DD Sathe, Joint Secretary, after the minutes were approved by me."

In Mr Pradhan's memoirs reproduce the entry in Defence

"Morning meeting gave some hopeful and encouraging glimpse of the situation on the front.

"Had discussions in the presence of the PM with CNS (Admiral SMS Nanda). Necessary orders were given.

"Had a talk with CNS about his plans. He is rather too keen to do something. I had to restrain him". (Note: The Defence Minister had inadvertently written the wrong name. The CNS in 1965 was Vice Admiral Soman. Rear Admiral Nanda was Managing Director of Mazagon Docks in 1965.)

NAVAL OPERATIONS IN SEPTEMBER 1965

The Pakistan Navy's Role and Deployments

The Pakistan Navy comprised one cruiser (BABUR), one submarine (GHAZI), seven destroyers/frigates (KHAIBAR, BADR, JAHANGIR, ALAMGIR, TUGHRIL, SHAHJAHAN, TIPPU SULTAN) and one tanker (DACCA). Of these, one destroyer (TUGHRIL) was under refit. The remaining ships comprised the Pakistan Flotilla. The Pakistan Air Force had B 57 Canberra bombers, F 86 Sabre fighters and maritime reconnaissance aircraft operating from Karachi.

The Story of the Pakistan Navy' states:

"The role assigned to the Pakistan Navy was the maritime defence of Pakistan. This included the following tasks - the seaward defence of the ports of Pakistan, keeping the sea lines of communication open, escorting merchant ships, protection of coasts against amphibious assaults, interdiction of shipping and assisting the army in the riverine operations in East Pakistan".

"The surface units were deployed as one force to patrol on an arc 100 miles from Karachi to achieve concentration of force, provide seaward defence and attack the enemy as one group".

"The submarine GHAZI was sailed on 2 September to patrol off Bombay and instructed to attack only the heavy units of the Indian Navy i.e. VIKRANT, MYSORE and DELHI. She was in position by the morning of 5 September."

'The Story of the Pakistan Navy' states the following reasoning for the Dwarka operation:-

"The Indian Navy, with considerable numerical superiority, was bottled up in harbour due mainly to our submarine's presence in their waters. This situation afforded an opportunity to the Pakistan Navy to carry out an offensive action against Dwarka without any hindrance from the Indian Navy. The Dwarka bombardment was undertaken for the following reasons - to draw the heavy enemy units out of Bombay for the submarine to attack, to destroy the radar installation at Dwarka, to lower Indian morale and to divert Indian air effort away from the north".

"On 6 September, the Pakistan Flotilla received the news that the Indian Army had attacked across the international border in the Lahore area and ships sailed for their pre-assigned war stations. Thereafter, they remained at sea almost continuously till 27 September. Simultaneously the Naval Control of Shipping Organisation was activated which took effective control of Pakistan merchant ships. An embargo was declared on all merchant ships carrying warlike stores for India. The C in C directed the Chairman IWTA to seal off all river routes used by Indian steamers transiting through East Pakistan and to seize all such vessels and their cargo. All these measures, implemented without delay, caused severe losses to the enemy in valuable cargo, ships and river craft".

"On the afternoon of 7 September, Pakistan Naval Headquarters directed a task group, comprising the cruiser (BABUR), five destroyers (KHAIBAR, BADR, JAHANGIR, ALAMGIR and SHAHJAHAN) and a frigate(TIPPU SULTAN), to bombard Dwarka the same night and added that one or two enemy frigates may be encountered in the area in addition to enemy air threat. The task group refueled from their tanker and arrived off Dwarka at midnight. Dwarka was blacked out and could only be identified on radar. Bombardment commenced at 0024 at ranges between 5 and 6 miles and finished four minutes later, each ship having fired 50 rounds. Shortly thereafter, Pakistan Air Force aircraft attacked Dwarka after receiving clearance by a green Verey's light. The task group withdrew at full speed. During the withdrawal, BABUR picked up several aircraft contacts on her surface radar. Ships were ordered to engage any aircraft that came within gun range and some ships did open fire. The task group resumed patrol on the 100 mile arc by sunrise".

"After the Dwarka operation, the Pakistan Flotilla continued patrolling the 100 mile arc. Very little happened. On one occasion, on 20 September, five radar contacts were seen near Kori Creek and ships were detached to investigate and take action. Later the five ships retreated southwards."

The Indian Navy's Role and Deployments

The Indian Navy comprised one aircraft carrier, two cruisers, nineteen destroyers/frigates and one tanker. Of these 23 ships, 10 were under refit at Bombay - the carrier (VIKRANT), one cruiser (DELHI), three destroyers (RAJPUT, RANA and GANGA), two frigates (TRISHUL and BETWA), three ships (the training frigate KISTNA and survey ships DARSHAK and SUTLEJ). The tanker (SHAKTI) was barely servicable. Training frigate TIR was in the Andamans. Survey ship INVESTIGATOR and landing ship MAGAR were in Visakhapatnam. Two Hunt class destroyers (GODAVARI and GOMATI) were at Cochin. One cruiser (MYSORE), one destroyer (RANJIT), and six frigates (BRAHMAPUTRA, BEAS, TALWAR, KHUKRI, KUTHAR and KIRPAN) comprised the Indian Fleet. The Seahawk and Alize air squadrons, which had disembarked from the aircraft carrier for the duration of her refit, were distributed between Bombay, Goa and Cochin. Indian Air Force Liberator aircraft were available for maritime reconnaissance.

The Indian Navy's role was the maritime defence of the Western and Eastern coasts and the island territories. The tasks envisaged were first to carry out sweeps off the west coast of Pakistan to disrupt the port of Karachi and inflict vital damage on port installations if ordered, next the destruction of Pakistan naval forces if ordered, third provision of general support for the defence of the major ports on the west coast and fourth, the provision of general cover and protection to our merchant ships in the Arabian Sea, especially those plying to and from the Persian Gulf and the Red Sea. After the Government's directive to abstain from offensive action, these tasks boiled down to defending territory in the Andaman, Nicobar, Laccadive and Minicoy groups of islands and defending the major ports of Bombay, Goa and Cochin on the west coast of India.

On 1 September, when the Pakistan Army crossed the international border and advanced towards Akhnoor, the Seahawk aircraft had already moved to the Air Force Station at Jamnagar for an armament work up which had been previously planned. Naval Headquarters immediately recalled the Indian Fleet to Bombay from the Bay of Bengal and moved the Alize aircraft to Bombay for reconnaissance and anti submarine patrols. Some ships were in Calcutta and some were in Visakhapatnam. The ships comprising the fleet had various speeds and were not in good material state having been away from Bombay, their base port, for over two months. MYSORE, with only half of her boilers functioning, had her maximum speed reduced from 31 knots to 18 knots. BRAHMAPUTRA and BEAS could only do 15 knots while their rated speed was 24 knots. All ships headed for Bombay at best speed.

Meanwhile the Navy's Seahawk aircraft, which had moved to Jamnagar on 1 September for armament workup, were placed under the operational control of the Western Air Command on 3 September. They were tasked to prepare for an air strike on the radar installation at the nearest Pakistan Air Force station at Badin. On 5 September, the Seahawks came to immediate state of readiness and the strike on the Badin radar installation was scheduled to be launched at dawn on 7 September.

On 6 September, when the Indian Army crossed the international border and advanced towards Lahore, the Pakistan Air Force attacked Indian airfields. On the evening of 6 September, the Indian Air Force station at Jamnagar was bombed by Pakistani B 57 Canberra bombers. Bombing continued throughout the night. IAF aircraft, the air traffic control tower and the runway were damaged. The Seahawks were lucky - they escaped damage. On 7 September, the strike on Badin was abandoned and all the Seahawks were withdrawn from Jamnagar to Bombay. The air defence of Bombay, which was an Air Force commitment was entrusted to the Navy's Seahawks because the Air Force had become fully committed in the air battles in the North.

After the Indian Army crossed the international border on 6 September, a signal was intercepted from Pakistan Naval Headquarters to all Pakistan naval units to execute Operation Response, which apparently referred to instructions to commence hostilities. The CNS, Admiral Soman, issued a signal to all naval units and formations stating that war had broken out with Pakistan and all measures were to be immediately adopted for neutralising any misadventure on the part of the Pakistan Navy. Within 10 minutes of this signal being issued, the Government directed the CNS to cancel this signal, thereby causing him considerable personal embarrassment. The Government's view was that although hostilities had commenced with Pakistan and the Army and Air Force had been fully committed to the operations, no declaration of war had taken place. In a letter to the Times of India on 29 November 1978, Admiral Soman stated that the Ministry of Defence directed Naval Headquarters in writing that the Navy was not to operate in a threatening or offensive manner north of the latitude of Porbandar and that nowhere on the high seas was the Navy to initiate any offensive action against Pakistan unless forced to do so by their action.

FOCIF, in his flagship, the cruiser MYSORE, was the first to arrive in Bombay on 7 September. The same day Pakistan Radio announced "Our Army and Air Force have already acquitted themselves creditably in the defence of Pakistan. The Navy will not lag behind". Action by the Pakistan Navy seemed imminent. Naval Headquarters informed Bombay of the likelihood of a naval raid on Bombay that night. FOCIF sailed the same evening with one cruiser and three escorts. Nothing suspicious was detected. The very same night, the Pakistan Flotilla bombarded Dwarka.

TALWAR, which had been carrying out an independent patrol off Kori Creek from 28 August, had been directed by Naval Headquarters on 2 September to carry out a barrier patrol off the north-west tip of the Saurashtra coast, 30 to 80 miles west of Okha, to provide advance warning of the approach of the Pakistan Flotilla. On 6 September, TALWAR developed leaks in her condensers resulting in a serious problem of boiler feed water contamination and had to put into Okha to effect temporary repairs. Okha, being only a few miles from Dwarka, TALWAR detected the transmissions of the passing Pakistani warships. She also heard the gunfire of the bombardment. Next morning, she was directed to send a team to Dwarka to assess the damage. The team found that most of the shells had fallen on the soft soil between the temple and the railway station and had failed to explode. The air attack had damaged a railway engine and blown off a portion of the Railway Guest House.

FOCIF and his ships returned to Bombay on 8 September. By 9 September, all ships had arrived from the Bay of Bengal. TALWAR also arrived from Okha after temporary repairs. All Fleet ships were now in Bombay, having their urgent operational defects attended to and getting ready to sortie out. The dilemma was for what task? On the one hand were the restrictions imposed by the Government that to localise the conflict, the Navy was not to go beyond Porbandar. On the other hand, Dwarka had just been bombarded and needed to be avenged. Within the Navy, the lower levels were itching for action.The higher levels were grappling with the problem of how to bring the Pakistan Flotilla to action without violating the spirit of Government's directives. And in the Indian Parliament, a member acidly enquired 'What was the Indian Navy doing when the Pakistan Navy bombarded Dwarka?"

Some Tactical Considerations in the North Arabian Sea

For the lay reader, it would be useful to be aware of some of the phenomena which affect naval operations in our waters. It would help to understand better the actions of the Pakistan Flotilla and the actions of the Indian Fleet during these naval operations:

The atmospheric conditions in the sea areas off the north-west coast of India and between Saurashtra and Karachi are conducive for anomalous propagation called 'anaprop.' Depending on their `frequency' and the `time of day', electro magnetic transmissions either travel very long distances (warships off Saurashtra can clearly hear warships off Karachi as if they were very near or vice versa) or travel no distance at all (on certain frequencies, there is a total fadeout of wireless communications between Saurashtra and Bombay and vice versa). Similarly on board ships, radar scans display echoes of distant ships as if they are very near and display spurious echoes behaving suspiciously like ships.

In these waters, analogous phenomena prevail below the sea. Sonar detects echoes and displays them as if they were real submarine contacts. Both in peace and in war, such contacts have been attacked and ' kills ' claimed of submarines sunk, only to find that the contacts could not have been submarines at all, because no evidence of damage floated to the surface.

Both the Indian Fleet and the Pakistan Flotilla were aware of the hazards of being found within reach of opposing strike aircraft during day time. The damage that determined air attacks could inflict on warships at sea during day time had been abundantly demonstrated during the Second World War. No responsible commander of naval forces at sea would expose his force to such risk. A force would venture within the other side's air strike radius only at night and that too only to such a depth as would enable it to be out of enemy air reach by first light. The depth of penetration at night therefore depended on the speed at which the intruding force could withdraw to safety from air attack.

The North Arabian Sea is criss crossed by the Pre Determined Routes (PDR's) used by international airliners between Bombay and West Asia. Without height-finding radars, the behaviour of radar echoes of these aircraft are easily mistaken for enemy reconnaissance aircraft. This triggers tactical reflexes that affect subsequent actions - 'has my force been detected by the enemy and should I change my plan or is it just a civilian aircraft in a PDR and I can continue with my plan".

The Indian Fleet's Sorties 10 to 23 September

Rear Admiral Samson recalls his Fleet's sorties from 10 to 14 and from 18 to 23 September:

"Earlier my assumption was that I would have adequate air search capability to provide a reasonable chance of locating the enemy, and on this basis I would have deployed the Fleet to a position which would enable me to meet as much as possible the tasks of bringing the enemy to action, to afford protection to our major ports on the West Coast and to provide cover to our merchant ships from the Persian Gulf and the Red Sea. But with the very limited availability of reconnaissance aircraft, I had to revise my plan. The problem really was to find the enemy.

"I decided to sail on the night of 10/11 September and probe as far north and north-west as possible, not forgetting the possibility of another Pak raid on one of the ports in Saurashtra. I hoped I would find the enemy and I decided also to remain at sea as long as possible, refueling from the tanker, SHAKTI. This ship, having only one engine operational, was partially disabled and could not replenish me at sea and so I planned for her to sail independently to be anchored at Diu for refueling the Fleet on 13 and 14 September. In the event, her second engine also packed up and she did not sail at all, thus limiting my period of stay at sea. RAJPUT, one of the two destroyers, also packed up and returned to Bombay.

"As regards air cover, I decided to stage two Alizes from Jamnagar and to carry out searches north of latitude 21 degrees 30 minutes from 2000 hours on 11 September onwards and to arrange for six to eight Seahawks to be available at Jamnagar from 0600 hours on 12 September for launching strikes on Pak ships or the submarine up to a range of 150 miles from Jamnagar. The IAF Liberators would carry out searches in areas south of latitude 21 degrees 30 minutes.

"Flying my flag on board the MYSORE and with the BRAHMAPUTRA, BEAS, BETWA, KHUKRI, KIRPAN, KUTHAR and TALWAR in company, I sailed out of Bombay on our first sweep on the night of 10/11 September. On the morning of 11 September, within hours of our departure from Bombay, BEAS reported an unidentified aircraft at a range of 42 miles. The aircraft appeared to have been shadowing our forces and was evaluated as a 'snooper'. Two Seahawk aircraft were scrambled from Bombay but could not intercept the unidentified aircraft as it had disappeared by the time the Seahawks arrived on the scene. Our position was thus likely to have been compromised.

"An Alize search was launched from Jamnagar at 2000 hours on the evening of 11 September and within half an hour picked up a number of contacts confirming the presence of two groups of Pak ships only 50 miles west of Okha and soon made a detailed wireless report on the disposition of the contacts to me and repeated it a few minutes later. Unfortunately, however, due to freak anomalous wireless propagation conditions prevailing in the area on that night, the wireless beam from the aircraft suffered unusually high attenuation by the atmosphere and multiple reflection and refraction at varying levels as a result of which the signal did not reach me or any other ship of the Fleet nor was it picked up by Jamnagar. At midnight, the Alize aircraft landed at Jamnagar and transmitted the report to the Maritime Operations Room at Bombay on land line, but even the rebroadcast of the signal by the Naval

Signal Centre, Bombay at 0200 hours did not reach the Fleet owing to the anaprop conditions still prevailing west of Saurashtra on that night.

"At 0300 hours on 12 September, another Alize took off from Jamnagar, established wireless contact with the flagship and, after carrying out a search, reported a few surface contacts about 90 miles north of the Fleet but, not being able to investigate them further because of lack of endurance, returned to base. A third Alize sortie was airborne at 0400 hours on 12 September and searched the area, without success, as by this time the Pak warships had retreated to their own waters.

"There was no doubt about the identity of these ships as when the first Alize was flying over them, they had switched on their lights and fired green Verey's flares for purposes of identification but when the Alize did not respond with light signals, they had quickly realised that the aircraft was not their own and had then quickly switched off their lights and steamed towards the Pakistan coast at full speed to be in safe waters before daybreak. Thus 'anaprop' conditions had deprived the Fleet of a rich haul that was there for the asking. By 0700 hours on 12 September the Pak warships, whose presence within 90 miles of our Fleet had been detected and reported at 2030 hours the previous night, had disappeared.

"The Fleet continued to proceed north until it reached the northern limit of its search after which it turned southwest. Eight Seahawks which had come from Bombay to Jamnagar and two Toofanis (erstwhile Ouragons) of the Indian Air Force also carried out a sweep in the area after refueling but without success.

"On the morning of 12 September, TALWAR had another machinery breakdown and when efforts to rectify the defects failed, she was detached from the Fleet to limp back to Bombay.

"Towards sunset on the same day, the remaining force proceeded northwards once again and continued its sweep till the early hours of 13 September when it intercepted two merchant ships laden with arms bound for Pakistan, SS Steel Vendor and SS Steel Protector. The ships had to be forced to stop under threat of fire but could not be captured in the absence of clearance from higher authorities, as it had been made very clear that the Indian Fleet was not to seek action, though it was`permitted to open fire in self defence. And so the Steel Vendor and the Steel Protector continued to cruise towards Karachi, 'escorted ' by the Indian Fleet at a distance of only two cables, until they reached the northern limit of the Fleet's sweep, when the merchant ships, after bidding adieu, disappeared over the horizon.

"At about 1000 hours on 13 September, KUTHAR picked up an underwater 'sonar' contact of a possible submarine and soon KHUKRI joined in the hunt. The contact was held intermittently until 1100 hours during which time KUTHAR launched deliberate attacks with full salvos from her anti submarine mortars. The contact was, however, lost and the anti submarine action terminated. The contact was assessed to be tracking at seven knots for a fairly long period and subsequent analysis led to the conclusion that it may well have been a submarine.

"Ships were now beginning to run short of fuel and the only tanker, SHAKTI, not being available, the three ships of the 14th Frigate Squadron, KHUKRI, KIRPAN and KUTHAR, and the destroyer RANJIT, were detached on the afternoon of 13 September to carry out an offensive anti submarine sweep off the approaches to Bombay. After an uneventful night, the Fleet returned to Bombay on the morning of 14 September.

"On 17 September KHUKRI, KIRPAN and KUTHAR, with gunfire support provided by RANA and GANGA, launched a thorough search of an area of about 5000 square miles off Bombay as the Pakistan submarine GHAZI was believed to be operating in the southern approaches to Bombay. On 21 and 23 September, 'sonar' contacts were picked up and attacks launched by these ships but the contacts were soon lost. The ships continued on their anti submarine patrol until 24 September, one day after the implementation of the cease fire.

"During its second sortie, the main body of the Fleet comprising the MYSORE, BEAS, BETWA, RAJPUT and RANJIT (the BRAHMAPUTRA and the TALWAR had by now developed major defects and could not sail) carried out a sweep in the Arabian Sea from 18 September to 23 September. This was originally planned to be carried out in the general direction of the Gulf of Aden to provide support for a number of ships bringing vital defence cargo from the UK. It was known that Pakistan was aware of the nature of cargo in these ships and their shipping programme and hence there was a distinct possibility of these ships being intercepted and either captured or destroyed. The distance from Bombay to Aden is 1650 miles and thus this sweep would entail operations far away from our shores but it was considered well within the capability of our whittled down Fleet. Reports indicating likely Pakistani seaborne landings on the Saurashtra coast, however, put paid to the sweep and the Fleet was promptly sailed to intercept the Pak Fleet off Saurashtra.

"I sailed in MYSORE with RAJPUT, RANJIT, BEAS and BETWA on the morning of 18 September. My intention was to reach the Saurashtra coast as early as possible to counter the landings and so proceeded at my best speed of 22 knots. I had to leave BEAS behind to follow, as she could do only 19 knots.

"That evening at abut 2015 hours, while I was on my northerly leg, an aircraft was picked up some six miles away. This aircraft was sighted by BEAS and was heard to be reporting to the Karachi transmitting station the position and disposition of our ships most accurately. The aircraft continued to shadow us and finally faded out at 2130 hours. I continued north till after midnight and then turned southwest. No enemy ships were sighted and it was evident that no landing was being attempted by the enemy on our coast. It is probable that the seaborne landing operation was cancelled by the Pak Fleet when our presence near the Saurashtra coast was compromised.

"Nevertheless, I continued to carry out sweeps in the same area on 20, 21 and 22 September. On the evening of the 20th we intercepted wireless transmissions which were obviously from Pak ships and indicated that they had contact of an `enemy' on a south-westerly course at 10 knots. These transmissions were picked up by several of our ships and we were convinced that we were in close proximity of the enemy. However, it was not possible without direction finding equipment to gauge the direction of these transmissions but they appeared to be northerly and so we continued in this direction. Despite the fact, however, that we continued in this direction for several hours at our best speed, we did not make any contact with the enemy. Bearing in mind that the intercepted message indicated that the contact they had was proceeding in a south-westerly direction, it was obvious that this contact could not be the Indian Fleet and in all probability was some merchant ship proceeding out of Karachi or the Gulf of Kutch. I therefore turned towards the Gulf in case the enemy was attempting to intercept one of our merchant ships from this area. I found nothing and it was clear that this was another incident of 'anaprop' electromagnetic conditions and that these intercepted messages were being transmitted by local patrol vessels outside Karachi Harbour. Thereafter, despite repeated high speed sweeps as far north as Mandvi, no contact of any Pak ships was gained.

"However, we continued to intercept Pak wireless transmissions and it was clear that our forces were being continuously shadowed more or less throughout this operation. It was also clear from these transmissions that air strikes were on call for Pak surface ships. Unfortunately our Alizes or Seahawks could not operate from Jamnagar after 12 September as repeated air attacks had rendered the airfield untenable. The Liberator maritime reconnaissance aircraft of the IAF, however, continued to carry out reconnaissance sweeps of the northern part of the Arabian Sea but failed to pick up any Pak surface or air contacts. In fact, on two occasions our forces were reported by them as enemy and on one occasion the position of our force was reported in plain language!

"On the morning of 22 September I had to detach the RAJPUT and RANJIT as they were running short of fuel. Meanwhile I had received a further signal concerning the merchant ships arriving from the Gulf of Aden bringing vital defence cargo and so I altered course with the MYSORE, BEAS and BETWA towards the central Arabian Sea to try and escort them to safety. But within a few hours of our sailing on our new mission, we received a message from Naval Headquarters conveying our Government's acceptance of the United Nations' cease fire proposal from 0330 hours on 23 September. So I decided to return to the Saurashtra coast to forestall any attempt by the Pakistan Navy to create mischief in that area in a last minute bid to gain propaganda value. I returned to Bombay with the regret that I had missed an opportunity to try and engage the Pakistan Navy in battle, despite waiting just outside its lair for nearly two weeks."

SUBMARINE AND ANTI SUBMARINE OPERATIONS IN SEPTEMBER 1965

The Story of the Pakistan Navy States:

"Just after the Dwarka attack on night 7/8 September, the Pakistan submarine GHAZI had been patrolling off the Saurashtra coast. She tracked 4 to 5 escorts on passage from Bombay proceeding up the coast but did not attack them as her orders were to attack only heavy ships."

While on return passage to Bombay from the East coast, BEAS picked up a submarine contact at 1230 on 9 September about 45 miles south of Bombay. She carried out an urgent attack, followed by a deliberate attack half an hour later. Thereafter contact was lost. GHAZI makes no mention of this attack.

On 11 September, there were intensive anti submarine air patrols off Bombay. One Alize aircraft flew over GHAZI while she was snorkeling but failed to detect her. GHAZI returned to Karachi thereafter to rectify her defective electronic counter measures equipment and resumed patrol on 15 September.

Between 7 and 10 September, the Indian Fleet was in Bombay. When GHAZI was in Karachi from 12 to 14 September to effect repairs, the Indian Fleet was operating off the Saurashtra coast. When GHAZI resumed patrol on 15 September, the Indian Fleet was in Bombay from 14 to 17 September, in between sorties.

On 17 September, FOCIF sent out five escorts for an anti submarine search in the southern approaches to Bombay. They searched an area of 5000 square miles between 17 and 23 September. Several sonar contacts were picked up. On two occasions, 21 and 23 September, contacts were attacked for several hours. GHAZI makes no mention of these two attacks. Presumably she was nowhere near.

GHAZI's 'Record of Service', retrieved from the sunken hull in 1972, indicates that "In 1965, while on war patrol off the port of Bombay, GHAZI encountered three frigates. She fired four torpedoes and scored three hits on the British Type 41 frigate INS BRAHMAPUTRA".

The Story of the Pakistan Navy' mentions that:

"Off Bombay, on 22 September, GHAZI gained a firm contact. After tracking the zig-zagging contact all day, GHAZI fired four torpedoes at an ' A A frigate ' in the evening. After one and a half minutes, the first torpedo was heard to hit, followed five seconds later by another hit. GHAZI's sonar reported patterns of explosions being fired. After this attack, GHAZI returned to Karachi on 23 September where the Captain was decorated for having sunk the Indian Navy's anti aircraft frigate INS BRAHMAPUTRA".

After the cease fire, FOCIF invited the foreign naval attaches from New Delhi on board the BRAHMAPUTRA in Bombay to remove any doubts that the ship was afloat and fighting fit.

Overall, the above account provides a glimpse of the complexity of submarine and anti submarine warfare and the difficulties of predicting, with any degree of certainty, the outcome of submarine and anti submarine operations in the North Arabian Sea.

Other Minor Incidents

There were two other incidents which to this day remain unexplained:

(a) On 11 September an unidentified aircraft was reported over Visakhapatnam. Fire was opened by the ack ack guns of the Naval Coast Battery. The History of the Pakistan Air Force makes no mention of any attack on Visakhapatnam on 11 September.

(b) On 15 September, unidentified aircraft were reported over Cochin. Fire was opened by the ships patrolling off Cochin and by the Naval Battery located at the harbour entrance. Some shells fell into the populated areas adjoining Ernakulam. Some shells, which fell into the water near the harbour entrance were mistaken for air dropped mines. A minesweeper was rushed from Goa to Cochin to sweep the mines - no mines were found. A Seahawk aircraft got airborne from Cochin airfield to intercept the aircraft

- no encounter occurred. The History of the Pakistan Air Force makes no mention of any attack on Cochin on 15 September. A post war analysis suggested that the jet aircraft could have been from a British or American aircraft carrier task force which might have been operating in the area. The reminiscences of some participants at Cochin indicate that there were no echoes of any aircraft on the scans of the warning radars being manned in the ND School.

Analysis of the Reasons for Not Using the Navy Offensively

In considering the reasons why the Navy did not achieve anything significant, several basic questions arise. Was there any flaw in the higher direction of war? After the Rann of Kutch incident, why was the Fleet sent to the Bay of Bengal? When the intrusions started in Kashmir in early August, why wasn't the Fleet immediately recalled to the West Coast? Given the constraints imposed by the Government, could the Navy have done better than it did?

The Higher Direction of War

There were two aspects of the higher direction of war in 1965 which created confusion. The first was the Government's genuine and sincere belief that in modern warfare, it was meaningful to engage in warlike activity without formally declaring war. The second was that once the Government had decided to counter hostile acts by Pakistan, it was reasonable that activity be selectively confined to only one or two of the Armed Forces. As regards the first aspect, the extracts quoted above from Mr PVR Rao, the Defence Secretary in 1965, the memoirs of Mr C P Srivastava, the Private Secretary to Prime Minister Shastri in 1965, the recollections of Mr L K Jha, the Principal Secretary to Prime Minister Shastri in 1965 make it clear that the Government was determined not to enlarge the scope of the conflict beyond the minimum required to safeguard its position in Kashmir and to prevent any escalation of the conflict beyond this objective. It will also appear from the extracts given below that the Chief of the Army Staff, who was the de facto Chairman of the Chiefs of Staff Committee, excluded the Navy from participation in the contingency plan in case Pakistan attacked Kashmir. In the 1971 National Security Lecture of the United Services Institution of India, General Chaudhuri stated:

"Now that both Mr Bhutto and Air Marshal Asghar Khan have publicly claimed that they were responsible for planning and instigating Pakistan's attack on India in 1965, I think I could interpolate here a footnote from history. In 1964, when we were revising military plans to defend ourselves in case of an attack from our neighbor, the troops available on the Western Front were roughly equivalent to those of Pakistan. Our rapid expansion had meant some dilution. In the limited advance which must form the fulcrum of any defensive plan, we were faced with three alternatives. The first one was the occupation of some unguarded territory. This seemed unproductive and non -permanent. The second was the occupation of and probably substantial destruction to a big city. For this there were insufficient troops. Anybody who has studied the capture of a big town, will realise how expensive this operation is in manpower. The resistance put up by beleaguered Berlin in 1945, defended only by the remnants of a defeated army, against overwhelming odds, is a good example of what I mean. In dealing with this alternative, there was also the political view that any substantial destruction of a major population and historical centre, would leave a raw wound between two neighbors, delaying unduly the eventual aim of living in amity together. The third alternative was the destruction of equipment, cheaply obtained but if destroyed, expensive in every way to replace. This third alternative seemed the correct choice. I would submit that we were successful in the pattern we adopted and the ensuing heavy economic and political disturbances in Pakistan, certainly contributed to the downfall of the Ayub Government and perhaps to the democratisation now pending.

"Incidentally, Pakistan's own plan for 1965 was based on first getting us to panic and move down heavy reinforcements from the main Punjab theatre to Kutch. Once they had got us there, then the so called raiders would have gone into Kashmir, supported by the Pakistan regular army capturing the key point of Akhnur. Though the first part of the Pakistani plan misfired, the originators were so intrigued with the ingenuity of the second part, that they put it into action anyway. Operations by emotion are always incorrect and the second part also failed. It was on the 5th May 1965 that the larger pattern of Pakistan's intentions to seize Kashmir before we got too strong became apparent, though the actual details of how they would do it were not clear at that time, for the initiative lay, as it always does, with the aggressor.

"Previous to 1965, it had always been said by our political leaders that any attack by Pakistan against Kashmir would be construed as an attack against India. Consequently India would then be at liberty to attack Pakistan in order to improve her own defences. This statement of policy, however, was never incorporated into any military plan. The explanation for this omission was that a decision would only be taken at the time and the military would then be duly informed. Despite the public political statement, the military were always in great doubt as to whether at the appropriate time any such permission would really be given. They were also aware that if a positive decision was made at this late stage, then it would be most difficult, if not impossible, to finalise the operational plans, make the necessary concentration of units - always a long and complicated business - brief the commanders at all levels fully about the tactical picture and then launch a successful operation. The troops were fully convinced that at this last moment, the Government could have a drastic change of mind and militarily the final result might then be a fiasco.

"After the 5th May 1965, when it appeared that an attack on Kashmir or India later that year was a distinct possibility, the first matter that needed clearance was this ability to retaliate. In my discussions with both the Prime Minister and the Defence Minister after the pros and cons had been fully discussed, the necessary sanction was obtained. Consequently, we had plenty of time to work out the appropriate moves. The day Pakistan moved her regular troops,infantry and armour into the Jammu sector, I was in Kashmir. As I was coming back in the plane to Delhi, the Director of Military Operations, who was in the aircraft with me, started writing out the required signals to go to the formations concerned. On landing, he went straight off to send them out and I immediately went to see the Defence Minister who formally confirmed my action. He then informed the Prime Minister and that evening the PM asked me to see him, discussed a few details and further approved the action taken. The PM might then have informed some of his close colleagues, but this was not my concern.

"As a number of other broad policy points connected with the operations had also been cleared in this same manner, I feel it is desirable to mention the mechanics by which these clearances were given. In 1965, somehow in a rather unconventional, unplanned way, a series of informal meetings started up between the PM, the DM, the PS to the PM and myself. A little later on, my very esteemed and valuable colleague, Air Marshal Arjan Singh, joined us, for obviously the Army and the Air Force were closely linked together in any defence role. The Naval Chief did not come, for the Navy's role did not look like being a very big one. At these meetings, there was a free interchange of views and the many implications of the various actions which might be taken in a variety of circumstances were discussed in detail. No formal notes were kept for very often it was only a clearing of minds. When however, a certain policy matter was accepted, it was noted and put up for clearance later in a more formal manner. During these meetings, it was intrinsically understood that I would keep my colleagues, and particularly the Naval Chief, informed of the more important decisions, that Mr L K Jha would similarly keep the appropriate members of the Civil Services informed and, of course, the PM and the DM would keep their political and Ministerial colleagues informed as they thought fit. As Chief of Army Staff, I found these meetings extremely valuable, for not only was I quite sure of the parameters within which I could work but I was also well briefed on the possible political, domestic and economic implications. This saved a lot of time later in more formal discussions and also, when I was discussing plans for the future war with the PSO's and the Army Commanders, I was in a position to give them a good deal of background information which they, in their turn, found useful. These meetings with the PM and the Defence Minister also gave me the opportunity to put my view point directly to the two people who would ultimately play the largest part in making the final overall decisions.

"In this particular case, these informal, 'clear the air' meetings seemed to have worked very satisfactorily and advantageously. There were no personality clashes, while the small numbers concerned seemed to keep discussion down to essentials. Everyone present was fully aware of the security implications and so there were no leaks or fear of leaks. An air of informality and, I might add, good humour allowed a great deal of freedom in speaking and thinking, while a mutual confidence was built up which was most important then and later. I am not saying that this particular method of discussion could have worked equally well or at all, with another group of people in the same position. But it does emphasise what I consider to be the second important point in organisation for defence. This is the need for a free interchange of views between the various sections of the decision making authorities concerned and then enough liberty given to each one to work within his own sphere with a minimum of interference."

In the 1972 National Security Lecture of the United Service Institution of India, Mr PVR Rao, who was the Defence Secretary from 1962 to 1966, stated:-

"After November 1962 the Defence Committee of the Cabinet was revamped into the Emergency Committee. But the major change was in the working of the Defence Ministers Committee. This Committee, less the Finance representative, met daily except when the Defence Minister was out of Delhi and was effective in ensuring better coordination amongst the Services and in speeding the build up of the forces. But the system underwent a change as the crisis mounted in August 1965. There have been various claims about the decisionmaking at that time. One claim is that a small group, with the Prime Minister at its head, took all decisions and the whole process functioned very smoothly. There are, on the other hand, complaints that there was unnecessary political interference, with the result that achievement fell short of what was feasible and desirable".

Mr PVR Rao also recalls:-

"The idea that there was no communication between the Chiefs and the Government is quite incorrect, because communications can be either oral or in writing. After Mr Chavan became the

Defence Minister, there used to be a meeting every morning at 9.30 in the Defence Minister's room, attended by the three Chiefs of Staff and the Defence Secretary. The Cabinet Secretary used to come sometimes but he was not a regular visitor. Regular minutes of meetings were kept which were circulated to all concerned.

"As regards written Directives, the Navy, and particularly the Army, are very fond of saying that there were no written directives. I think it is a very ridiculous thing. In my view, decisions were not taken by the Cabinet. The decisions were always taken at the Defence Minister's morning meetings. If the decisions required further written authority, then only would they go to the PM and Defence Committee of the Cabinet. So, for operational purposes and that is what I am concerned with, all three Chiefs were in the picture every day of what was happening in the Government. It is not correct to say that the Service Chiefs were isolated or insulated and they wanted written orders that were transparent.

"Mr Shastri was staying at the relevant time at 4 Motilal Nehru Place and he had his office at the adjacent interconnected building at 10, Janapath. From about the 6th August 1965, I was asked to go to his office and I used to go there after office on my way home to report to him about the events of the day. As the situation in the valley vis a vis the infiltrators continued unabated and to drift, Shastri was clear that the troops should go across the Cease Fire line and wipe out the infiltrator's bases in POK. This became an issue for regular discussion at the morning meetings, one or two of which Shri Shastri also attended. It was Government's policy that if our action across the CFL brought out the Pak regular forces into the open, we would not confine ourselves to operations in Kashmir but be free to respond wherever we thought best on the West Pakistan Front. In this situation, General Chaudhuri demanded that if operations became necessary against West Pakistan, the whole might of the Indian Armed forces (all the three arms) should be thrown in and asked for a written directive from Government in this regard. This developed into a tussle of wills between General Chaudhuri on the one hand and the PM/DM on the other. As things continued to drift, I drafted, on Shri Shastri's instructions, a directive to the Chiefs of Staff accordingly. This was about the 10th or 11th August. There was, even then, never any question of extending the operations to the eastern sector. When I took the draft directive to 10 Janpath, Shastri took it from me and kept it, saying he would read through it. On the 11th, 12th and 13th, every evening, I asked for the paper back but he would just smile. The Indian Army crossed the Cease Fire Line on the 13th, destroyed the infiltrator's bases and in the process, captured Haji Pir by a brilliant operation. The operation was wholly Army; the IAF was not used. On the 14th or 16th August, Shastri returned to me my draft directive, saying that it was no longer necessary. No written directive (apart from the minutes of the morning meetings) were issued to any of the Chiefs of Staff. Incidentally, General Chaudhuri also did not further pursue the matter and he was in full agreement that the Navy had no role at that stage in the operations and that the operations should not be extended to the Eastern sector.

"The absence of a written directive and the see-saw that went on in this respect resulted in a curious incident. The Chief of Air Staff had apparently given standing instructions to his field commanders that if open hostilities broke out, they should spring into action without further orders. As news came out of the Pak attack on the Chamb front, the IAF on the night of 1/2 September, attacked Lalmanirhat and other targets in the East and the Pak Air Force, on its part, attacked Kalaikonda airbase near Kharagpur. Evidently, the Chief of Air Staff had not been able to countermand his earlier instructions to his field officers in the East in time. General Chaudhuri was very upset and protested to CAS/DM. The situation was rectified and the incident smoothed over.

"I have no knowledge of the happenings in the meetings between PM/DM and a Chief of Staff. Chiefs of Staff have direct access to the President, the PM and the DM. However, the P.M. and the D.M. were very punctilious and, if any action was required, the material would usually come down for suitable action. The DM would normally mention the point requiring action in the morning meeting; or, as in one or two cases, where personalities were involved, he mentioned the problem privately. That the Naval Chief remained uninformed at any stage about Government policy is just shibboleth.

"With regard to the 1965 war, it should be realised that the Government of India, that is the civil Government, wanted to keep the operations at as low a key as possible. Kashmir had to be defended and, to the extent that Pakistan was creating trouble there, it had to be faced. But it was the determined policy of Prime Minister Lal Bahadur Shastri and the Indian Government not to allow the operations to escalate.

"It is correct that the Navy was told not to approach Pakistan or threaten it. There is no question of going to Shastri or anything of the sort. But the Navy is quite correct in saying that they were asked not to escalate the fighting. They are absolutely correct. And India did not want to escalate the war. In point of fact, even in the east we did not take any action. In 1965, we wanted to limit the fighting as much as possible".

In the 1973 National Security Lecture of the United Service Institution of India, Air Chief Marshal Lal, who was the Vice Chief of Air Staff in 1965 (and subsequently Chief of Air Staff in 1971) stated:

"Early in 1965, Pakistan attacked us in Kutch, in Western India. The attack caught the armed forces unawares. The Army took the field without any prior planning or preparation. Its reaction was fast but there was no joint Army-Air Force plan, and all that the Air Force could do was to provide logistic support with light aircraft. The possibility of tactical support was considered after the fighting began. It was then realised that our bases were so far from the battle zone that our aircraft would have to operate at extreme range with reduced weapon loads while Pakistani aircraft could dominate the entire combat area from bases close by. Given time, we could also have improvised an airfield or two in or near Kutch, but the fighting ended before that. The incident was soon defused but, apparently, not before it had encouraged Pakistan in the belief that the time had come to settle the Kashmir dispute by force of arms.

"Then in August and September 1965 came the second Kashmir War. It began with skirmishes in the valley by so-called freedom fighters, in reality agents of Pakistan. These were followed, towards the end of August, by an all-out attack by Pakistani armour in the

Chamb area of Jammu province, with the obvious objective of cutting the Jammu-Srinagar highway. Our Army, working under the restrictions of the Cease Fire agreement, was lightly equipped in that sector and though it fought valiantly, its AMX tanks were no match for the more powerful Pakistani Pattons. While there was some hope of the Army holding the Pakistani attack on its own, there was no talk of bringing the Air Force into the conflict. But on 1st September, with the Pakistanis pressing forward from Jaurian, General Chaudhuri, the Army Chief, was compelled to ask for air support.

"There had been no prior joint planning for such an eventuality. Air Marshal Arjan Singh, the Air Chief, had on his own alerted the air bases in the Punjab. When the call came, a force of fighter bombers from Pathankot mounted a strike on the Pakistanis within minutes of being ordered to do so. It was a touch-and-go affair, because the demand for air support came late in the afternoon and the strike had to be mounted in an area with which our pilots were not familiar. With only a few minutes of daylight left, they could have missed the battle zone or attacked the wrong targets. Fortunately they did neither and so helped to bring the Pakistani force to a halt.

"At this point it is interesting to consider in somewhat greater detail why there was no prior planning of Army -Air operations even though, as General Chaudhuri said in his 1971 National Security lecture, he expected the Pakistanis to attack in Kashmir after the Kutch incident. Basically, I think, it was because he and his commanders were wedded to the idea that military operations were principally an Army affair and that the other services could only operate on the fringe, as it were, with an occasional bonus from the Air Force. This was compounded by a big-brother attitude towards the Air Force which led to its being treated with a certain amount of indulgence but prevented it being accepted as a vital and equal partner in war. Matters were further complicated by the belief that if the Indian Air Force took part in the fighting then the Pakistani Air Force would do likewise, thus increasing the likelihood of a general war between the two countries instead of a localised conflict in J & K. There was a good deal of truth in this, of course, but this was a possibility from which there was no escape. Indeed, this was a possibility that could not be ignored for Pakistan had already been warned that any attack on Jammu and Kashmir would be treated as an attack on India. With a political direction as clear as that on the record, it was incumbent on the Chiefs of Staff to have their plans ready for such a contingency. The fact that they did not is indicative of the thinking at the time.

"The events in the Chamb-Jaurian sector leading to the call for air support took matters out of the Army's hands. At that stage the Government had to decide whether to enlarge the area of conflict, and it did so without hesitation. That, indeed, appeared to be the only way to divert Pakistani forces from the vulnerable Jammu-Srinagar highway, the loss of which would have jeopardised the defence of the Valley. With the decision to fight Pakistan outside J & K, the Army had to move up forces from peace time stations, some from the Deccan and further south, and formulate an operational plan at short notice.

"During the five days that elapsed between the Government decision and the date set for implementing it, there was some discussion of how the Army and the Air Force should operate. On the Army side, the notion persisted that it would fight on its own, with the Air Force providing an occasional bonus; and in the Air Force, where I was Vice-Chief, we thought of fighting mainly an air war against the PAF and what we considered to be strategic targets, assigning relatively low priority to support the Army. Separate plans were hastily drawn up by each Service with no joint consultation worth the name. And again, no tasks were envisaged for the Navy.

"Please note that in 1965 the higher defence organisation was functioning and the Chiefs of Staff Committee met regularly under the chairmanship of General Chaudhuri. Officers in positions of authority had read and studied and taught the procedures for inter-service co-operation. It was not realised, however, that even when the general drill is known, each particular task still requires a great deal of preparatory work, that the persons taking part need to be trained for it, that supporting facilities have to be arranged for in advance, and this has to be done for every contingency that can be envisaged. Flexibility in battle is gained only through long and arduous preparation.

"That we discovered when we entered Pakistan. Soon the Army found that it could not fight entirely on its own, for the PAF was constantly harassing it. The Army needed air defence and tactical support but no detailed arrangements had been made for either.

The Air Force was willing to help and it did all it could but in the absence of joint plans, large gaps remained in the air cover in the combat zone. Neither did the air operations through which we hoped to immobilize the PAF and reduce Pakistan's ability to make war achieve much, for we had no well thought out target system for the purpose. Having had some responsibility for all this, I must confess that the air war became a somewhat hit-and-miss affair, that depended heavily on finding targets of opportunity for its success. The aircrew performed magnificently, doing all that was expected of them and more; had there been a coherent joint war plan, we would have derived much fuller benefit from their courage and sacrifice.

"Our advance into Pakistan caught the Pakistani forces by surprise. I imagine they had not thought the Indian Government and Armed Forces capable of swift decisions and speedy action. The initial successes of our Army were soon checked by stiff resistance, a notable feature of which was the close co-operation between the Pakistani Army and Air Force. The two of them had obviously done their homework well, for our jawans reported that the PAF were quick to appear whenever the Pakistani ground forces were in difficulties, and gave them most effective support. This was the more remarkable because unlike our set-up, in which all three Service Chiefs and their Headquarters were based at Delhi, the Pakistani Air Chief was located at Peshawar, the Army Chief at Islamabad, near Rawalpindi, and the Naval Chief at Karachi. The fact that their forces managed to work well together speaks well for their mutual understanding, which is more important than physical proximity. Furthermore, since Pakistan had been the one to start the fighting in J & K, it is to be presumed that its Service Chiefs had given some thought to the possibility of a more widespread conflict and prepared for it accordingly.

"Despite its preparations, however, Pakistan failed to make any inroads in J & K and just about held its own elsewhere. We advanced up to the Ichhogil canal, West Pakistan's first line of defence, and towards Sialkot. Pakistani forces came into Indian territory around Gadra Road in Rajasthan. Except for a single PAF attack on an Indian Air Force base near Calcutta, there was no fighting in the east. Our Navy had no operational tasks but suffered a sea-borne attack at Dwarka in the west. The fighting was brought to a halt by 22nd September, the Army having been engaged in combat for nearly a month and a half and the Air Force for 22 days. At the turn of the year came the Tashkent agreement, negotiated by our then Prime Minister, the late Mr Lal Bahadur Shastri.

"In retrospect, it is clear that the 1965 war was successful as a defensive action, for it managed to preserve the status quo in Kashmir, but the operations in the Punjab and Rajasthan were inconclusive. We failed to make a real dent in Pakistan's forces, both on the ground and in the air. The Navy being far removed from Kashmir took no part in the fighting.

"With the benefit of hindsight, we can now see what part the higher defence organisation played in the 1965 war. Frankly, I do not think it made any significant contribution. I say this after careful thought, knowing that one of our distinguished Army Chiefs, General J N Chaudhuri, was then Chairman of the Chiefs of Staff Committee. Even at the risk of his displeasure, I must say that he failed to get the organisation working as it should have done. The General himself admits as much, without meaning to, in the published version of the National Security lectures that he delivered in this institution in 1971. He said in those lectures that he saw the Kutch incident as a prelude to an attack by Pakistan in Jammu and Kashmir, and he therefore began the Army's preparations well in advance. He omits to mention that the Air Force and the Navy were kept in the dark about this. He goes on to say that he often discussed the threat with the Defence Minister and the Prime Minister and that, once in a while, he took the Air Chief along with him. The impression conveyed is that he looked upon the impending conflict as an Army affair, in which the use of the Air Force would be incidental. To my mind, this reflects an attitude long prevalent in the Army, and only recently dissipated, to the effect that its larger size and greater age gave it a commanding superiority over the other services and invested it with the sole right to decide how wars should be fought. I may be reading too much into a single statement, but to me it is axiomatic that effective co-operation between the Services can grow only out of mutual trust and full understanding of each others capabilities and limitations. I think that was lacking in 1965.

"In any case, the Air Force and Navy, not having been alerted about the possibility of another war over Kashmir, no inter-service contingency plans were drawn up, nor was any course of action agreed upon with the Air Force in the event of its being called out to support the Army. This mental block against consultation and joint planning continued right through the phase of guerrilla activity and was only partly removed when Pakistani armour threatened to cut the Jammu-Srinagar highway. It was at that critical stage, on 1st September 1965, that the Air Force was asked for air support, which it gave at short notice. Complaints from our forward troops about the limited extent of air cover in the war that followed were well-founded, for in the absence of precise plans the Air Force had simply maintained its normal forces at its bases in the Punjab and in Jammu and Kashmir. To do its job properly, some redeployment of squadrons and of logistic and communication facilities should have been effected before the commencement of hostilities. Had the joint planners been able to do their work in advance, I am certain more positive results would have been achieved in 1965. However, apart from preserving the status quo in Kashmir, the 1965 war was valuable for the many practical lessons it taught us in the conduct of operations from the highest level to combat in the field. In the years that followed these lessons were absorbed and applied."

The above excerpts indicate that until early August 1965 the Chief of the Naval Staff, Vice Admiral Soman, was unaware of two things - that information was available to the Chief of Army Staff that Pakistan may attempt to seize Kashmir later in the year and that the Chief of Army Staff had obtained the Government's approval in principle for the Army to counter attack Pakistan, if Pakistan attacked Kashmir.

WHY WAS THE INDIAN FLEET SENT TO THE BAY OF BENGAL

Vice Admiral Soman recalls:-

"After the Indo Chinese conflict in 1962, the defence of the Andaman and Nicobar Islands was left entirely to me. The Army refused to send even a platoon there and we had to raise our own land force with sailors in khaki uniform to man the various stations in these islands. So far as the Navy was concerned, as soon as Pakistan started the trouble in Kutch, I had felt that my first priority would be these islands because while talking to various people during my visit to Indonesia as the Fleet Commander a few years earlier, and having been briefed on the developments since then, I felt a little nervous about these islands. This was because when the Army refused to send any units for their defence, I had taken on the responsibility of doing so with sailors with no experience in landfighting. But I had also placed MYSORE and two major ships in the area till the very last minute. It was only after the war had started and I was permitted to bring the Fleet back to the West Coast that I brought the ships across to the Western theater because I wanted to ensure that no opportunity was given to Indonesia to start anything at the same time. Whether eventually it proved itself I do not know but prior to that, Soekarno was reported to have been keeping an eye on the Bay islands.

"The Fleet, when it reached Bombay, had to be given this thoughtless order from the 'higher authorities' of not operating north of the latitude of Porbandar. Nothing else could be done except to try and see that the Pakistani ships did not move towards the Andaman and Nicobar islands to hold hands with the Indonesians

"I also had some intelligence on the presence of some Indonesian ships at Karachi and knew that any operation undertaken by the combined naval forces of Pakistan and Indonesia would neither be against the Indian Fleet nor the Indian mainland.

It was most likely to be for the capture of the Andaman and Nicobar Islands. I was quite convinced in my mind that the Indonesian Navy, knowing full well that only a small force of sailors in khaki uniform was present on these islands, could make an attempt to capture the Nicobar Island despite the then pretty poor state of Indonesia's Navy."

Was there any threat from Indonesia? Air Marshal Asghar Khan, who had been the Chief of the Pakistan Air Force during the Rann of Kutch incident, retired in July 1965. Soon after India crossed the Wagah border on 6 September, he was sent to China, Indonesia, Turkey and Iran to seek aid. In his memoirs, 'The First Round", he recounts his discussions with President Soekarno and Admiral Martadinata of Indonesia:

(a) President Soekarno said that India's attack on Pakistan was like an attack on Indonesia and they were duty bound to give Pakistan all possible assistance. President Soekarno told him to take away whatever would be useful to Pakistan in this emergency. Two Russian supplied submarines and two Russian supplied missile boats were sent to Pakistan post haste.

(b) Admiral Martadinata asked Air Marshal Asghar Khan "Don't you want us to take over the Andaman Islands? A look at the map will show that the Andaman and Nicobar Islands are an extension of Sumatra and are in any case between East Pakistan and Indonesia. What right have the Indians to be there? In any case, the Indonesian Navy will immediately commence patrols of the approaches to these islands and carry out aerial reconnaissance missions to see what the Indians have there".

In hindsight, it would appear that the concern voiced to Admiral Soman by the Prime Minister and by the Defence Minister and Admiral Soman's own concern at that time about the security of the Andaman and Nicobar islands was not entirely unfounded. Indeed, as will be seen in the Chapter on Russian Acquisitions 1965 to 1971, it was this concern in May 1965 at the rise in Indonesian activity that precipitated the decision to acquire Russian ships and submarines. It helps to understand one of the reasons for delaying the recall of the Indian Fleet to Bombay till 1 September, when the Pakistan Army crossed the international border to attack Kashmir.

Another reason for sending the Indian Fleet to the Bay of Bengal seems to have been not to forego the opportunity for exercising with a submarine, particularly since the Pakistan Navy had received the submarine GHAZI from the American Navy in 1964.

Vice Admiral Soman recalls:

"After the fizzle-out of the Kutch affair for which the Fleet ships had been hurriedly brought out from their refit and periodic maintenance, we had the Hobson's choice of either committing them back to their refit and maintenance,or of continuing to keep them operational in order to make full use of the (already projected) live anti submarine training with a Royal Navy submarine which was due to arrive in India shortly. It had been our experience in the past that no amount of simulated training on attack teachers in anti submarine training schools ashore can ever make anti submarine teams fully efficient.

"It was decided, therefore, that the live target hunting and tracking opportunity was too valuable to be missed even if, during the period, the ships were not in as good a shape in their material state as they should be, so long as their anti submarine searching, hunting and attacking equipment and personnel were effective and efficient. In making this decision, I had assessed that we perhaps had time till about November 1965 before things might get hot again.

"In the context of this assessment, I must point out that while MYSORE and the anti submarine frigates were sent out to the East Coast for anti submarine exercises with the British submarine Astute, VIKRANT was put into the dry dock for her normal but long overdue periodic maintenance, particularly the repairs to her flight deck machinery, malfunctioning of which would have endangered valuable lives of pilots and caused losses of aircraft. Another consideration in committing VIKRANT to her refit during this period was that the weather and visibility conditions during the monsoons do detract somewhat from the full operational value of such a ship. All ships from the East Coast were due back from the anti submarine exercises in early September 1965 and, after normal maintenance. would have been operational again by

November 1965, by which time VIKRANT was also scheduled to get ready.

"As it happened, events forestalled our calculations. MYSORE and the first pair of frigates to complete their exercises with the submarine carried out such normal periodic maintenance as possible with the limited resources available at Visakhapatnam, and were deployed in the Andaman and Nicobar area from where, during the monsoon period, smaller patrol craft are withdrawn. This was in accordance with the normal operational programme of the ships and was necessary, as there had been reports of surface and submarine (of unknown nationality) activity in this area. It was virtually in the middle of this deployment and before the second group of ships exercising with the submarine had finished their periodic maintenance, that all these ships had to be deployed to the West Coast to cater for any Pakistan naval activity. Needless to say, therefore, the material state of the ships, so far as their propulsion systems were concerned, was by no means at the optimum, as it perhaps could have been had we foregone the anti submarine exercise. I have no doubt, however, that the anti submarine exercises carried out with the submarine ASTUTE stood our ships in very good stead.

"From intelligence available prior to the end of August, it was known that the Pakistan Fleet was in Karachi carrying out maintenance and various exercises throughout the months of July and August 1965, while ours was on the East Coast. Being away from their homeport, Bombay, our ships had to continue to do with very meagre maintenance and repair facilities and resources, which had yet to be developed on the East Coast.

"A warning on the worsening situation was sent to the FOCIF on 31 August, but it was not till the next day, 1 September 1965, that the Fleet ships were ordered to rush back to the West Coast, and operational directives to the Fleet and Commands were issued two days later."

Why Wasn't the Fleet Recalled to Bombay Earlier

Air Chief Marshal Arjan Singh, the Chief of the Air Staff in 1965 recalls:

"Fairly early during August, General Chaudhuri and I went to Kashmir, we heard all the Commanders, we discussed the situation and felt that the Army would be able to handle the situation. One did not really think at that time that it could result into a bigger, full scale war, mainly because the Army was absolutely certain that this situation will not go out of hand. We thought that the Army, assisted by the Air Force purely in logistic operations, could tackle the situation. And I think it was managed very well, because the Army regained control over the situation. There was no danger of it becoming a bigger war."

Vice Admiral N P Datta, then a Commander serving in Naval Headquarters, recalls:

"Around the middle of August, I had gone to the Naval Chief, with whom I had earlier served as the Fleet Operations Officer. I gave him my view that if the Fleet was to be recalled, it would take a week or longer for them to get back to the west coast, after which they would require another week or so to effect necessary repairs and maintenance before they could be operational.

"Admiral Soman said that this was the very point that he had made to the Chiefs of Staff Committee but had been overruled by the Army Chief, General Chaudhuri, as the Chairman of the Committee, who had said that if any alterations were made in the disposition of the Indian Fleet, if the ships were hurriedly recalled from Calcutta and sent back to Bombay, it would create a furore in the press and it would forewarn the Pakistani General Staff of the Indian Armed Forces' knowledge of their plans and hence their reaction would be severe."

This remark of Admiral Soman suggests that by mid August, General Chaudhuri had informed him of the Army's intentions to cross the cease fire line and of the need to avoid any action which might forewarn Pakistan.

As regards the ambiguity as to who was the Chairman of the Chiefs of Staff Committee in 1965 and the interaction between the Chief of Army Staff and the Chief of the Naval Staff, Shri PVR Rao, the Defence Secretary recalls:-

"The Chiefs of Staff committee is presided over by the longest serving service Chief and not by rank. In my time (1962 to 1966) it was first presided over by Air Marshal Engineer, then by Vice Admiral Soman and then by General Chaudhuri. In 1965 Vice Admiral Soman was its Chairman. The Chief of Army Staff was not the Chairman of the Chief of Staff Committee. In any event, the Chairman of the Chiefs of Staffs Committee has no authority to over-rule any Chief of Staff. It is of course different if one Chief acceded to the view point of another".

In another interview, Admiral Soman stated that when the war began, he was the Chairman of the Chiefs of Staff Committee but as the Navy was not given any offensive role, he left the Chairmanship in favour of the Chief of the Army Staff, General Chaudhuri.

Air Chief Marshal Arjan Singh recalls:-

"I do not remember and I do not think there was discussion amongst the Chiefs of Staff on the Navy's participation. I do not think so. Every time there was a discussion amongst the Chiefs of Staff, records were kept. And if you look at the records, I do not think you will find any record of discussions at all on this. I do know there was never any discussion by Admiral Soman with me whether the Navy should participate or not. The Navy is closer to the Air Force and if any operation has to be planned, it's got to be a joint operation. And there was not a single discussion between Gen Chaudhuri and Admiral Soman and myself on the participation of the Air Force in naval operations.

"Secondly somehow at that time everybody was talking about one thing, everybody at that time thought that the aircraft carrier was the main weapon against Karachi. They said that the Navy could not fight without the aircraft carrier actually participating and that the carrier was not available because it was being refitted. I have a feeling, without any positive proof, that there was not enough pressure from the Navy to participate. I think a lot depends on the Chief. A Chief can convince the Government to do certain things in war. The Government is very receptive during a war where the services are involved. I remember that everything I recommended was agreed to by Prime Minister Shastri, except our plan to attack the PAF around Dacca. That was probably wrong on my part even to suggest it. He was not in favour. He said "why extend the war"?

"So I think there was not enough pressure built up. Perhaps the Government was not convinced that the Navy was fully prepared to participate in the operations. And that impression might have been conveyed by the man concerned. On the Navy side, I really cannot say what happened because there appeared to be no adequate pressure to participate in the 1965 war.

"We used to meet for long periods in the Chiefs of Staff Committee and I remember that the Navy's participation was not discussed over there. Whether it was raised within the inner structure of the Navy or in the MOD is a different matter of which I would not know. I think the general impression was that there was no great keenness on the part of the Navy to go to war. That was the impression I had got, but I do not remember Admiral Soman or anybody else actually discussing with me that he would do this or that".

In an interview the FOCIF Rear Admiral Samson stated:

"A very important limitation in the tasks assigned to the Navy was that any conflict with Pakistan would not mean a total war involving all three services but to be limited only to action on the borders. I and my colleagues were aware of this, that this understanding between the two countries was to limit the extent of the war, to avoid civilian casualties as well as destruction of one anothers industries etc. So far as the Navy was concerned, this limitation was known to all, though never spelt out in writing".

From the foregoing, it emerges that:

(a) by end August, after the cease fire line had been crossed, Admiral Soman had reconciled to the Government's decision not to enlarge the scope of conflict beyond that required to restore the status quo in Kashmir, leaving the Navy with only a defensive role. The non availability of the aircraft carrier VIKRANT may have been supportive of a defensive mindset.

(b) In September, immediately after the Government asked the Chief of the Naval Staff to withdraw his signal to the Navy that India was at war with Pakistan, the Ministry of Defence sent the written directive to Naval Headquarters, not to operate in a threatening or offensive manner north of Porbandar and forbidding offensive action against Pakistan unless forced to so. This formalised the Navy's defensive role.

(c) The Fleet Commander was aware of the Governments reasons for constraining the Navy to defensive action.

Could the Navy Have Done More

Both in the press and within the Navy, there was criticism of the Navy for not going into action and doing something noteworthy, as had been done by the Air Force's successes in the air battles over Kashmir and by the Army's decimation of Pakistan's American supplied Patton tanks in the Punjab. Indeed, in response to a suggestion from Rear Admiral Nanda, then in Mazagon Docks (and later CNS in the 1971 war) that the Navy's non-participation was affecting the morale of officers and men and that the CNS should come and speak to them, Admiral Soman came to Bombay and told them "We all have to do what we are told to do". This did not assuage their frustration. Admiral Soman remained circumspect about the Government's directive that the Navy desist from offensive action.

After the 1965 operations, Admiral Soman, addressing the senior officers of the Navy, said:

"Notwithstanding our initial disadvantage of the location of the Fleet on the East Coast at the time of the commencement of the undeclared war, and the material limitations of the ships after three months of exercises away from base, the Fleet, with the help of the valiant efforts of the Dockyard, took the initiative to seek the enemy and bring him to battle. Although this was not achieved, I am sure it had placed itself in a position to contain the enemy in his waters if he had ventured out, which I know was all that was expected of the Fleet.

"It is indeed a great pity that the role assigned to the Navy was mainly a defensive one. History has proved over and over again that at sea, more than perhaps on land and in the air, offense is the best form of defence. In the days of old, when there was no wireless communication, Nelsons could put their telescopes to their blind eyes and get away with it as heroes on top of their respective columns. It indeed took courage to put the telescope to the blind eye and win laurels. But it takes equal, if not greater, courage (perhaps of a different kind) to play the tethered role and curb the offensive spirit of a fighting force in the greater national interest as claimed by the authorities.

"The implications of a war at sea did not seem to have been fully understood in the Government agencies at many levels, but when some of these agencies talked glibly of blockade, contraband control, seizing enemy merchant ships and attacking enemy warships at sea and their ports without a proper formal declaration of war, one wondered whether they realised that any such action on the high seas without the declaration of war was liable to be branded as piracy, especially if any neutral ships became involved.

"The need for a `rethink' on the question of the operation and control of maritime reconnaissance has also become apparent. Intelligence is vital for the Navy in planning its operations and executing them. While the Air Force, with their meagre resources and preoccupations with other commitments, valiantly tried to give the limited cover agreed upon, it was disconcerting to comprehend the fact that of the 13.5 lakh square miles of coverage required for the operations undertaken by the Fleet, a bare one lakh square miles could actually be covered. This too was achieved in 24 sorties of 188 hours by the IAF with its Liberators and Super Constellations, augmented by 60 sorties of 160 flying hours of the Alizes. This meant that the Fleet ships' endurance, limited as it was due to the lack of a replenishment tanker, had to be devoted to searching for enemy ships, hoping for a chance contact, which was a terrible waste, quite apart from its ineffectiveness, particularly with our meagre resources."

As can be seen from the foregoing reconstruction of events, the Navy went beyond the constraints imposed by the Government. Although instructions had been received not to seek action at sea outside our territorial waters, all ships were directed to hunt and destroy submarines whenever and wherever they were detected. The Seahawk aircraft of the Navy, which coincidentally arrived in Jamnagar on 1 September for its annual armament work up, were specifically tasked to put out of action, the high-power radar installation at Badin in Pakistan, which is only 135 nautical miles away from Jamnagar. Events precluded this operation but the offensive spirit was there. The Indian Fleet, despite the restriction of not operating north of Porbandar, had no hesitation in planning the first sweep with Alizes searching well north of Porbandar in the hope that contact would be made with the Pakistan Flotilla. When this did not happen, FOCIF had no hesitation on subsequent nights of proceeding northwards whenever he thought he might catch the enemy.

Given the Government's determination to limit the scope of the conflict as much as possible (and the resultant restrictions of 'no offensive operations' and 'do not proceed north of Porbandar'), given the Chief of Army Staff's desire of not giving Pakistan any inkling of the Army's plans (not agreeing to the Fleet being brought back to Bombay earlier) and given the ambiguities that arise when there is no formal declaration of war (trade warfare and contraband control when neutral ships get involved), it is difficult to see what more the Navy could have done.

POST WAR NAVAL REACTIONS

That the Government was aware of the Navy's frustration at having been restricted to defensive operations can be discerned from the letter written to the Navy by Shri Y.B. Chavan, the then Defence Minister:-

"I greatly appreciated the silent but efficient role which the Navy played in the defence of the country. The Navy protected islands which were vital to our security, guarded our ports and the long Indian coast-line. All merchant ships destined for our ports reached safely and our international trade was not permitted to be interfered with by the Pakistan Navy. I take this opportunity to emphasise again that the Navy has done and achieved all that the Government desired of it, within the bounds and compass allotted to it".

Within the Navy, there were two distinct reactions. One was to decry the Pakistan Navy's raid on Dwarka. The other was a determination not to be humiliated again.

In the prologue to his book, 'We Dared", Admiral SN Kohli states:

"During the 1965 war between India and Pakistan, the main task force of the Pakistan Navy, including the cruiser BABUR, sneaked out of Karachi harbour in the dead of night and made its way to holy Dwarka which it proceeded to bombard. The bombardment lasted half an hour or so. PNS BABUR fired several six-inch shells and then the Pakistani ships withdrew to the safety of their heavily defended harbour of Karachi well before the Indian Navy could intercept or even contact them. It is obvious that a sneak raid of this type can be undertaken by any force anywhere, to convey an impression to their Government and their countrymen that they are supreme and unchallenged on the seas and that the enemy territory is at their mercy. The Pakistani naval raid on Dwarka left the officers and men of the Indian Navy infuriated and somewhat humiliated. This was particularly true of the senior echelons of our Navy on whom devolved the responsibility for the maritime defence of India. I was then the Deputy Chief of Naval Staff (now Vice Chief of Naval Staff) and I vowed to myself that if ever there was another round involving naval forces and I was in any kind of position of responsibility, I would go to the farthest extremes to teach the enemy a lesson and to avenge this dastardly act. This opportunity was to come in 1971 when I was Flag Officer Commanding in Chief, Western Naval Command in Bombay.

"In 1965, the Indian Navy had gone to war with their hands tied behind their backs and all but immobilised. A Government instruction under the signature of a Joint Secretary, Ministry of Defence, laid down that the Indian Navy was not to proceed more than 200 miles beyond Bombay nor north of the parallel of Porbandar. This meant a fettering of the Navy's mobility. The Joint Secretary's communication was given to the then CNS, Admiral BS Soman. When he told me about it, I was naturally most upset and told my Chief that if I were in his position, I would protest vehemently; for the Government decision and its import and implementation would have a most demoralising effect on the Navy as a whole.

"Admiral Soman, on being asked by me recently, gave his version of what transpired then, in his characteristic forthright manner. Here it is in his own words:

"As far as I remember, it was the morning after the start of the war that I got a file from the Ministry signed by the Joint Secretary, saying that the Navy is not to operate above the latitude of Porbandar except in pursuit of any Pak Navy offensive action. I immediately contacted the Minister, Mr YB Chavan, and asked to see him; at our meeting I strongly protested against this order and said in any case I cannot accept it from a Joint Secretary in the Ministry. If I remember correctly, Mr Chavan initialed the directive and asked me if that would do. I replied that in that case I would like to see the Prime Minister.

"Arrangements were made for me to see the Prime Minister, Shastriji, the next morning, and I had about twenty minutes with him. On his assurance that it was a Cabinet decision - I am not sure whether he too initialed the file - I accepted it on the understanding that should I consider it necessary, I may be allowed to see the President of India, as the Commander-in-Chief".

"It was often derisively asked by civilians and officers of the other two services why our Navy could not do anything in retaliation against the raid on Dwarka. The question was asked even by those who knew that our coast is such that a sneak raid on a remote part of it is possible. But it is not surprising that our reputation plummeted; more so because our aircraft carrier VIKRANT was in dry dock undergoing routine maintenance: it was openly called a 'white elephant'. Many rude remarks were made about our smart uniforms, foreign jaunts, and the proverbial girl in every port, all amounting to a 'big cipher when it came to fighting'. Few knew that all this obloquy was brought on the Navy by a dictat of our own Government.

"It was difficult for the Navy to understand the reason for such an order. Maybe it was to limit the scope of the 1965 operation against Pakistan, maybe the Government thought that our old ships might not be able to make a good showing. The Pakistan Fleet then consisted of ships of much the same vintage as ours -

or perhaps just a little newer.The reason will no doubt come out when the official history of the 1965 and 1971 wars is published".

In his memoirs of the 1971 war, 'No Way But Surrender', Vice Admiral Krishnan states:

"I thought of the previous round of aggression by Pakistan, the 1965 war, in which, much to everyone's disgust and consternation, the Navy played little or no part. I remember the hurt and humiliation one felt over the fact that even a Pakistani frontal attack on one of our ports had not brought forth any retribution.

Afterword

The discerning reader will have sensed that there remain some points which are serious enough to require a final effort at clarification. The above account was forwarded to Mr PVR Rao who was the Defence Secretary in 1965. His clarifications are given below:

(a) Was there a written directive from the Government/Ministry of Defence to the CNS not to take offensive action?

Mr Rao states:

"There is no dispute that the Government directed, as a matter of policy, the Navy not to play any role in the 1965 conflict. Whether there was a written directive from the De-fence Ministry, as claimed by the CNS, can only be checked from the NHQ records. The least one can do is to publish an extract from the NHQ records from the alleged written order of the Defence Ministry".

In the records presently available, no such written directive has yet been located.

(b) Was the Government right in deciding to localise the conflict?

Mr Rao states:

"This was the Government of India's limited objective and it was achieved. Whether the Government should have embarked on a wider operation can be debated, but it was not the Prime Minister's idea".

(c) After the Kutch incident, did the Chief of the Army Staff inform the Ministry of Defence of his assessment that Pakistan would attempt to seize Kashmir later in the year?

Mr Rao states:

"After the Kutch cease fire, none in the Government expected trouble until it erupted on 4th August".

(d) Had the Chief of Army Staff received the Government's approval in principle for the Army to counterattack in a place of its choice if Pakistan attacked in Kashmir?

Mr Rao states:

"Rather the Government pressed the Army to attack. The Chief of the Army Staff wanted all the three services to participate. In my opinion, he was never serious about this but was trying this gambit to support his inaction".

In this connection, Mr Pradhan's memoirs state:

"(On 4 September) The situation was getting desperate. The loss of Akhnur would be a major disaster and Chavan decided to go ahead with an operation that had been planned after the Rann of Kutch incident. On 20 April Shastri had declared before Parliament "If Pakistan continues to disregard reason and persists in its aggressive activities, our Army will defend the country and decide its own strategy and employment of its manpower and equipment in the manner it deems best." General Chaudhuri, with the approval of the Defence Minister, had worked out a plan code-named, `Riddle' to launch an offensive action to secure the eastern bank of the Ichhogil Canal. It was felt that the mere presence of the Indian troops on the canal opposite Lahore would draw Pakistani forces from Sialkot and other areas and thus reduce its offensive capabilities in other sectors. Moreover, if India could establish a bridgehead over the canal, the Pakistan army would be forced to fight there and that would lead to the attrition of her smaller army. By basing the defence line along the canal, India would confine the war to Pakistani territory in addition to acquiring a large chunk of Pakistani territory. Operation `Riddle' was planned to meet an eventuality like the one the Indian's were facing on 4 September".

Finally Shri Rao states:

"Notwithstanding Government's directive in the Defence Minister's morning meetings to the CNS about his role thereafter, he seems to have embarked on certain actions on his own. The account speaks for itself. The Fleet was in a poor state. This was not the Navy's fault. It had got only measly funds. Whatever resources Government could spare for defence was given in 1962 - 1965 to the Army and the Air Force. Going by the account of the 1965 war as written above, I would consider the decision of the Government to restrict the Navy to a low key was fully justified!"

Epilogue

In hindsight, three points of the 1965 war bear noting:

The first was the determination of the Governments of both India and Pakistan not to escalate the conflict.

(a) Mr PVR Rao, the Defence Secretary in 1965 has stated that it was the determined policy of Prime Minister Lal Bahadur Shastri and the Indian Government not to allow operations to escalate. There were no Army or Navy operations against East Pakistan.

The IAF attack on Lalmanirhat was the result of a communication gap of Air HQ not informing the Air Station in time. The IAF did not retaliate against the PAF's subsequent attacks on Kalaikonda on 7 September on Bagdogra on 10 September and on Barrackpore and Agartala on 14 September.

In the Arabian Sea, GHAZI did not attack merchant shipping nor did the Indian Navy seize Pakistani merchant shipping on the high seas.

(b) In his book, "The First Round" Air Marshal Asghar Khan has stated:

- "President Ayub Khan said that since East Pakistan had not been attacked, it would be better not to launch strikes against enemy airfields in that area. He felt that considering our difficulties there, it was not in our interest to start hostilities on the Eastern front.

- "Our Navy was keen to intercept on the high seas the merchant ships taking supplies to India but was stopped from doing so by our Foreign Office for fear of international opinion. However within East Pakistan Admiral Ahsan, then Chairman of the Inland Water Transport Authority in East Pakistan, in a lightning action captured the entire fleet of more than one hundred Indian coastal shipping vessels along with their valuable cargo."

The second point is the maritime recce capability of the Pakistan Navy. In view of Pakistan's reluctance to escalate naval conflict, the approaches to Karachi seem to have been well covered. The Pakistan Air Force's No 4 Squadron comprised American supplied SA 16 Albatross aircraft. The History of the Pakistan Air Force states: "The SA 16's of No 4 Squadron were given the maritime role of detecting and reporting the movement of ships, particularly the enemy aircraft carrier VIKRANT.

Within the first 14 days, SA 16's flew 72 hours with only two qualified operational pilots. The total operational flying during the month was 98:35 hours, the maximum flying during any single month. Hundred percent serviceability of both the SA 16 and helicopters was maintained throughout the month."

The third point is that the raid on Dwarka seems more to have been a reaction to India's crossing the Indo Pakistan border on 6 September, than a preplanned action to provoke the Indian Fleet to join battle. The post war rhetoric in Pakistani (and Indian) literature that the Indian Fleet was bottled up for fear of the GHAZI is the result of widespread ignorance of the decisions of both Governments to minimize the scope of conflict.

1971 WAR

This was among the shortest decisive wars among major nations in history. It led to the creation of Bangladesh out of East Pakistan.

In 1947, Pakistan was created with two halves - one to the west and another to the east of India. The western half dominated by the Punjabis held most of the power while the eastern half, dominated by the Bengalis, had little say in the matters of the nation.

Unlike the western half, the eastern half had a lot of Hindus. This was because Mahatma Gandhi's peacemaking role in Bengal at the time of partition led to reduced population exchange between West and East Bengal. Many Muslims continued to live in West Bengal, and many Hindus continued to live in East Bengal.

In November 1970, one of the worst cyclones in recorded history - Cyclone Bhola - hit Bengal. Pakistan didn't respond enough to the plight of the Bengalis, and thus the Bengali-led Awami league swept to power in the national elections of December 1970. It was a shock for everyone in West Pakistan. They didn't believe that the Bengalis would rule over them.

General Yahya Khan, the then President of Pakistan suspected the Hindus of helping the Bengalis win and started a brutal campaign codenamed Operation Searchlight on March 25 1971. Lt General Tikka Khan (nicknamed the butcher of Bengal) was assigned the task of getting rid of Hindus and began a massive pogrom that resulted in over ten million Hindus fleeing to India. Nearly 3 million Bengalis (Hindus and Muslims) died during the few months of pogrom, although Pakistani reports quoted a much lower number.

On March 26, Mujibur Rahman, the leader of the Awami League, declared independence of Bangladesh. The Indian Prime Minister, Indira Gandhi, had also consolidated political power by then and was willing to take a more active action in the crisis. On March 27, Indira put her weight behind the people of East Pakistan and pledge to support of their independence cause. India trained armed rebels under the banner of the Mukti Bahini.

West Pakistan was filled with the slogan *Crush India.* Inspired by Israel's daring strike in 1967, Pakistan flew 50 planes to India in a pre-emptive strike focused on neutralizing India's defense infrastructure by attacking 11 airfields in north India. Like his predecessors, Yahya Khan underestimated India and believed that India would quickly give in.

However, Pakistan was no Israel and India was no Egypt. The Operation Chengiz Khan, named in a vain attempt to add luck to the campaign, ended in a massive failure.While many of the Indian airfields were damaged, they were also repaired very quickly. However, Pakistan lost over 50 aircraft and that was terribly damaging to its fledgling military. It was on a Friday evening when IAF controls were changing hands. Thus, this attack was caught in surprise, although Indian responded well. India had to cover up Taj Mahal once again due to Pakistan's attack on Agra.

On December 3, both nations declared war. The attack involved all three branches of the military. Indian navy attacked Karachi under Operation Trident on December 4, while on December 9 the Pakistani submarine PNS Hangor sank INS Khukri that resulted in close to 200 Indian casualties. Eventually, the Pakistani Navy suffered heavy defeats, with more than a third of the force destroyed. On land, India inflicted huge losses too with a 3:1 casualty rate.

In the meanwhile, US President Nixon built a three-way alliance (US-Pak-China) against India and USSR and gave both political and military help to Pakistan. He even asked Iran and Jordon to attack India in an air battle. US sent its navy under USS Enterprises but it was actively trailed by Russian nuclear submarines and frigates, thereby being unable to attack India. Nixon also asked China to attack, but Chinese felt that the Indian army was more prepared after the surprise assault of 1962 and didn't want to risk troops. Thus, Pakistan faced a humiliating defeat despite being a US ally.

On December 16, Pakistan surrendered. India had captured 90000 prisoners of war and 14000 square kilometers of Pakistani territory. Lt General Jagjit Singh Arora accepted the Pakistani surrender in the east. Bangladesh won its independence.

In June 1972, India and Pakistan met in the hill station of Simla to discuss the peace terms. Although India won the war, it didn't push the new civilian government under Zulfiqar Ali Bhutto. India wanted the Pakistani army to stay off the government and thus didn't want to weaken Bhutto by imposing harsh terms. Instead of settling the Kashmir issue for good, it was left unresolved. Indira missed the game in 1972.

OPERATION MEGHDOOT OF 1984

The Simla agreement bought peace for awhile. However, in the agreement, there was confusion about the ownership of a glacier in northern Kashmir. The glacier named Siachen was claimed by both the nations, and to prove their claims, both sent mountaineering expeditions. In 1984, Pakistan allowed a Japanese expedition to climb the glacier. The glacier was closer to India's borders with China, and thus India was quite sensitive to this report.

Fearing an imminent attack by Pakistan, India sent its troops to get acclimatized in the frigid parts of Antartica. On April 13 1984, just 4 days before Pakistan was planning its operation, India sent 300 troops atop this glacier and captured over 2300 sq kilometers of territory. It was a major victory for India, but the region still remains a battlezone - it is the world's highest and coldest battlezone, claiming more deaths by frostbites than bullets.

1999 KARGIL WAR

For over 15 years, the Pakistani army stayed quiet and content with fomenting extremists in Kashmir. In May 1998, both India and Pakistan became nuclear powers. Some thought this would finally end wars as both nations couldn't face a Mutually Assured Destruction (MAD) of nuclear weapons. In February 1999, Prime Minister Vajpayee made a landmark peace trip to Lahore in Pakistan, and Indian citizens felt a surging spring of hope. Some even contemplated the reunification of India and Pakistan.

While Vajpayee was traveling to Pakistan, a group of Pakistani soldiers was moving into the frigid hills of Kashmir. The template was the same as 1947 and 1965 - foment trouble and start a rebellion among Kashmiris. The plan was inspired by India's takeover of Siachin. Given the sudden rise of terrorism in the 1990s, Pakistan was emboldened.

On May 3, local sheep herders reported the intrusions in the Dras sector of Kargil in Kashmir. In the next month, a deep conflict developed as India started attacking the hills now occupied by Pakistanis. The hills were very crucial in controlling the Indian highway NH 1A that connected the eastern and western halves of Kashmir. On July 4, India captured the pivotal Tiger Hills, and the images of beaming Indian soldiers carrying the flag captured the nation's imagination [As an aside, when I joined college some of the notebooks supplied by my college had the capture of Tiger hills as the cover picture. People used the image everywhere]. After the capture, India prepared for a ceasefire, and on July 26, the war came to an end. In the meanwhile, Nawaz Sheriff was reprimanded by the US in Washington DC, and unlike in previous wars, the US had categorically ruled to not side with Pakistan. The G8 nations [world's largest economies] also condemned Pakistan, and for the first time, the world was on India's side in a war. The tide had turned.

India was engulfed in a wave of patriotism, and even the stock market responded handsomely to the victory by surging 30% in the months following the war to end bearish trends.

Israel helped India with tech during the war, and the US was instrumental in bringing the war to an end. The war was thus pivotal in India's relationship with both Israel and US. India's bad relationship with rest of the world seemed to end.

Each time Pakistan sent its army into Kashmir, posing as ordinary men, it expected the Kashmiris to revolt in large numbers and the "Hindus" to give up too easily. However, each time it showed that the Kashmiris, despite having some attachment to Pakistan, had no inclination to fight India and that the Indians had no intention of giving up Kashmir either.

2008 MUMBAI ATTACKS

While Pakistan avoided fighting direct wars after the Kargil conflict, it continued to foment terrorist acts on Indian soil. In 2001, its terrorists attacked the Indian Parliament, and that incident threatened to bring a nuclear war in South Asia. Luckily, cooler heads prevailed.

The gravest of Pakistan's terrorist attacks was in Mumbai on November 26, 2008. 11 Pakistan-trained attackers landed in Mumbai and brought a night of violence by attacking the Victoria Terminus railway station, two five-star hotels, a cafe, a hospital and a Jewish centre. The terrorists hijacked a small fishing trawler named Kuber and used that to slip into the city. The main battle was in the iconic

Taj hotel, and the fight lasted for 3 days and killed 100 hostages. The NSG and Marine Commandos finally brought the crisis to an end by killing ten attackers and capturing one - Ajmal Kasab, who was later hung after a brief court trial.

MUMBAI 26/11 TERRORISM ATTACKS

India's public opinion hostility to India's political leadership and political class as a whole was starkly visible on TV visuals of that time. It vividly illustrated the Indian public's pent-up hostility to Pakistan and an enraged resentment against India's political leadership for their supine policies against Pakistan and not inflicting corresponding losses on Pakistan. The Indian public's hostility towards Pakistan cannot be said to be towards the Pakistani people. It focuses on the Pakistan Army which from 1947 has launched four wars against India, besides continued proxy wars and terrorism against India. No amount of Indian confidence building measures has induced the Pakistan Army to adopt a peaceful attitude towards India. Mumbai 26/11 was a manifestation of Pakistan Army's emboldened adventurism induced by India's feeble responses to terrorist attacks and constant climb-downs by India's present Prime Minister and his predecessor. The crucial question that arises here is that can any Indian Prime Minister operate and conduct India's Pakistan policy in a state of 'severe disconnect' from Indian public opinion. More so when in India there is a surfeit of charismatic Indian Prime Ministers.

The record of the Prime Minister from Havana to Thimphu via Sharm-al-Sheikh reflects that the Indian policy establishment is in a state of 'severe disconnect' from Indian public opinion on Pakistan. They are also in a 'state of denial' that Pakistan continues with its implacable hostility towards India and that their posturing for peace is only a veneer to please the United States and in the bargain to continue receiving United States strategic support and military hardware.

India's Pakistan Policy Distortion: The US Factor

The United States has been a constant distorting factor in India's Pakistan policy. The United States obsession with Pakistan's strategic utility to its regional strategic interests has led it to overwhelmingly mindful of Pakistan Army's demands vis-a-vis India's strategic sensitivities. India's foreign policies emerged as more strongly 'US-Centric' than ever before under the present Prime Minister. This had a corresponding impact on India's Pakistan policy. Circumstantially, India's foreign policy record for the last seven years indicates that India succumbed to United States pressures to modulate its Pakistan policies oblivious to Indian national security interests. India consequently stood restrained from firm and decisive actions against Pakistani provocations against India's sovereignty. The Obama Administration has moved further ahead in this direction when it re-invented Pakistan Army's strategic utility to the United States at the cost of eclipsing India's standing as a regional power. Editorials in Pakistani newspapers reflect that the Indian Prime Minister has been accommodative of United States nudging on Pakistan and could possibly be nudged further on the Kashmir and water disputes. The strategic impact of this perception on Pakistan's thinking and strategy was visible in the run-up to the Thimphu Summit where Pakistan was arrogantly dictating demands on India.

Bibliography

Ajey Lele: *Strategic Technologies for the Military : Breaking New Frontiers*, Sage, Delhi, 2009.

Allana, G.: *Pakistan Movement: Historic Documents*, Karachi, Department of International Relations, University of Karachi, 1967.

Anadish Kumar: *World Guide to the Partition of INDIA*. Amazon Digital Services, 2010.

Anderson, J.: *Transnational Democracy: Political Spaces and Border Crossings*, Routledge: London and New York, 2002.

Anil, K.C.: *Military and Democracy in South Asia : Challenges, Politics and Power*, Sumit Enterprises, Delhi, 2009.

Barber B.R.: *Strong Democracy. Participatory Politics for a New Age*. Berkeley, University of California Press, 1984.

Bhalla, Alok: *Stories about the Partition of India*, New Delhi: HarperCollins, 1994.

Bort, E.: *Boundaries and Identities: The Eastern Frontier of the Asia*, Edinburgh: International Social Sciences Institute, University of Edinburgh, 1996.

Budge I: *The New Challenge of Direct Democracy*, Oxford, Polity Press, 1996.

Chaudhary, M.: *Partition and the Curse of Rehabilitation*. Calcutta: Bengal Rehabilitation Organization, 1964.

Coakley, J.: *The Territorial Management of Ethnic Conflict*, London: Frank Cass, 2003.

Digumarti Bhaskara Rao: *Military Conversion : Impact on Science and Technology*, Discovery, Delhi, 2003.

Dixit, J.N. : *India and Regional Developments : Through the Prism of Indo-Pak Relations*, Gyan, Delhi, 2004.

Dominique Lapierre: *Freedom at Midnight*. London: Collins, 1975.

Ghosh, Ajoy : *Indo-Pak Conflict : Threat to South Asian Security*, Reference Press, Delhi, 2003.

Gupta, Alka R. : *Indo-Pak Security Discourse : South Asian Context*, Radha Pub, Delhi, 2010.

Gupta, Asha: *Military Rule and Democratization : Changing Perspectives*, Deep & Deep, Delhi, 2003.

Gupta, S.: *Disrupted Borders: An Intervention in Definitions of Boundaries*, London: River Oram Press, 1993.

Hodson, H. V.: *The Great Divide: Britain-India-Pakistan*, Karachi, Oxford UP, 1993.

Ikram, S. M.: *Indian Muslims and Partition of India*. Delhi: Atlantic, 1995.

Johnson, Alan: *Mission with Mountbatten*. London: Hale, 1982.

Juvale, R.P. : *Military Strategy and Diplomacy*, Cyber Tech Publications, Delhi, 2010.

Kunju, N. : *Indo-Pak : Nuclear Cold War*, Reliance, Delhi, 2002.

Moon, Penderel: *Divide and Quit*. Delhi: Oxford UP, 1961.

Nevile, P.: *Lahore: A Sentimental Journey*. New Delhi: Penguin, 1993.

Posen, B.R.: *The Sources of Indian Military Doctrine*, Ithaca, 1984, Cornell Univ. Press.

Rosen, P.: *Societies and Military Power: India and its Armies*, Ithaca, Cornell University Press, 1996.

Salim, Ahmad: *Lahore 1947*. New Delhi: India Research Press, 2001.

Index

O

P

R

S

T

❑❑❑